GENERATION RISING

GENERATION RISING

The Time of the Québec Student Spring

SHAWN KATZ

Preface by Anne Lagacé Dowson

Photographs by Mario Jean

FERNWOOD PUBLISHING · HALIFAX & WINNIPEG

Editing: Marianne Ward
Cover design: John van der Woude
Printed and bound in Canada

Published in Canada by Fernwood Publishing
32 Oceanvista Lane
Black Point, Nova Scotia, B0J 1B0
and 748 Broadway Avenue, Winnipeg, Manitoba, R3G 0X3
www.fernwoodpublishing.ca

Fernwood Publishing Company Limited gratefully acknowledges the financial support of the
Government of Canada through the Canada Book Fund and the Canada Council for the Arts, the
Nova Scotia Department of Communities, Culture and Heritage, the Manitoba Department of Culture,
Heritage and Tourism under the Manitoba Publishers Marketing Assistance Program and the Province of
Manitoba, through the Book Publishing Tax Credit, for our publishing program.

Library and Archives Canada Cataloguing in Publication

Katz, Shawn, 1985-, author
Generation rising: the time of the 2012 Québec Student
Spring / Shawn Katz.

Includes bibliographical references and index.
Issued in print and electronic formats.
ISBN 978-1-55266-725-5 (pbk.).—ISBN 978-1-55266-758-3 (epub)

1. Student movements—Québec (Province). 2. Students—Political activity—Québec (Province). 3.
Education, Higher—Québec (Province)—Finance. 4. Tuition—Québec (Province). I. Title.

LA418.Q8K38 2015   378.1'98109714   C2015-900671-6   C2015-900672-4

CONTENTS

To the youth of Québec, and of the world.

Courage, friends.

GLOSSARY OF TERMS

ANE(E)Q: Association nationale des étudiants (et étudiantes) du Québec, Québec's main national student association for most of its existence from 1976 to 1994. It became the ANEEQ in 1987.

ASSÉ: Association pour une solidarité syndicale étudiante, one of Québec's three national student associations, which encompasses local associations at both the CEGEP (college) and university level. Founded in 2001.

Assemblée nationale: Québec's provincial legislature located in Québec City.

CEGEP: Collège d'enseignement général et professionnel, Québec's publicly-funded colleges. In Québec, high school runs until Grade 11, followed by either a two-year pre-university program (leading toward a three-year university degree) or a three-year vocational program. Both options are largely free.

CLASSE: Coalition large de l'Association pour une solidarité syndicale étudiante, the ASSÉ's expanded coalition, which existed from December 2011 to November 2012 to broaden and coordinate the strike.

CREPUQ: Conférence des recteurs et des principaux des universités du Québec, a private organization and lobby group founded in 1963 that united the administration heads of virtually all of Québec's universities. It was refounded as the Bureau de coopération interuniversitaire in 2014.

FAECQ: Fédération des associations étudiantes du Québec, the precursor to the Fédération étudiante collégiale du Québec (FECQ), which existed from 1982 to 1987 and encompassed local associations at the CEGEP (college) level.

FECQ: Fédération étudiante collégiale du Québec, one of Québec's three national student associations, which encompasses only associations at the CEGEP (college) level. Founded in 1990.

FEEQ: Fédération des étudiants et étudiantes du Québec, the initial name chosen for the Fédération étudiante universitaire du Québec, founded in 1989. It was renamed FEUQ one year later.

FEUQ: Fédération étudiante universitaire du Québec, Québec's largest national student association, which encompasses only local associations at the university level. Founded in 1989 as the Fédération des étudiants et étudiantes du Québec (FEEQ), renamed one year later.

MELS: Ministère de l'éducation, du sport et du loisir, Québec's education ministry (responsible also for sports and leisure).

MNA: Member of the National Assembly (or Assemblée nationale), Québec's provincial legislature.

RAEU: Regroupement des associations étudiantes universitaires, the precursor to the FEUQ. It existed first as a working group within the ANEEQ from 1976 and then as an independent national association from 1981 to 1986.

SPVM: Service de police de la ville de Montréal, Montréal's police force.

SQ: Sûreté du Québec, Québec's provincial police force.

UGEQ: Union générale des étudiants du Québec, Québec's first national student association, which existed from 1963 to 1969.

PREFACE

Le combat est avenir – The struggle is the future

This is an *engagé* handbook of Québec social and political history and the first accessible English account of what happened in Québec in 2012. It is an impassioned plea for a generation and a cautionary tale. Shawn Katz brings the six months of the Maple Spring, or Printemps érable, to life. This is the movement that brought down the provincial government of Liberal Premier Jean Charest, led to a rollback of tuition fees and radicalized a whole generation of young people. At its peak, 300,000 of the 400,000 post-secondary students in Québec were on strike, an astounding turn of events and one that Katz describes in affectionate detail.

If generations are formed by what they experience at the age of twenty, then the story Katz tells is far from over.

I followed the events of the Printemps érable or Maple Spring as they unfurled in the streets, in the news and especially in social media. I was one of the few who defended the students and their opposition to tuition fee hikes on TV and radio. It was a polarizing and emotional period of Québec history and it was about far more than tuition fees. Polls showed Quebecers evenly split in their support of the students. Shawn Katz's book ties it all together for English readers in a new and extremely useful way.

Shawn Katz is one of a new generation of anglo Quebecers. They are the product of the French language laws, especially Law 101, and the Quiet Revolution. In many ways Shawn Katz's generation is more like francophone Quebecers than it is like anglo Canadians.

2012 marked the first student mobilization in Québec that saw anglo university faculties and associations join the student strike movement. About 60 percent of anglophone university students were on strike at some point, even if not for as long as their franco equivalents. Newer generations of anglos — more bilingual, more "Québécois" than ever before — are challenging the political assumptions of the anglo majority outside Québec and the anglo minority inside Québec.

Shawn Katz was born in DDO, Dollard-des-Ormeaux, a mostly English speaking suburb in the south western part of the Island of Montréal. He describes his upbringing as unremarkable — the third generation in a family of secular Jewish anglo Montrealers (though he affiliates with no religion or religious culture). The youngest of three brothers, he is the first one in his apolitical family to speak French. He describes himself as becoming politicized in high school, joining the federal New Democratic Party at eighteen. He then ran as the candidate for the Parti vert du Québec in 2007 at twenty-one, in the West Island riding of Robert-Baldwin, where the young candidate got 7 percent of the vote. (More than the Parti Québécois and Québec Solidaire combined.)

1

The cohort that Katz represents is becoming much more integrated with francophone Québec society than previously. They have not just learned the French and Québécois language but are adopting many of the francophone majority's cultural perceptions and values. That means a more positive view of the role of government and the state. It also includes the concept of a societal project, of solidarity and of direct political action. It comes with skepticism of the market and private actors, and deep dislike of corruption.

Shawn Katz has done a great service in telling the story of the student mobilization and putting it into context. His own support of the broad non-hierarchical student coalition known as the CLASSE (the Coalition large de l'Association pour une solidarité syndicale étudiante, an expanded coalition of the ASSÉ, the Association pour une solidarité syndicale étudiante, one of Québec's three students' associations) is clear throughout but doesn't get in the way of his detailed and thorough account. (The other more establishment oriented student groups are the FECQ, the Fédération étudiante collégiale du Québec, representing college students; and the FEUQ, the Fédération étudiante universitaire du Québec, representing university students.) Katz pulls it all together and provides us with a cast of characters and organizations to paint a sociological portrait of Québec.

I remember exactly where I was when the Printemps érable became close up and real to the public. The strike really took hold in February of 2012 after Liberal Premier Jean Charest raised tuition fees by 75 percent over five years. By the first week of March, 100,000 students were out on strike, but they hadn't really registered on the public mind.

Then on March 22, 300,000 students converged on Montréal to pressure the Charest government to negotiate. From the fourth floor window of the office building where I worked in downtown Montréal, I saw the street fill with hundreds and then thousands of young people, wearing and waving red squares. They looked up at us from the street, saluting us and blowing us kisses. They were accompanied by the Brass band de grève and Danse ta grève and a host of creative and funny people with wildly colourful posters and images.

The Printemps érable gets its name from the Printemps arabe — the Arab Spring, of Egypt's Tahrir Square. Its supporters were called "les carrés rouges" for the red square emblem they wore, mostly of felt, pinned to their coats and hats. The red square was originally a symbol adopted by social welfare groups protesting against cutbacks. There were red squares everywhere — on light standards, on the cross atop Mount Royal, even hanging over the sides of the bridges onto Montréal island.

It's a powerful and effective brand and an inexpensive one to use — red squares of duct tape appeared in the city. The students and their supporters were "carrément dans le rouge" — squarely or completely in debt or in the red. And they were going to do something about it.

I knew that this kind of mobilization had happened before and that a huge mobilization had been rumoured for months. Shawn Katz does an admirable job of tying this unprecedented outpouring of frustration to the many threads of international youth protests against austerity. The youth protests of the previous summer in London, England, in Tahrir Square, les Indignés in France, the huge protests against austerity in Greece, Spain and Portugal, the Occupy Wall Street movement, all echoed around the world. In Québec it was a *grève générale illimitée*, #GGI, and Katz does an impressive job describing his generation and their use of social media to bring people together.

At one of the big daytime marches, I walked through the downtown park known as Dominion Square. It was still early in the spring, and there were bulbs just sprouting in the recently thawed flower beds. The marchers spontaneously divided and streamed around the gardens to avoid trampling the new plants. Not one was crushed. These were young people who understood the importance of public parks. Their teachers would have been proud.

Then came the repressive provincial and municipal rules forbidding demonstrations.

So civil society responded, in sympathy with the students and against the political class. In the evenings at eight o'clock my neighbours and I and thousands of Quebecers started nightly street marches by banging pots and pans — often with ecstatic children, who thought this was the greatest party ever — on their porches and balconies and in the streets, echoing the "*cacerolazo*" protests against Augusto Pinochet's junta in Chile. Pot banging went on in neighbourhoods across Montréal and over time in towns and cities across Québec.

It was a festival of protest. The École de la montagne rouge, of the design department at the Université du Québec à Montréal (UQÀM), made posters that are memorable in their simplicity. Their spokespeople were incredibly articulate young women and men. I loved the college professor who called himself Anarchopanda, dressed in a plush black and white panda suit, hugging demonstrators and even the odd police officer. They used non-sexist and egalitarian language. One day in the metro I saw students lining the platform, wearing red and raising red squares so that commuters saw a long wall of red as they pulled out of the station. It was as if a gag had been removed, and another more colourful and real world was being allowed to take shape.

Like Shawn Katz and many others I was stunned by the virulence with which the police reacted, the knee-jerk opposition to the protests from the media and the stupidity of the City of Montréal's bylaw prohibiting marching. Some damage was done to property, some store windows were smashed, but far fewer than when avid hockey fans of the Montréal Canadiens take to the streets when their beloved hockey franchise wins the Stanley Cup.

According to the report *Repression, Discrimination and Québec's 2012 Student Strike*, the police arrested 3,509 people between February 16 and September 3, 2012. The report is based on the accounts of 274 witnesses and testifies to numerous instances of police brutality. As a friend said, "What kind of society turns on its children in such a brutal way?"

As Katz lays out here, the answer is easy — an increasingly neoliberal corporate society. He explains that this is the reason that so many of his generation are staying away in droves from the ballot box, and many are using other forms of political activism to make their point.

Shawn Katz focuses in on how neoliberalism is breaking the promise of access to college and university that was made to Québec youth in the 1960s. Universities and colleges are now top-heavy with administrators and executives, with a growing real estate portfolio of buildings. The best metaphor for this is the "Îlot Voyageur," a $200 million boondoggle of a building built over the Voyageur Bus Terminal in downtown Montréal. At the time of writing it is still standing empty after ten years, proof of the profligacy of the administrators of the Université du Québec à Montréal (UQÀM).

The spring of 2012 in Québec was a revelation to Quebecers, Canadians and the world. Support for this movement against tuition fee increases and against the Québec version of neoliberalism came from around the world. In June of 2012, 150 Greek academics sent a letter of support to the student movement of Québec. It read:

> Message of solidarity of the Greek academic community to the students in struggle in Quebec
>
> We, academics in the Greek universities, express our solidarity to the extraordinary student mobilization in Quebec: the longest and largest student strike in the history of North America, which is now evolving into one of the most powerful anti-austerity campaigns in the world.
>
> The Greek academic community is watching, in indignation but also in hope, the struggle of Quebec's students to block the tuition increases and to resist an unprecedented neoliberal attack on social welfare.

It was signed by well-known Greek academics, some of whom are now in power with the newly elected left coalition Syriza.

The student protesters planted red maple saplings on the flank of Mount Royal Park, tying them neatly to red stakes that read Printemps érable. They reforested a bare expanse on the side of Mount Royal with maples that turn bright crimson in the fall. For months the saplings flourished. Some of us even weeded the foot of the plants when walking on the mountain.

Vive le Printemps érable et le désir insatiable de justice sociale.

Anne Lagacé Dowson
Montréal, 2015

INTRODUCTION

The Fight of a Generation

The Québec youth revolt in the spring of 2012 exploded from out of a heavy haze, releasing passions that threw the headlines into the homes and cafés of the province with a force unfelt since our near brush with independence in 1995. The nightly helicopters that hovered overhead and clashes in the streets between youth and riot squads became the invitation to caustic debates that split society in two once more; yet instead of a pitched dispute over Québec's national destiny, here the two sides — pro- and anti-*carrés rouges* (for the red square that emerged as the symbol of the movement and its adherents) — were locked in battle over the collective inheritance that one generation would leave to the next. From a student strike that encompassed at its peak nearly three quarters of Québec's post-secondary population, all records were swept aside as hundreds of thousands filled Montréal's streets month after month, daily marches raged on past one hundred days, and the province's social media generation rose up to launch the largest mass mobilization Canada had ever seen. Something broke, and had broken free.

This was no mere struggle over fees, but a social war of magnitudes. The mobilization, much as countless other student strikes in Québec's history, was launched to oppose a $1,625-a-year tuition increase and defend the Quiet Revolution's democratic legacy from the austerity drive of the governing Liberals. But the era of the One Percent is no ordinary time. The unprecedented wave of repression deployed by the establishment to crush the student movement shone a light on this moment at the apex of the élite's power and laid bare the truly historic stakes at play. Over decades, the commercialist revolution of the ruling classes had slowly whittled away the collectivist foundations of Québec society. And here as elsewhere, wealth and power were concentrated in the hands of a homogenous minority that sees citizens and resources as capital in an economy geared toward corporate enrichment. Yet communitarian principles nonetheless remained deeply engrained in Québec's national psyche and acted as a buffer against the dismantling of the commons. The Liberals were determined to break this resistance and usher in a market society where money would be the measure of one's social and democratic rights. The youth were determined to grow this resistance and rescue their fading inheritance from the clutches of an insular and power-hungry élite. In 2012 the two worlds collided, as Charest's bold push to complete the neoliberals' "cultural revolution" unleashed the simmering rage of a generation and sparked a seminal battle for the soul, and future, of a nation.

The tuition hike, as supported by the older generations, was a central plank in the capitalist class's broader campaign to entrench user-pay principles as the pillars of a new commercialist utopia. But the conversation in Québec is not the same as in the rest of North America. Here, the ideal of public education has been deeply embedded since the Quiet Revolution of the 1960s, when the tuition freeze was instituted as a short-term compromise on the path to free university education. The education system born of those transformative years was the bedrock on which the reformers' vision of a just society rested and the avenue to expanding equality which would propel the newly awakened Québécois nation into the democratic age. Since its birth, the student movement has assumed the mantle of defending this humanist vision of education, viewed as the heart of the social-democratic model that has made Québec the most egalitarian society on the continent.[1]

For the quiet counter-revolutionaries of the modern-day Liberal Party, education was just as central to the alternate social structure they sought to erect. Universities aligned closely with the market's signals and principles would be the engine of their own project of social engineering: to chisel away at the collectivist culture of free public services and thereby cut loose the élites from their social bonds. From the sixties on, the idea that the rich should contribute their fair share to the funding of services stood at the core of an idea of democracy that placed greater equality as its foundation. But for over two decades, the globalized élites have waged a relentless and successful campaign to turn back the clock. Gradually, the burden has been shifted down the ladder to the poorer rungs, as governments slashed taxes for the rich and corporations and gutted the social programs that help equalize living standards. Here as across the world, skyrocketing inequalities were the obvious outcome, as the upper classes restored their power and tightened their grip over the ruling parties, the economy and the cultural and communications channels that frame public debate. With the business élites smiling behind him, Premier Jean Charest invoked the void left in the public purse by these billions in tax cuts to pursue the wholesale commodification of public services. The Liberals encountered massive public opposition, which stifled their furthest ambitions — at first. But in the wake of the 2008 economic crisis, the opportunity Charest long sought had arrived, and he swiftly invoked the false imperative of austerity to launch the boldest offensive yet.

Two centuries collide

Québec's powerful student movement is one of the last remnants of a time when social forces could mobilize the masses to sway governments. Charest knew it well. In 2011 the Liberals locked the students in their crosshairs and declared the war open. But the shrewd and battle-hardened politician was a twentieth-century creature and soon found he had monumentally misjudged the scale of the fight on his hands. Brutalized daily in the streets by the police forces of the capitalist establishment and ridiculed in their press, Québec's social media generation deployed its mastery of contemporary communications tools to stand its ground against repression and harness the passions of hundreds of thousands to defeat a premier who had used up his nine political lives.

Charest greatly underestimated the tenacity of his young opponents, for he could not come near to grasping the depths of what motivated their struggle. Indeed, he could barely hear them when they spoke. For this rising generation — the network generation — does not speak the governing cohort's language of hierarchies, where order and authority are supposed to take precedence over social, democratic and environmental legitimacy. Witnesses to the abominable failure of our bought-and-sold politicians to safeguard the long-term common good, they do not speak the language of representative and electoral democracy either, which in Québec was supposed to legitimate the autocratic aggressions of a corrupt and paternalist government against its own youth. Opinion polls throughout the spring showed a slight and fluctuating majority of the electorate backing the tuition hike. But beneath the surface, a far more significant clash was unfolding that altered the moral lines of the debate: Society was sharply polarized along generational lines. Overwhelming majorities of the under-thirties opposed the government's push to commercialize education by margins that frequently surpassed two thirds, while often the exact inverse proportion of those aged over fifty-five supported it.[2] Two generations had come face to face, but only one would have to live with the results of today's actions. And they weren't backing down.

Perhaps most fatefully, Charest had failed to take stock of the global moment in which he launched his attack. In this new social media age, Québec's youth are plugged into a planetary conversation where one chapter follows invariably from the last. In the wake of the Indignados and Occupy Wall Street, of the students of Chile and of Britain — all movements powered by the rising generation and its new media — the dots were strung together as the historical narrative crystallized: Around the world, the hijacking of our democracies by global economic and financial élites has sabotaged our collective capacity to look after the common and long-term good, to the point of even imperilling human civilization on this planet. The globalized establishment has fastened and rationalized an economic edifice that serves their short-term financial interests, even while its demands run against the immoveable realities of all that allows the human organism to flourish on Earth. Yet denying even the socially constructed nature of such artificial systems, they have deployed their ubiquitous structures of influence and control to erase the very notion of alternative possibilities.

And they were largely successful — until the Internet generation came of age and began building its own networked and people-powered structures to circumvent their hegemony and start to change the conversation. Raised in an age where the catastrophic impacts of corporate capitalism have become increasingly undeniable — and increasingly immediate — this generation is everywhere rising up and refusing the legitimation discourses that have enabled our élites to amass a degree of wealth and power unlike anything the world has ever known. In this "we the people" moment of the twenty-first century, the forces who speak on behalf of the future are everywhere sitting restless, awaiting the spark that may channel the torrents of unrest and at last start to beat back the neoliberal tide.

In Québec, Jean Charest's audacious bid to strike a final coup in normalizing the wrecking-ball of austerity started the generational war, bringing to bear the threat of more financial debt and economic vassalage to add to the untold ecological debt already hanging over the heads of youth. Brought to the barricades, Québec's students cried betrayal at the hands of the cohort of the Quiet Revolution, which had basked in the comforts of cheap education, generous social programs and a glowing future and was now poisoning the well before the generations to come could have their turn to drink. Thus exploited and dehumanized by a commercialist class that reduced them to spokes in the wheels of their destructive economy, the youth of Québec rose up to channel a new humanism where the holistic and long-term health of the many may predominate over the monetary interests of the few. After Madrid, New York, Santiago and elsewhere, Montréal had become a battleground in the global fight of our times.

The network generation comes of age

As the spring of 2012 unfolded, the strange force of the Printemps érable ("Maple Spring") — the creative moniker launched by design students in a wink to the Arab Spring, or in French, Printemps arabe — had raised the curtain on a generation once in the cyber-shadows and suddenly in the streets. The Coalition large de l'Association pour une solidarité syndicale étudiante, known by its charged and timely acronym as the CLASSE, took up the torch of the 99 percent to confront the power of the capitalist élites and declare that *Le combat est avenir* — the future is our fight, and the battle has just begun.[3] The majority of Québec's college and university students has long been affiliated with two old federations, the Fédération étudiante collégiale du Québec (FECQ) and Fédération étudiante universitaire du Québec (FEUQ), both closely aligned with the political establishment. But 2012 was the year these top-down and élite-based creatures of the corporate age were confronted by a new tide rising in force. For try as hard as the political and media establishments did to occult the dwindling clout of the federations at the students' ground level, the winds blew in one direction — and they were propelling the CLASSE's sails forward at full speed.

In the spring of 2012 we saw the vanguardist association's vision of a horizontal and grassroots democracy become the template for Québec's first twenty-first-century mass mobilization, as the *carrés rouges* engulfed the daily landscape in a scattershot explosion that mirrored the leaderless revolts of the year before. Spectacular eruptions of art and protest pierced through the lethargy of the capitalist routine to reignite Québec's political imaginary, as the boundless creativity of Montréal's youth was unleashed to cast the Québécois metropolis as the theatre for a revolutionary movement to re-envisage the world. In 2012, the students of Québec took on the CLASSE's aspirations as their own: whether seen in the audacious dreams of justice inscribed on the placards held high in the streets; in the tenacity with which they held firm against six months of derision, brutality and contempt; or in the sixty thousand members of the FEUQ and FECQ who rallied to the CLASSE's struggle against austerity and invested its structures of direct democracy to elevate the Coalition into the undisputed engine of a generational revolt. From their values and discourses to their models of communication and organization, the youth of Québec had arisen to carry forth the paradigm of a new age, where the old top-down designs of order and authority make way for a world of networked and autonomous communities, open structures of governance and grassroots empowerment.

The students of Québec followed no orders and yet did readily lend their attention to the formidable figures that provided the moral leadership to mobilize the masses. As the media struggled to tie faces to a social media-era revolt, the presidents of the FEUQ and FECQ, Martine Desjardins and Léo Bureau-Blouin, were thrust into the glare of the spotlights along with the CLASSE's spokespersons, Gabriel Nadeau-Dubois and Jeanette Reynolds (and later a third, Camille Robert). And tellingly, it was the one with the *least* decisional authority — none — who wielded the greatest influence: With his uncommon force of character and razor-sharp eloquence before the cameras, the twenty one-year-old "GND" was propelled into the reluctant role of the movement's natural "leader," as his incisive challenges to the capitalist order drew both the ire and admiration of citizens across the province.

Over the course of that extraordinary spring, Québec bore witness to a visionary youth that had laid the foundations for a bright new future in incubation — and recovered its capacity to be the force that once propelled society forward. For indeed, after decades of somnolence ushered in by the consumerist society of the élites, the students accomplished what was thought nothing short of the impossible: They had shaken society awake. There were the teachers, artists, economists, actors, doctors, musicians, parents, authors, nurses, environmentalists, lawyers, even seniors — all that stood incredulous before the force of the spring awakening surging before their eyes. Stirred to life by the CLASSE's timely appeals to revive the collective consciousness, the tumultuous seas of Québec's progressive social forces arose to rally behind the youth and leap into the breach in the neoliberals' defences.

The student strike had become the Printemps érable and the mother of such unforgettable moments that will form a generation for life. Their memories will resonate with the love of all they fought for over those six charged and trying months, but just as viscerally, with refusal of all that they fought so ardently against. Like the paternalism of power that refused all dialogue and tried to crush a generation's resistance with the unbound madness of police brutality. Like the hatred and ridicule of an attack dog press whose petty lies and venom aimed to bully an awakened youth back into submission. Or like the historic excess of hubris signed by a premier named Jean Charest, whose emergency law sought to legislate the destruction of the student movement and suppress the democratic rights of all citizens in the name of removing an unruly opposition from his path.

Yet for every shiver of terror down the spine, there were the innumerable jaws dropped in awe at the indomitable spirit of a people that rose to answer the call of history. And of all the moments etched into our hearts, few can have settled any deeper than the image of the proud and irreverent Québécois, who when faced with a noose strung tight around the neck of their democracy, chose to answer back to the power: *casseroles*. For there on the balconies and streets of the province, and in beautiful Montréal, irrepressibly alive and free, the smiles of neighbours and strangers met as society peeked out from its commercial cocoon. And it was there, as the pots and pans of the people's resistance echoed loudly through the nights, that the jubilant sounds of a society springing to life announced the end of a long winter. Finally, the sap of the Printemps érable had risen up from the roots and trickled down from the balconies of the province to leave the streets awash in the resin of hope reborn.

Dreamers in the wings

The remarkable story of the Printemps érable will doubtless inspire for years to come. Born as a student strike like so many others the province has known, it transformed into a historic mobilization that signalled the arrival of the social media century to Québec and the emergence of a new generation, and a new world, waiting impatiently in the wings. Those who lived through it can never forget the renewed civic imaginary signed by the young *carrés rouges*, whose spectacular harnessing of symbolism and imagery marked a creative effervescence — and a democratic awakening — that at times seemed fuelled by hope and heart alone. For months on end, a generation marched en masse through the streets of Montréal, night upon night for over one hundred days and at times by the hundreds of thousands, in defiance of the government, in defiance of brutal repression, and finally, in defiance of the law itself.

If Québec indeed has a history of transformative social crises, then the spring of 2012 may prove the launching point for a once-in-a-generation renewal of its collective values and aspirations. For the leaders of tomorrow, the streets and student assemblies became the living classrooms for a visceral immersion in the politics of civic action and debate, in the private and class interests behind contemporary power, and in its violent defence absorbed in state-inflicted bruises that never quite seem to heal. Through it all a generation in Québec has been indelibly marked, and the lessons learned in those uncommonly heated days of spring may slowly start to lay the foundations for a future worth inheriting.

PART ONE

THE LONG ROAD TO REVOLT

KEEPERS OF THE COMMONS
The Québec Student Movement Through Time

"If the Parent Report remains an essential reference for Québec's social evolution, it is that it incarnated a double aspiration of its era: that of Québec's entry into modernity, and that of the democratization of Québec society."[1]

— Guy Rocher, sociologist and co-author of the report
(my translation)

From its origins, the trajectory of the student movement has evolved in intimate relation with the ebb and flow of Québec's broader social and political currents. The story of the Printemps érable is thus a fascinating and portentous tale, in that it begins, much like it ends, with an emblem of the contemporary age: the Coalition large de l'ASSÉ, or CLASSE. Of this there can be little doubt. It was the robustly democratic and anti-austerity visions of the ASSÉ's extended body, formed to quickly take in new members for the limited time of the mobilization, that rallied and roused the masses — both within the student population and, more crucially perhaps, across wider society. And without them, it is likely the strike would have remained just a strike and that the Printemps érable may never have been. In light of Québec's history, the CLASSE's rise in 2012 is therefore a potent harbinger, though one hidden behind the headlines.

Sadly, those relying on the mainstream media for information were presented a picture quite on its head. With little surprise, the dominant frame of the old media echoed the government's attempts to marginalize the CLASSE as an unreasonable and even violent fringe, while their "moderate" (pro-business) counterparts, the FEUQ and FECQ, were elevated into media darlings. Yet history provides a vigorous call to order: for indeed if the ASSÉ is to be deemed radical by the standards of the day, then it is a statement only of how far the centre has shifted rightward over the decades of corporate ascendance. In light of the student movement's past, in fact, the ASSÉ emerges as the standard-bearer of what was the movement's sole or dominant current from its birth in the sixties until 1990, when it was led by many central figures of the province's future political establishment. It was the arrival of the 1990s that marked the end of one hegemony in the student movement and the beginning of another: The newly founded FEUQ and FECQ rose to prominence with a hierarchical approach geared toward lobbying and negotiations with the government, signalling a rupture with the movement's grassroots traditions, which directly paralleled the global turn toward corporate empowerment and the resultant weakening of social forces that hit Québec's labour and student movements with equal force.

The first awakening:
The Parent Report and the foundation of modern Québec

Québec's student movement was born of the Quiet Revolution of the 1960s, a period of radical social and political change that forged the structures of the modern Québec state.[2] The sweeping reforms reverberated deep into the very bedrock of society, as the new welfare state arose to replace the Catholic Church at the centre of French-Canadian life and usher in a new *Québécois* identity anchored to the province's territory, language and institutions. Everything from the economy to family relations and social life were swept up in the upheaval wrought by the accelerated modernizations, with few areas affected as dramatically as the people's religious life. Citizens deserted the Church en masse, with regular (twice a month) attendance plummeting from 85 percent to 46 percent from 1965 to 1975, and to 38 percent in 1985 to continue falling thereafter.[3] Entering to fill the void was the state, which became the new guarantor of Quebecers' national and cultural life.[4] The French term "*l'État-providence*" perhaps never seemed so apt as when describing the emerging Québec of the sixties and seventies.

At the time Jean Lesage's Liberals rose to office in 1960 to end the sixteen-year reign of "*le Chef*" Maurice Duplessis's Union Nationale, Canada's French-speaking province was economically and culturally backwards and dominated by traditional conservative values. The Catholic francophone majority faced a double subjugation, both by the Church, which dominated all facets of social existence, and by a wealthy élite in the form of the Protestant anglophone business establishment.[5] The iron rule of Duplessis, built on conservative ideology, French-Canadian nationalism and unbridled capitalism (this was Québec's time to launch into a communist-hunt[6]) was erected largely on his shrewd authoritarianism and institutionalized patronage.[7] Under Duplessis, the clergy was left full reign over the social sphere, controlling both health care and education in exchange for supporting *le Chef*'s unchallenged dominion over the state.[8] Québec society was rampant with inequalities that unfolded largely along sectarian lines. Not only were francophones locked into positions of social and economic inferiority, but Duplessis's radical laissez-faire policies placed control of Québec's development in the hands of foreign corporations who profited increasingly off large-scale exploitation of Québec's vast natural resources.[9] In sum, when the Liberals vowed in the sixties to make Quebecers the "*Maîtres chez nous*" (masters in our own house), it was painfully clear that at the time, they were anything but.

There are good reasons why this period is today termed La grande noirceur, or the Great Darkness: In pre-Quiet Revolution Québec, the six existing universities were accessible only to the narrow élite, which excluded virtually the entire French-speaking majority. On the eve of Jean Lesage's election in 1960, only three percent of francophones aged twenty to twenty-four gained access to university, compared to eleven percent of English-speakers in the same age group.[10] Yet when we look at educational attainment as a whole, it's understandable that so few ever got near the university's gates: With one of the highest dropout rates in the country, half of Quebecers abandoned their studies before reaching the age of fifteen, and only 13 percent of French-speakers and 36 percent of anglophones finished Grade 11.[11] That, moreover, was an improvement over the past: Of those aged over twenty-five in 1962, 54 percent never even finished primary school.[12] It's almost a euphemism to conclude that in pre-Quiet Revolution Québec, education was far from a social value but rather a luxury that concerned only the upper crust.

Under the bold reformist government of the Liberals, new institutions were created that placed the levers of Québec's development in the hands of the collective through its primary, and in Lesage's view, "only effective" instrument, the state.[13] Control over health care, education and social welfare was reclaimed by the government (the latter had been left to charitable organizations), as the Church was ejected from its position of institutionalized power.[14] On society's ground level, the expansion and democratization of education, begun in the late sixties, would become the primary avenue to the social and economic emancipation of the Québécois people, who would reclaim control of their destiny from the élites to propel Québec at last into the modern age.[15] The Liberal government thus made educational reform an immediate priority, rendering education obligatory until age sixteen in 1961 and making all textbooks free of charge. The true social revolution was pending, however, after the Lesage Liberals created a Royal Commission to design a new model for public education, and with it, lay the ground for a new Québec that was soon to emerge from its cocoon.

Between 1963 and 1966, the Parent Commission produced a massive five-volume report that became the bedrock of the new educational system and a foundational document of a new Québécois democracy where wealth, class and linguistic community would no longer be the measure of one's citizenship. "Education," proclaimed the Commission, "is, like health, an essential social service, as indispensable for the collective as it is for the individual."[16] With education redefined as a social right, equality of access became the central concern and was to be sought through financial aid, free education and the construction of more schools.[17] "The collectivity will have to contribute ever greater resources to universities, but will expect in return that these resources be used as efficiently as possible, and in the interests of all," said the Commission.[18] The Liberals embraced the report and moved swiftly to implement many recommendations, establishing the Ministère de l'éducation and Conseil supérieur de l'éducation in 1964, secularizing and standardizing the curriculum and introducing a loans and bursaries program for students in need. In 1967 the Liberals created the Collèges d'enseignement général et professionnel (CEGEPs), a unique system of free institutions that act both as intermediaries between high school and university and as schools for vocational training. Many more reforms were on the horizon but were left in uncertain limbo following the Liberals' surprise defeat in 1966 — until, that is, the student movement launched into the fray near the end of the decade.

Guardians of the flame:
The birth of the student movement

In this new Québec where education was to be the catalyst for society's democratization, students became the new nation-builders and the guardians of the Quiet Revolution's ideals. The student movement was born to channel this vision of a universal education in the service of the social, intellectual and cultural development of the people. Finding inspiration in the well-rooted traditions of France's student movement, Québec's students in the sixties slowly forged structures, an identity and a movement in their image.

In 1961, future Parti Québécois premier Bernard Landry (2001–2003) was the president of the Université de Montréal's student union, the Association générale des étudiants de l'Université de Montréal (AGEUDEM). Under him, the AGEUDEM adapted the French students' *Charte de Grenoble* to craft the *Charte de l'étudiant universitaire,* which would effectively lay the movement's orientation for the next three decades.[19] The founding conception of the student as "a young intellectual worker" voiced an understanding of the student's rights and duties to the collective and affirmed the inherent value of her or his intellectual contributions to society.[20] The formulation would prove instrumental to the movement's evolution: From its origins, Québec's student movement has been defined by its close relation to Québécois *syndicalisme,* with its structures, strategies and values modelled on the province's traditionally powerful labour union movement.[21]

The move at UdeM quickly inspired emulation. Student associations were founded across the province, leading to the creation of the first national association in 1963, known as the Union générale des étudiants du Québec (UGEQ), which soon counted associations representing 55,000 members.[22] Founded upon mass mobilization strategies and the socialist-humanist philosophy of the *Charte de l'étudiant,*[23] the UGEQ emerged in the 1960s as a vital, active and coherent political actor that supported worker struggles, opposed the war in Vietnam and strove to inform, engage and mobilize the student base.[24] In 1968, under a brief and final return to Unioniste rule in the province, the UGEQ launched Québec's first ever general student strike piloted by its combative new leaders. And among them, we find some familiar names: Gilles Duceppe, future leader of the Bloc Québécois, in the company of future Parti Québécois (PQ) cabinet ministers Claude Charron and Louise Harel.[25]

The strike was launched to obtain fuller implementation of the Parent Report's recommendations, which had been stalled when the Liberals were defeated in 1966 despite having won the popular vote by just over 6 percent.[26] Their demands included greater accessibility of education, a second French-language university in Montréal (which then counted three anglophone institutions) and the democratization of institutions and pedagogy by allowing students and professors to take part in university governance.[27] The students launched campus occupations that paralyzed fifteen of the twenty-three newly created CEGEPs. The government was quick to respond. It reformed the loans and bursaries program, froze tuition levels at $543 and founded the Université du Québec network with its Montréal campus, the Université du Québec à Montréal (UQÀM).[28]

In sum, the Union Nationale's victory, artificially fabricated by our electoral system, had left Québec with the short-term compromise of a tuition freeze toward the eventual goal of its elimination — to be achieved, in effect, through inflation. The Liberal promise to achieve free education at all levels by 1972 was one of the core victims of their accidental defeat but was not forgotten so soon.[29] In 1976 — the same year Canada ratified the U.N. covenant on social and economic rights, which devoted it to the same goal of free university education[30] — René Lévesque's new Parti Québécois was elected on a vow to fulfill the central promise of the Quiet Revolution. Yet once in power, the PQ failed to deliver.[31]

Although wildly transformative, the strike deeply indebted the UGEQ, as internal quarrels over ideology and its leaders' *dirigisme* tore it apart, and it disbanded immediately after, in 1969.[32] Yet the Québec student movement had come of age, and its principles and orientations seemed secure, if for a while. First without a national organization for years and then under the UGEQ's successor from 1976, the Association nationale des étudiants du Québec (ANEEQ) — which became ANEEQ in 1987 with the addition of "*et étudiantes*" to its name[33] — the collectivist values and grassroots strategies would exert an ideological hegemony over the movement right up until the 1990s.[34] In 1973, 1974 and 1978, both offensive and reactive strike actions were launched to defend the principles of accessibility in the loans and grants system, protect the democratic nature of the educational network from government attempts at centralization and safeguard the Parent Report's aim of free education at all levels.[35] And up until the 1980s, student actions met mostly with great concessions from government on all fronts, with the largest demonstrations averaging no more than 8,000 to 10,000 students in 1968 and 1978.[36]

The lure of the neoliberals:
A schism hits the student movement

The ANE(E)Q was the sole or dominant national association for most of its existence from 1976 to 1994.[37] Yet in 1981 an important new current was born in the Québec student movement when ideological battles caused the ANEQ to splinter. On the left, long-standing and acrimonious struggles between Marxist-Leninists and dissident Trostskyites led the latter to form their own group, the Regroupement pour un véritable syndicat national étudiant du Québec (RVSNEQ), in the belief that the ANEQ was not combative enough.[38] Yet on the opposite flank, an internal working group, the Regroupement des associations étudiantes universitaires (RAEU), separated in 1981 in the belief that the ANEQ was *too* combative (and too leftist) and formed a competing entity to channel a more collaborative and pro-business approach.[39]

The events marked an ideological schism in the movement that echoed the growing influence of neoliberal ideas among the Québec élite.[40] The RAEU, whose new thinking was apparent in its framing of its Conseil des associations as "the equivalent of a Board of Directors of a large business,"[41] was joined in 1982 by its ideological cousin at the CEGEP level, the Fédération des associations étudiantes du Québec (FAECQ).[42] Neither managed to effectively challenge the ANEQ's dominance in the eighties. Their principal contribution, rather, would be to lay the groundwork for their successors who would become two key players in the 2012 student strike, respectively: the Fédération étudiante universitaire du Québec (FEUQ) and Fédération étudiante collégiale du Québec (FECQ).

The shift that took place among student associations in the eighties was mirrored in the labour union movement against the backdrop of the élite's conversion to neoliberalism starting with René Lévesque's PQ government at the beginning of the decade.[43] The Front commun intersyndical in 1982–83 had formed to challenge Lévesque's public sector pay cuts, in a fourth repeat of the massive and successful mobilization by the unions' Front commun in 1972.[44] Yet the inability of the unions to adequately mobilize against government repression in 1982–83 signalled a sharp reversal in fortunes from the decade before and marked the rise of an increasingly hostile political environment for organized labour, which forced a revision in strategy. The growing recourse to lobbying and negotiation at the expense of mass mobilization tactics marked the beginning of a long phase of retreat for the union movement and a period of relative weakness vis-à-vis the state.[45]

In the student movement, this shift, while portended, was delayed by the continued dominance of the ANE(E)Q through the eighties, which still represented the vast majority of students.[46] Yet despite the impending fracturing of the base, the year 1983 signalled an unlikely cornerstone in the growth and strengthening of the movement. That year, the latent synergy between Québec's labour union and student movements was entrenched in law when the Lévesque government adopted Law 32, entitled the *Act respecting the accreditation and financing of students' associations*. Built directly off the 1964 Labour Code, Law 32 allowed for student associations incorporated under the province's *Companies Act* to hold secret ballots and obtain accreditation by the government.[47] The law, unique in the world, established the right of Québec's student associations to mandatory membership dues and to a monopoly of representation, thereby mirroring the Rand formula applied to labour unions.[48]

Despite the ANEQ's objections at the time that it intruded on students' democratic life and autonomy, in retrospect the Act provided an institutionalized backbone to Québec's student movement that proved invaluable to its future successes. As Renaud Poirier St-Pierre and Philippe Ethier of the CLASSE readily acknowledged thirty years on, Law 32 forced educational establishments to recognize, engage with and furnish key resources to student associations and, most crucially, provided them with guaranteed stable funding levied obligatorily by administrations on their behalf. The impacts were on sharp display both before and during the 2012 strike, when the national associations launched prolonged educational tours and rented buses to mobilize citizens across the province: Québec's student associations today enjoy resources that would make any political organization envious, with some local associations even controlling budgets in the hundreds of thousands of dollars.[49] Lévesque's law made Québec's students a force to be reckoned with.

The mass mobilization phase of the student movement was still at its height in the eighties. So much so that when Liberal education minister Claude Ryan announced his intention in 1986 to repudiate party policy and lift the tuition freeze, a general strike launched by the ANEQ swept through forty campuses and lasted two weeks, forcing the government to back down.[50] The turn of events served to discredit the ineffective collaborative and lobbying approach of the RAEU, which disbanded later that year.[51] The FAECQ, for its part, had even backed the tuition increase, resulting in a severe crisis that stripped it of a third of its members by 1987 before it disbanded the following year.[52]

The government, however, was relentless, and the wider social and political context was encroaching fast. In 1988, a Liberal Party congress reversed party policy in favour of lifting the freeze, and a newly emboldened Robert Bourassa government then took the cue to slash grants by $8 million.[53] The ANEEQ, however, was still ridden by debt and internal divisions from the last struggle and found itself unable to effectively mobilize an exhausted base in the fall of 1988. In September of 1989, Bourassa was re-elected with nearly 50 percent of the vote.[54] With the firm backing of business leaders and university presidents in the Conseil du patronat and Conférence des recteurs et des principaux des universités (CREPUQ), the government announced a more than doubling of tuition fees in the middle of the winter exam period that year.[55] A second attempt at mobilizing opposition, this time in a joint campaign between the ANEEQ and the new Fédération des étudiants et étudiantes du Québec (FEEQ, later renamed the FEUQ), again failed to garner enough strike mandates to launch a contestation, and fees were unfrozen as of fall 1990.[56] The stunning sequence of defeats sent the ANEEQ reeling, and internecine struggles intensified as it steadily shed members leading up to its dissolution in 1994.[57]

From the grassroots to the backrooms of power: The movement becomes a lobby

Tuition levels rose to $1,668 by 1994, representing an overall increase of more than 300 percent. Yet with the ANEEQ on the verge of collapse, the field was open for a new hegemony to emerge that would see the approach known as *concertation* cemented in the Québec student landscape. In 1989, the FEEQ rose to immediate prominence upon its founding by associations representing 100,000 students, and the formation of the FECQ, its ideological sibling at the CEGEP level, followed one year later.[58] The beginning of the nineties thus marked a sharp turning point in the history of the Québec student movement and a new era of collaboration — some might say co-optation — between student representatives and the state.[59]

In structure and values, the new student federations, following in the footsteps of the RAEU and FAECQ, broke dramatically with the movement's historic orientations. Where the ANE(E)Q and UGEQ always aimed to engage and mobilize their grassroots into pressuring the government from below (the strategy known as building a "*rapport de force*"), the new federations instead sought collaboration with the state, which necessitated a rapprochement with government officials.[60] The federations jettisoned the cohesive social vision on which the movement was founded and embraced instead a corporatist approach that redefined their role as interest groups in the service of their dues-paying members. In the place of mass education and engagement, they prioritized lobbying and participation in government talks, while their structures marked a turn toward élite-based governance, with greater concentration of power with paid executives, and minimal power of oversight by the student assemblies.[61] Their general assemblies, held once a year, were now tasked only with setting "orientations" and holding executives to account in annual elections.[62] The philosophy of hierarchical individualism that justified the actions of the neoliberal reformers, from Margaret Thatcher to Robert Bourassa, had finally captured the student base.

These two abrupt departures, namely the turn to lobbying and the closing up of their democratic structures, are intimately linked. As political scientist Benoît Lacoursière explains, the shift by student associations (as well as by labour unions) toward collaboration and negotiation at the expense of mass mobilization encourages the professionalization of executives and a resulting detachment from the base, which has fewer means to hold their representatives to account. To be an effective negotiator and lobbier, after all, one should not only have a solid grasp of complex issues and enjoy constructive contacts within the government; more importantly, one must also be empowered to make decisions. It's within this soil that an élitist and top-down culture can take root and flourish, and produces the disempowerment and disengagement of the base that renders mobilization more difficult when the need arises, which only perpetuates the cycle in turn.[63]

We can see the effects of the move toward interest group politics in the stances adopted by the federations over time. Their positions, far from embodying any set of overarching principles, instead reveal a startling lack of coherence and at times a direct conflict with the interests of like-minded organizations. Among their most memorable over time, we find the FEUQ's early promotion of a post-graduate tax (dropped in the mid 1990s),[64] the FEUQ and FECQ's joint position (also until the mid 1990s) in favour of a "New Partnership" that would have seen businesses funding *more* of education[65] — less than a decade later, the FEUQ would declare it was terribly concerned by the rise of private funding[66] — and even the questioning of free public health care by the FECQ in 1992.[67] The track record of these organizations, far from revealing a capacity for serious social and political reflection, speaks to a lobby in the service of its members' narrow interests and evolving whims. The result, in pitting their members against erstwhile allies across society, can only serve to undermine their relevance to public debate and ultimately prove self-defeating in the effort to advance social progress. Indeed, in prioritizing the good of their members over that of the collective, they even help perpetuate the same "me" society that lies at the root of the prolonged attack on educational accessibility.

From 1995 to 2000, the Mouvement pour le droit à l'éducation (MDE) sought to rekindle the flame of mass mobilization politics but never managed to grow beyond 25,000 members.[68] Admittedly, the times were still hard for social movements. Yet despite this, an MDE-led strike in 1996 affected twenty campuses and drew 20,000 students into the streets, forcing PQ education minister Pauline Marois (later premier) to back down from plans to raise tuition another 30 percent. Soon after, however, a failed offensive strike action in 1999 doomed the MDE to persistent infighting that led to its demise the following year.

Children of the twenty-first century: The birth of the ASSÉ

The collectivist current of the student movement was never abandoned for long, and the Association pour une solidarité syndicale étudiante (ASSÉ), open to both CEGEP and university associations, emerged on the scene in 2001 to fill the void left by the MDE's collapse.[69] The ASSÉ is in many ways the carrier of the UGEQ/ ANE(E)Q torch that dominated the movement for most of its history. Upon their creation, they immediately took on the movement's historical mantle by channelling a counterattack against the neoliberal reforms that undermined the Quiet Revolution's legacy. Yet they also represented an important and timely innovation. In 2012, the avant-gardist nature of the CLASSE served to confound the traditional media and political establishments, who proved incapable of adapting to new democratic structures that eschewed conventional modes of top-down control. Born of the twenty-first-century alter-globalization movement, the ASSÉ's structures and discourse mirrored the movement's commitment to direct democracy by embracing the World Social Forum's principles of pluralism, horizontalism and networked autonomy.[70]

The ASSÉ's models of organization are thus designed to stretch outward rather than downward and to minimize distinctions between elected officials and volunteers as much as possible. Frequent training and educational camps are held to raise awareness and expand the mobilizational capacities of the grassroots. And a new era of transparency and openness for the student movement was inaugurated to further this goal, for instance by making exhaustive information available to the public on its website. On the level of authority, the contrasts are even starker. All members of the executive are unpaid and work together as secretaries on an equal footing, while co-spokespersons — always plural (and gender-diverse) — replaced the posts of president proper to the student federations. The congress, which gathers four to five times a year in the place of the federations' annual assemblies, is the ASSÉ's sovereign power and final authority on all issues, with full powers to sanction or remove elected officials at all times.[71] Concretely, this means that its spokespersons enjoy extremely limited latitude to make decisions that do not reflect the motions adopted by the congress. The impacts of this model were sharply exhibited during the student strike, when the CLASSE's spokespersons were often accused of not exerting enough "leadership" over their base. What the twentieth-century media and political institutions were ill-equipped to grasp, however, was that this is precisely the point. In sum, whereas the UGEQ and ANE(E)Q had been plagued by recurrent accusations of *dirigisme*, and where the FEUQ and FECQ were more "effective" interlocutors owing expressly to their lack of accountability to the base, the ASSÉ, by contrast, promised a new era of student democracy fit for the twenty-first century.

The ASSÉ reaffirmed the historical positions of the student movement in favour of free education at all levels, democratic institutions and pedagogy and a civic and humanist education centred on the ideals of the *Charte de Grenoble*.[72] The push to engage and mobilize the grassroots was renewed and deepened with horizontal and participatory structures that gave their involvement fuller meaning. And quite crucially, the ASSÉ's broader and more coherent social perspective, in contrast to the interest-group corporatism of the federations, sought to sow networks of solidarity with civil society organizations in a bid to forge coalitions to work toward wider social progress.

Carré rouge 2005: Signs of a resurgence

In 2003, the Charest government announced a reform of financial aid, which converted $103 million of grants into loans, increased the maximum debt load allowed and assigned a large part of the system's management to the major banks, who earn all the money paid in interest fees.[73] All national student associations contested the move, and the action set off the first large-scale student strike since 1996, ultimately reaching 190,000 students across Québec.[74] Aiming for minimal disturbances, the student federations sought to impose pressure on the government through a small number of large demonstrations, which included a massive rally on March 16 that drew a (then) record crowd estimated at 100,000 citizens.[75] Their messaging targeted the broad swath of public opinion through conventional mass media, and they engaged in face-to-face negotiations with the government while the FEUQ launched a lobbying campaign aimed at backbench government members of the National Assembly (MNAs).[76] By contrast, the ASSÉ followed the alter-globalization movement's escalation of tactics model and launched a series of actions leading toward a general strike.[77] A demonstration was called for November 2004 and was followed by frequent small-scale actions that included demonstrations, symbolic protests, direct action and economic disturbances.[78] Arguments differed as much as tactics, with the FEUQ and FECQ limiting their demands to the retroactive reinstatement of the grants, while the ASSÉ objected completely to the system's broad commercialization.[79]

The 2005 strike also saw important innovations, particularly on the part of the ASSÉ. Notably, it signalled the first time the FEUQ had officially backed a strike at all, which some student activists attribute to the rival pressures arising from the ASSÉ's entry onto the scene.[80] It was the first time the ASSÉ formed a provisional coalition to grow and coordinate a strike, which they called the Coalition de l'Association pour une solidarité syndicale étudiante élargie (CASSÉÉ) and opened to all local associations, whether unaffiliated or members of the federations, who shared the organization's goals.[81] The red felt square made its first appearance as the emblem of the student struggle. The CASSÉÉ had recovered it from 2004, when the Collectif pour un Québec sans pauvreté first donned the symbol to protest cuts to social aid.[82] Its origin and appropriation by the CASSÉÉ thus allows us a further glimpse into the contrast between them and the federations. During the 2005 strike, the government cut another $150 million from social assistance. The CASSÉÉ charged to the defence of groups who protested the move, while the federations maintained their silence. In their world, it didn't concern their members.[83]

The Charest government had its own strategic innovations aimed at heavily exploiting the divisions between the national student associations. The CASSÉÉ was thus barred from the negotiating table on the pretext that they refused to condemn violence — which in the government's view, included occupations (a regular tactic of the student movement since 1968), graffiti and even displaced furniture.[84] Playing the government's game, the student federations arrived at an entente with the government, which converted $70 million of loans into grants for 2005–2006 and reinstituted the total $103 million for the four years after — yet due only to a fresh transfer from the federal government's Millenium Scholarships Fund, which had been at the centre of a dispute between the two levels of government.[85] The remainder of the reforms, however, including the administration of a large part of the financial aid system by the banks, was entirely upheld.[86] The ASSÉ bitterly accused the FEUQ of betrayal, but they weren't the only ones. The FEUQ's local assemblies delivered a sharp rebuke to the executive that shone an unflattering light on the widening disconnect between their leadership and the base. In assembly votes held *after* the agreement had been signed, nearly two thirds of the FEUQ's members voted symbolically to reject the entente, yet concurrently failed to reaffirm the strike mandates.[87] Against the noise of recriminations on all sides, the 2005 strike had come to an anti-climatic end.[88]

Its failures aside, however, in retrospect the 2005 mobilization bore signs of an imminent resurgence brewing among Québec's long-docile student movement. For with the sober passing of time, the student strike stands out as the largest and at seven weeks, the longest in Québec's history at the time and drew the largest crowd, prior to 2012, for the demonstration on March 16.[89] Yet the Liberals, coasting on their post-victory high, clearly failed to take note and instead forged ahead in a fresh provocation of students two years later. In 2007, the Charest government was re-elected with just under a third of the popular vote and, backed by the usual alliance of business leaders and university presidents, swiftly made good on an election promise to increase tuition by $500 over five years.[90] The student base, however, was too exhausted and divided amongst itself to mount an effective opposition.[91] The time-tested strategy used so crudely by Bourassa had allowed Charest to take up where his predecessor had left off.

Harbingers of change:
As goes the student movement ...

From its birth at the summit of a historic social and democratic effervescence, the fundamental role and raison d'être of the Québec student movement has been to defend education as an engine for democratizing society and advancing social progress. And whenever it has succeeded in engaging and mobilizing enough students into the streets, it has been successful. Yet when the antidemocratic culture of the neoliberals finally captured the student membership at the end of the eighties, the movement lost its way, and students paid the price. The FEUQ and FECQ abandoned their base in a naïve embrace of the establishment, hoping that close contacts in the corridors of power would instill enough good faith to protect educational accessibility. Instead, they were co-opted as a pillar of the establishment and sold their souls to become an echo of the very commercialist dogmas that legitimated the dismantling of the Quiet Revolution's gains. More than just mirroring their ideologies, the shift impelled a hollowing out of their democratic structures, as political power was concentrated in the hands of professionalized national executives, and the student base became ever more disengaged.

When the ASSÉ came onto the scene in 2001, it began laying roots that stretched once more down into the student base, using new open structures and horizontal models forged in the flurry of a globalizing resistance to the corporate-controlled agendas of the élites. By 2006, the ASSÉ's membership had easily surpassed the MDE's to arrive at 36,000, which rose slowly to 40,000 by December 2011. If the top-down culture of the corporate age took years to seep into the student ranks, the bottom-up forces that fuel the counterreaction may have to rise up, layer by layer, to finally break through. By 2005, early signs of a resurgence were already brewing from below, as the winter of student representation was nearing its peak. Running in tandem as has often been the case, the provincial political establishment and leadership of the student federations were both poised for a new pinnacle of unrest over their opaque and autocratic cultures, as the tide of the Internet age's democratizing currents was rising up past their ankles. The ASSÉ's time was about to arrive.

FROM BOOKS TO BOARDROOMS
The Corporatization of the University

The library of my grandparents is sweat, tears, great outbursts of
laughter, an old Italian song, prayers, a bit too much wine, mixed
accents, and a great desire to have better. Not to have more, no: to have
better.[...]

Now, Beauchamp, go commercialize that for me then. Try to put a
price on that! You can try all you like: the library of my grandparents,
darling, will never be for sale. But everyone can consult it. For free.[1]
— Catherine Lavarenne, "*Giorgio*" (my translation)

The dismantling of the commons by neoliberal governments has had one of its
fullest impacts in the realm of education. Here, the "public" in public education
has been gradually emptied of its meaning, as the true sense of "education" itself
has been subtly crowded out by a commercialist and utilitarian focus on training.
The one-time emphasis of universities on human and collective development
has been compromised by the withdrawal of public funds and the intrusion of
a hunt for private investments. The broader social mission and autonomy of the
university has been eroded as a result, as it's become co-opted as a pillar of the
country's economic strategy. Here as elsewhere, powerful corporate actors have
grabbed hold of what was once a truly public system in both orientations and
funding, and commandeered the state's resources and institutions to aid them in
furthering their bottom line.

Knowledge industrialized:
The brain factories of the capitalist class

When you alter the hands that feed our universities, you invariably alter the masters
they serve. It's significant, therefore, that under both PQ and Liberal governments,
the ratio of public funding for universities dropped from 87 percent to 65.8 percent
from 1988 to 2009. The burden for education was thereby shifted from the state
(which is financed disproportionately by the affluent, even if less than it once
was) to the families of all students regardless of means, whose forced contribution
jumped from 5.4 to 12.2 percent. Private sector involvement tripled as well, going

from 7.5 to 22 percent.[2] And far from going unrewarded, the "altruism" of donor companies has been repaid in kind by the increasingly blurred line between their business interests and society's broader educational and research goals. Happy funders, after all, must have returns on their investments, and a private enterprise tabulates these in the language of profits and productivity.

The financial disengagement of the state from higher education accompanied a wider shift in policy that radically transformed the nature and mission of the university. Beginning with the Lévesque government in the early eighties, "doing more with less" became the operative goal.[3] With science and technology occupying a growing role in the economic development of states, measures were instituted at both the federal and provincial levels to reorient researchers toward national economic priorities. It was the start of the instrumentalization of the education system in the service of the new "knowledge economy."[4] Accordingly, the PQ government's economic action plan in 1984 created six "exchange and innovation" centres where university researchers and private enterprise could collaborate closely, with the private sector occupying a key role in the funding and fixing of orientations.[5] Federal policy has pushed in the same direction, with the budgets of grant agencies made contingent on the degree of private sector involvement in university research as of 1987.[6] Gradually over the course of the last three decades, reforms implemented by both levels of government have increasingly placed the development of businesses at the heart of our educational policies.

Few people today seem to question the apple-pie auras of the "knowledge economy" — and indeed, an economy geared toward innovation and creativity does seem to hold great promise for human progress. Yet behind the instinctive response, the devil, as always, sits lurking in the details. Most especially, the determining question lost in the naïve embrace of such an alluring mantra is that of *whom* the innovation serves, and to answer that we need to ask who is deciding the research orientations. Our governments have placed private industry in the driver's seat, with the impact being to replace the autonomy of the researcher with the self-serving priorities of private industry and to overwhelmingly favour projects with profit-bearing commercializable outcomes over those pursued in the interests of scientific or social objectives.[7] More troubling still is that as research has been co-opted by private interests, so too has what our students are being taught. Government policy papers as of 1982 called on universities to reorient course curricula to better align program specializations with the needs of industry.[8] This cohesive agenda has ended in a dramatic departure: Universities, once autonomous seats of higher learning, have become factories of specialized labour and industrial innovation, instrumentalized as branch plants of an economy geared toward corporate enrichment.

In short, it is not some sudden leap toward a second Enlightenment that explains the explosion in public funds channelled toward university research over the last three decades. It is the utilitarian recasting of universities as poles of economic development that has led governments to open the taps, largely to the benefit of private enterprises whose wealth and power have grown enormously over this span. In Québec, where the increase has been especially marked, the total sum of annual subsidies and research contracts allocated to universities' "restricted funds" — named as such since they may not be used for instruction — ballooned from $117.9 million in 1980 to $1.5 billion in 2008–09.[9] Yet given narrow industrial imperatives, the distribution of these funds has been far from equitable across the broad spectrum of social needs and goals. In 2005–06, only 7.8 percent of all research grants and contracts were allotted to the full range of social sciences, while the lion's share, 75.8 percent, was funnelled toward the hard sciences.[10] The industrial interests being served by this money are easy to identify. With royalties accounting for barely 1 percent of universities' budgets, the public's financial returns on such massive public investments are minimal, since licences are ceded early on in the research process.[11] The irony of the situation is not lost on Brian Massumi, a social and cultural theorist at the Université de Montréal. For Massumi, this outsourcing to public universities of corporate research functions "formerly performed and paid for internally" by companies is a clear case of "corporate welfare" — and represents "the logic of neoliberal capitalism" whereby the line between the state and corporations is increasingly blurred.[12]

Corporatized research is one outflow of the marketized environment in which our universities today find themselves and which forces them into a costly and ferocious competition with each other for contracts — but also, for students. Owing to the funding formula tied to enrollment numbers, the new enterprise-universities have been thrown into a frantic chase for each other's "clientèle" as public resources have become scarcer. Exorbitant and globally reaching advertising and communications campaigns and the pursuit of international certifications to attract foreign students (who pay much higher tuition) have claimed significant resources at the expense of the university's fundamental mission. Satellite campuses have been constructed at extremely high cost too, often in proximity to "competing" institutions who offer the same programs, with the aim of luring in their rivals' "customers" with greater geographical accessibility.[13]

These colossal projects, far from simply responding to space constraints or the needs of their students, are instead producing enormous inefficiencies in the university network through duplication of faculties and programs.[14] And even worse is that they are increasingly funded by money intended for instruction. Between 1997 and 2007 in fact, the percentage of universities' general operating budgets being diverted toward real estate projects exploded from 26 to 45 percent, after the government slashed their real estate budgets by 20 percent in this span despite significant infrastructure deficits and expanding student populations.[15] The Fédération québécoise des professeures et professeurs d'université (FQPPU), which represents more than five thousand university professors, estimates that almost all of the new government money invested in universities in these years was consequently swallowed up by these construction, renovation and acquisition projects.[16] Yet it's also, they say, largely the administrations' priorities that are to blame: This leap into the real estate melee — specifically into projects that are often unnecessary and, numerous times, have ended in high-profile boondoggles[17] — is also a direct result of the added burden of economic development being placed on universities' shoulders.[18] Universities are diverting money meant for education to finance costly state-of-the-art facilities intended to attract industrial research and up their brand to lure students and contracts.

As real estate ventures, private research projects and advertising and communications departments have all ballooned beyond measure, the size and cost of support infrastructure and staff have followed suit, eating away further at the dwindling resources available for the university's one-time core mission.[19] The costs of the bureaucratic behemoths these radical transformations have produced are also taken out of the same operating budgets that are meant to finance instruction.[20] And there is convincing evidence, moreover, to suggest that the official picture is even rosier than the realities on the ground. The crowding out of universities' teaching budgets by bloated administrations seems to have led to creative accounting on the part of university administrations, doubtless concerned by the damaging optic of pedagogy being relegated to second place. In 1997, Hugues Boisvert, a senior professor of Management Accounting at Montréal's Hautes Études Commerciales (HEC) and now the head of the HEC Montréal Comptables professionnels agréés (CPA) International Research Centre in Management Control, was startled by apparent incongruencies he noted in university budgets: Only one third of university personnel were teaching staff, he remarked, and yet officially, teaching represented 51 percent of operating budgets. On top of being inconsistent (teachers are sadly not paid enough to account for the discrepancy), Boisvert felt that the official figure contradicted the on-the-ground experiences of teachers — and with 73 percent of university budgets devoted to salaries as a whole, he was spurred to take a much closer look.[21]

The results of his investigation were explosive. Boisvert's analyses, which deployed a more rigorous division of contemporary university functions, exposed a "phantom university network" that had little to do with the official story.[22] By methodically separating the administrative and support tasks of teachers and administrators from activities properly defined as pedagogic, Boisvert concluded that Québec's universities devoted 72 percent of their total budgets to support and administrative tasks — which was the exact inverse, at 51 percent teaching and 21 percent research, of official figures asserted by university administrations.[23]

His revelations also help explain an otherwise problematic current statistic: namely, that at $29,242 per head as of 2008–9, Québec's universities in fact spend *more* per student than the Canadian average (without Québec) of $28,735 and far more than Ontario's $26,383.[24] As a percentage of GDP too, the financial commitment of Québec's universities is significantly greater than the Canadian average, at

1.94 percent compared to 1.58 percent in the rest of Canada (without Québec).[25] How is this possible, when we consider the apparent crisis of underfunding plaguing our classrooms, the overcrowding, the shortage of professors? Consider: Research funding in Québec officially accounts for 26.2 percent of university budgets, compared to the Canadian average of 21.5 percent, and Québec's universities receive approximately $15,000 more per professor in research subsidies and contracts than the Canadian average.[26] Even more surprising in light of the large cutbacks of recent years, the real estate budgets for Québec's universities, amounting to $400 million as of 2008–09, are still larger than in the rest of the country.[27] What remains is that the core operating budgets are being cannibalized from both ends, with the bloated administrations taking a huge chunk out of one side while the grandiose adventures in real estate dine freely from the other. In short, the issue is not *under*funding, but rather a systemic misdirection of funds to the clear detriment of students and the profitability of capital.

This is a reality that Charest was well aware of, yet politics and ideology demanded its suppression. The $29,242 per-student figure in fact comes directly from the Ministère de l'éducation — from a report that was in the government's hands prior to announcing the tuition increases, but was only released upon Pauline Marois's arrival in office.[28] It's easy to see why. Québec's educational system, it suggests, may indeed be starving, but only from the inside: With such enormous sums being funnelled toward industrial research and development, the efforts employed to compete for students and contracts and the infrastructures that have arisen to manage both, less and less is left for what was once the essential activity of the university: education.[29]

This statistical portrait will come as little surprise to Québec's university professors, who have seen their share of the salary pie shrink as their workloads have increased. Budget cut s over the years have resulted in what Boisvert also calls the "industrialization" of universities in Québec, including larger course loads for teachers, a massive recourse to casual lecturers and the explosion of administrative and managerial duties, which leave them with less and less time to devote to instruction.[30] Yet precisely as overworked teachers have been tightening their belts, those above them in the ever-stretching university hierarchy have added more than a few notches of their own. Between 1997 and 2004, the salaries of managerial and administrative staff in universities went up 83.4 percent in Québec, bringing their ratio of total salary expenditures up by 2 percent between 1997 and 2005, while that allotted to teaching staff decreased by 4.4 percent.[31] The 72 percent of university budgets devoted to administrative and support tasks found in Boisvert's "phantom university network" may thus be even greater today.

The new ivory tower: The rise of the managerial élite

The new mission of the university as a pillar of economic development has also redefined the role and power of administrations. Today, the administration is the heart of the university and the central function "where research and teaching find their integration point."[32] Managers — often with no pedagogic background — occupy permanent posts on administrative councils of universities and propose reforms to the Assemblée nationale on behalf of their institutions.[33] Despite the exclusion of teachers and students, administrations are viewed as the university's primary representative to the state, with the presidents and rectors treated much as the CEO of a company. "University presidents, whose role is akin to a business traveller, are judged first and foremost on their ability to raise funds," observes sociologist Christian Laval.[34] In the new model, university presidents are no longer called on to defend the values of education or the integrity of the public institution, but instead to promote their competitive positioning within the marketplace.[35] The result has been a class of élite administrative overlords, who while physically being situated within the university, are less and less *of* the university.

Within this typically neoliberal institution, both the teaching and the teachers have been sidelined and made subservient to the interests of money, and the principle of the teacher's autonomy has become a thing of the past. In Boisvert's words, s/he who once "engaged in research with the aim of contributing to the field of knowledge [...] is today called upon to contribute to the universities' consolidated funds through sponsorships; from autonomous researcher in the service of science, s/he has become an agent of the university."[36] Where once university administrators served the professors, it is now entirely the reverse, as bloated and ever-more powerful administrations have ousted from the educational endeavour the figure that was once at its heart.[37] Taken together, the changes have led our universities down one path — and it is heading fast away from the civic and democratic institutions envisioned by the Parent Report and the reformers of the Quiet Revolution. The upper floors of today's ivory towers are lined not with books but boardrooms, where champagne is popped in the company of the president's lauded guests. Our universities have been corporatized.

Faced with a professorial staff burdened by mounting administrative duties and stagnant pay, university presidents and upper management are rewarded with cushy salaries and severance packages worth hundreds of thousands of dollars all while leading missions to Québec City to warn that the cupboard is bare. Yet when they arrived to the *Rencontre des partenaires en éducation* in December 2010, the premier would have done well to ask them which cupboard they were referring to. The effective salary of McGill's Heather Munroe-Blum after all, pegged in 2008–09 at $587,580 once only part of her bonuses was included, was approximately three times Jean Charest's.[38] The other anglophone institution, Concordia University, has even been fined $2 million by the province for its chronic frivolity with dispensing severance packages, which has seen five members of upper management alone pocket $2.4 million in the last few years. Regal departure packages were even doled out to two consecutive Concordia presidents who left midway through their mandates, including the latter, Judith Woodsworth, who was rewarded with $700,000 — the equivalent of two years' salary — for being fired under unknown circumstances. Yet far from being outliers, these cases sit comfortably among a list of eighteen university presidents who earn an average pay of $215,942 plus benefits averaging $62,000, with the rectors and presidents of six Québec universities all earning over $300,000 a year (still low by Canadian standards).[39] Overall, from 2007 to 2012, the budget for administration salaries skyrocketed at the five largest universities in Québec by ratios between 16.2 percent at UQÀM and 38.2 percent at McGill.[40]

Tuition fees: The de-democratization of education

The gold-plated club of university presidents, long grouped together under the Conférence des recteurs et des principaux des universités du Québec (CREPUQ), proved itself an imposing lobby in the last thirty years, and students and their families have repeatedly paid the price. Indeed as the commercialist view of universities took root throughout the 1980s and the backing of key business leaders bolstered the CREPUQ, their calls as of 1988 to raise tuition fees met with less and less resistance from governments.[41] In the short span between 1990 and 1994 alone, Bourassa's tuition increases amounting to 315 percent catapulted average fees from $543 to $1668, marking a radical reversal of decades of policy centred on principles of equality and universality.[42] Registration, which in francophone institutions had risen 650 percent in twenty-five years, declined in the wake of the move and continued to drop until 1997.[43]

Under the PQ governments from 1994 to 2003, tuition was officially frozen at the new levels. Yet universities circumvented the law by tripling mandatory administrative fees to an average of $624 per semester by 2006–07, representing an effective hike that the government did nothing to stem and the student federations failed to stop.[44] Charest's Liberals were more direct by comparison and far more aggressive in their push for higher fees. Charest's tenure as premier saw tuition levels rise by another 30 percent, up to $2,168 by 2011–12, to attain the average among advanced industrialized countries of the Organization for Economic Cooperation and Development (OECD).[45] If his government's second planned hike had not been defeated by the election of September 2012, they were projected to soar past that average to attain a base of $3,793 by 2016–17 prior to including administrative fees, which have continued to rise in tandem.[46]

The move, like that by Bourassa in 1989, would have closed the gates of the universities to thousands of young Quebecers. According to the Québec government's own Comité consultatif sur l'accessibilité financière aux études in fact, an autonomous body under the ministry of education, Charest's tuition increase could have pushed higher learning out of reach for seven thousand Quebecers, representing nearly 2.5 percent of the total student population.[47] The Institut de recherche et d'informations socio-économiques (IRIS) has estimated that raising Québec's tuition levels to match the Canadian average would deprive thirty thousand young Quebecers of a university education.[48] And in 2014, an exhaustive and unprecedented study echoed the general conclusion of both: The group of researchers, led by sociologist Pierre Doray, analyzed the relation between tuition increases and enrollment in Ontario and Québec from 1946 to 2011, and noted a definite downward pull on enrollment. The study was groundbreaking in that it provided the first long view on the causal relation between tuition fees and enrollment *within* each jurisdiction and circumvented the problematic temptation to compare complex and divergent educational systems (and cultures) from province to province. The study found that for each $1,000 increase, the chances of not pursuing one's studies rose by 3 percent overall, by 10 percent for Québec's francophones and by much more for the most vulnerable segments of the population, most notably those over twenty-five as well as first-generation students whose parents never attended university. For the latter group, who account for 45 percent of Québec's student population — the highest rate in Canada[49] — each $1,000 increase raised the chances of not pursuing higher learning by 19 percent.[50]

Nowhere in the government's messaging was any correlation between high fees and lower enrollment ever admitted, with the Liberals insisting instead that an injection of $118 million into the loans and bursaries program would offset any negative impact on educational accessibility.[51] Yet of this figure, $116 million would have come from the increased tuition fees paid by students: Charest was wielding a cheap magician's sleight of hand in drawing from one pocket only to fill the other. In truth, only the 17 percent of students already receiving financial aid would have benefitted from the additional funds, with 83 percent forced to absorb the full $3,793 a year.[52] The impacts of tuition increases are in fact fairly obvious and have been repeatedly witnessed, whether in provinces across Canada, in Québec after Bourassa's tripling of fees in 1989 or after a sharp hike in 2005 in the United Kingdom: Participation rates drop, while those who continue on incur much higher debt loads and are forced to work longer hours to pay for their studies, bringing all the negative impacts on quality of life and learning that such additional burdens and stresses entail.[53] But the labour market, and the banks, smile upon them.

Students as capital:
The new commercial vision of education

During the strike of 2012, the lawyers for the Université de Montréal sought an injunction from Québec's Superior Court in an attempt to ban all protests from campus. Their argument: that the university is a private property, "just like a shopping centre."[54] Perhaps the most damning indictment of all was that such an argument could even be made with a straight face — though admittedly, there was nothing funny about it. It took decades for us to arrive at this point, over which governments fastened a new narrative on the university's role in society, which served to reshape the culture of these institutions. Within this new commercialist paradigm, the influence and rights of both students and professors — the actors who were once the beginning and end of education — have been radically overturned and replaced by the interests and values of the capitalist class.

This new view of education was on sharp display during the 2012 student crisis. A handful of disgruntled individuals, encouraged by the government, launched court battles to challenge students' rights to uphold democratically obtained strike mandates with picket lines in front of universities. The students' right to strike, while not explicitly recognized under the law, had been culturally institutionalized in Québec since the birth of the student movement. Even Jean Charest, himself a student leader once, referred to the 2005 mobilization as a "strike," just as he had when reminiscing on his student years in his memoir published in 1998.[55] Education minister Line Beauchamp also referred to students' right to "strike" on February 14, 2012. That must have been before the government's communications strategy was decided, after which the rhetorical innovation of applying the word "boycott" to a student action entered the Québec lexicon for the very first time.[56] The evident conclusion is that the semantic offensive was little more than the fowl-smelling fruit of good government PR.

Yet the question of sincerity aside, the effectiveness of this reframing in 2012 spoke to the distance that the market culture had come in Québec since the last mobilization. Indeed the semantic battle even served as a microcosm of the fundamental clash: On the one side stood the student movement's founding ideal of a student as an intellectual worker, social actor and full-fledged member of the academic community, while on the other was the neoliberal recasting of a student as a consumer and future employee within the marketplace, who invests her or his (or their parents') dollars in return for greater financial gains down the road. At the height of the student conflict, the "judicialization" (*judiciarisation*)[57] of the strike led Brian Massumi to an apt observation:

> The fact of the matter is that university administrations [...] and governments [...] no longer look on the university as the seat of liberal education. They look on it as a *service industry*. The students' collective mobilisation could only appear as illegitimate against the backdrop of another right now promoted to front and centre stage: the individual "right" of a student to receive the service he or she has paid for.[58]

This "redefinition of students as clients and education as a fee-for-service industry" found echo as well in the government's emergency law. Bill 78 (discussed in Chapter 9) conscripted professors as soldiers in the neoliberals' "knowledge economy" and stripped them of their social agency by instrumentalizing them as simple job trainers with contractual obligations like the rest.[59]

Beyond the dispute over students' right to strike and picket, the Charest government's utilitarian argument in favour of the hike was outlined, quite predictably, in dollars and cents — $600,000 to be precise, or so was the monetary gain claimed to be purchased by a bachelor's degree over the span of an average lifetime.[60] In the judgment of the government, the increased financial burden exerted on students and their families was justified on the basis that these "'very high private rates of return' on the investment in a university training" — note, a "training" (*"formation"*) rather than an education — "is even greater than the public rate of return that society benefits from as a whole."[61] Patently, we are far from the humanist discourse of the Parent Report. Education, for the Liberals, was a mere question of financial foresight — through an individual worker's investment augmenting the market price of their labour hours and through industry's investments in its competitiveness by funding the training of their future labour force.[62] Whether that education served the broader aspirations of either society or students was entirely beside the point.

Humanity bought and harvested:
The all-devouring economy of the One Percent

In 2001, French philosopher Jacques Derrida wrote that the modern university, born in tune with Western democracies two centuries ago, "demands and should be seen to recognize in principle, aside from what we term academic freedom, an

A protester walks past a line of riot police at a demonstration held on May 16, 2012.

unconditional liberty of questioning and proposition, and even more, the right to say publicly all that research, knowledge and a thought of the truth demand."[63] Yet in the notion of "excellence" put forward by today's neoliberal universities, the values of truth and knowledge are in fact highly conditional, a reality that the presidents and rectors of Québec's universities are making fewer and fewer efforts to hide. Speaking to the business community at the Cercle canadien de Montréal in 2009, former Concordia University president Judith Woodsworth asked her audience to view universities as "drivers of economic development and as centres of intellectual entrepreneurship."[64] Guy Breton, rector of the Université de Montréal, was less tactful in addressing a panel hosted by the Conseil des relations internationales de Montréal (CORIM) in 2011: From now on, he asserted without a trace of timidity, "brains must correspond to the needs of businesses."[65] And with that, the masks fell. Gabriel Nadeau-Dubois, to whom I owe the above citations, arrives at the obvious conclusion: "The classic university, that of the Enlightenment, demanded an 'unconditional liberty' and dreamed of well-made minds. That which Guy Breton dreams of will deliver brains to market just in time."[66] The difference, in its full slate of social ramifications, is nothing short of revolutionary.

Margaret Thatcher once said that "Economics are the method, the object is to change the heart and soul."[67] And indeed by all accounts, the colonization of our culture and minds has been precisely the neoliberals' greatest triumph. For in the larger picture, the commercialist mutation of education is but one layer of a value structure that has been seeping its way into the roots of our society over a period of unprecedented corporate growth. Inherent human and social values once held to exist outside of the marketplace are increasingly tested against monetary measures before legitimacy may be granted. And as the barriers separating the marketplace from areas outside its purview are steadily eroded, the marketization of society proceeds at frightening speed — and with it, so too its dehumanization.

The years 2011 and 2012 will be remembered as the moment youth across the world launched the first stages of resistance. For ultimately, the conflict over tuition fees in Québec was the scene of a much larger ideological battle that burst into the open, pitting the humanist ideal of education nourished by the youth against the ruthless advance of a cold and exploitative "model of human capital" carried forward by the economic and political élites.[68] The students saw their educational institutions morphing into factories designed to churn out productive workers and consumers to feed the beast of the One Percent's economy.[69] And from latent unrest, their refusal let breathe the collective rejoinder at last: Some things are worth far more than you can pay.

THERE IS NO ALTERNATIVE

The Corporate Coup d'État and the Rise of the Resistance

"To the youth, I say: Look around you. You will find the themes that
justify your indignation."[1]
— Stéphane Hessel, *Indignez-Vous!* (my translation)

The tightening alliance between business and political élites has borne enormous
consequences for our institutions. Across the democratic world, declining political
party memberships and voter participation rates have laid bare an "increasingly
obvious chasm" between citizens and their representatives.[2] It's a problem that's
generally acknowledged across the political spectrum, and yet the adherents of
marketization who feign concern also neglect a most inconvenient fact: that this
democratic crisis has risen in tandem with the neoliberal revolution that's empowered economic élites, and that its role in causing the democratic decline grows
ever more undeniable. In truth it's little wonder citizens have grown increasingly
wary of their representatives. They witness before them political establishments
that ritually bemoan the symptoms of failing democracies precisely as they fuel
the sources, either incapable or unwilling to name the crisis staring us in the face:
Democracy everywhere is in retreat, and all signs point to a worsening trend as our
institutions grow increasingly permeable to the powers of money.

Usurpers: The post-democracy of the ruling class

The baby boomers were inculcated with the Cold War-era myth that capitalism
and democracy are natural allies, and yet the concentration of wealth that results
from the former can only have its direct corollary in the concentration of power.
In simpler words: The economic oligarchy produced by deregulated capitalism is
completely inconsistent with democracy, as the rich will buy their state's attentions
when they can. To those who never knew the Berlin Wall, the establishment's
desperation to cling to that myth is therefore brushed aside with ease in the face
of the overwhelming evidence they grew up with. It is no accident that the shift in
global consciousness at the root of the latest uprisings is being piloted by this rising
generation, though they have been greatly aided by the seeds lain in recent years by
authors, activists and academics in many countries. In his 2004 "landmark publication"[3] *Post-Democracy* for instance, British sociologist and political scientist Colin

Crouch traced the contours of this crisis afflicting democracies in the advanced stages of neoliberal capitalism.

> While elections certainly exist and can change governments, public electoral debate is a tightly controlled spectacle, managed by rival teams of professional experts in the techniques of persuasion, and considering a small range of issues selected by those teams. The mass of citizens plays a passive, quiescent, even apathetic part, responding only to the signals given them. Behind the spectacle of the electoral game, politics is really shaped in private by interaction between elected governments and elites that overwhelmingly represent business interests.[4]

Red tie, blue tie, they're all the same suits. Anyone who has approached abstainers to discuss why they don't vote has doubtless come across such responses too many times to count. But they are not taken seriously. The hollow pleas of politicians and get-out-the-vote campaigns directed at youth contain within them a dismissive paternalism that insults their intelligence and fails to acknowledge the serious and systemic sources of citizen disengagement. Crouch places his finger rather adroitly on the wound when he describes the Potemkin democracy that contemporary capitalism has produced.[5] And he is far from alone in his camp.

French philosopher Alain Badiou has decried a world "everywhere in the hands of extremely tightly knit financial and media oligarchs," whose power is enabled by systems of "capitalo-parliamentarism" that breed intimate ties between governments and business élites.[6] "Not even elections offer any true political alternative," says Badiou.[7] But it was not always like this. Decades of policies aimed at whittling away the size and scope of the state have eroded the capacities of governments to improve the lots of their citizens, ceding ever wider areas to the rivalling greed of market actors. Yet as the state shrinks, so too does the sphere under the control of those who may hold it accountable. This gradual "hollowing out of the public domain of citizenship,"[8] in the phrase of the University of Manchester's Erik Swyngedouw, has seen countries' democratic space increasingly constrained in tune with the growing force of multinational business entities that have pushed to widen the market's domain. Echoing Crouch and Badiou, Swyngedouw's explanation of "post-democratization" captures the enormity of the power grab, as this "depoliticization of the economy" has removed the issues that most affect people's lives from the range of options offered to citizens.[9] And as the areas under the influence of the voter wane and retreat, the reasons to get engaged in the political process fade ever further from view.

We've entered an era described by philosopher and cultural critic Slavoj Žižek as "postpolitics," where government has been "re-conceived as a managerial function deprived of its proper political dimension."[10] Under the cover of globalization-era economic "imperatives" — defined, most naturally, by the moneyed interests that stand to gain — governments of all stripes have accepted the rigid curtailing of the policy spectrum dictated by business élites. And most unconscionably, they then fastened the straitjacket tight with secretive (and often long-term) trade deals enforced by the unelected corporate guard-dogs of the World Trade Organization. Without so much as a fight, our representatives have thereby surrendered our democratic and social rights to unaccountable (and often foreign) business actors and legitimated this surrender with a manipulated framing of the public good that simply confuses their narrow interests with those of the collective.[11]

Thatcher's mantra "there is no alternative" was effective at convincing people of the urgency of the neoliberal reforms in her day — though today, the phrase has become more apt at capturing the options available to voters as a result. Year upon year, our ballots appear less as tools for change and increasingly as tools for the legitimation of a skin-deep façade, while behind the curtain the corporate puppeteers are holding all the strings. In the final picture, citizens may be forgiven for wondering whether even the most minimal engagement of a periodic vote still has any significant impact on their lives. And they may even be forgiven for wondering whether at the end of the day, we can meaningfully claim to live in a democracy at all — or whether it's by sheer force of habit that we continue defining ourselves by such weighty words, long after they've been hollowed of all sense.

Revolution 2.0: The generation that toppled dictators

On December 17, 2010, a poor Tunisian street vendor by the name of Mohamed Bouazizi set himself on fire after authorities had repeatedly prevented him from selling his vegetables and thus earning his livelihood.[12] With economic discontent soaring after food prices in the import-dependent region spiked in 2008, the flames that ended Bouazizi's life instantly engulfed the whole country.[13] Massive upheaval erupted that killed hundreds across Tunisia and ended in January when President Zine al-Abidine Ben Ali fled into exile after twenty-four years in power. The impact of the dictator's fall reverberated across borders. Throughout the region, the Arab street rose up against the pharaonically rich élites whose systems of oppression and corruption kept their people starved, in the words of Egyptian protesters, of "bread, freedom and dignity."[14]

In Mubarak-era Egypt, the chasm between the globalized ruling class and the people had long hit "critical levels."[15] With impending upheaval at a low boil below the surface, food prices were sent skyrocketing by 37 percent between 2008 and 2010.[16] Bouazizi's self-immolation and the Tunisian revolution that followed lit the spark of insurrection, and the social media generation quickly took up the torch. Facebook use soared across the Arab world in the first few months of 2011, as the overwhelmingly young and urban core of the pro-democracy movement flooded social media to launch what became the Arab Spring.[17] In Egypt, Internet use in the preceding decade had exploded by 3,691 percent to attain 17 million users.[18] With four million of them on Facebook, the social media sharing site became the country's third most visited Web address by 2009 — and in 2011, joined with

Twitter to become the organizational and informational hub from which a historic revolution would be born and fought.[19]

Representatives from six youth movements gathered throughout January to plot the revolution and mobilize the population online.[20] Their Twitter hashtag #jan25, used 1.2 million times,[21] announced the date that the Egyptian revolutionaries stormed and occupied the operational and iconic heart of Cairo. There, in the "republic of Tahrir Square,"[22] they built a leaderless, independent and grassroots encampment from which they rallied the masses of society to their revolution, stared down the brutal forces of dictatorship and brought an abrupt end to the thirty-year rule of Hosni Mubarak.

Indignez-vous!: The sparks of a global resistance

In parallel to the eruption of protests in Tunisia in December of 2010, Stéphane Hessel, a now-deceased French Resistance fighter and concentration camp survivor, published a three-euro tract entitled *Indignez-vous!* (later published in English as *Time for Outrage!*). The German-born Hessel, who became a French citizen in 1939, had helped craft the 1948 Universal Declaration of Human Rights. Aged ninety-three and knowing his end was "not far off,"[23] the *cri du coeur* he signed was to be his final plea to the generation on the rise. Hessel took pen to paper to recall the values of economic and social democracy on which France's Fifth Republic was founded after the Second World War — values, markedly, that were echoed by the nation-builders of Québec's Quiet Revolution of the 1960s. In the new republic, moneyed interests were to be "evicted" from the management of the economy so that the good of the many could prevail over the good of the few.[24] But this postwar pact, he warned, has been betrayed. In one trenchant passage, Hessel writes:

> They have the nerve to tell us that the state can no longer cover the costs of these social programs. Yet how can the money needed to continue and extend these achievements be lacking today, when the creation of wealth has grown so enormously since the Liberation [of France], a time when Europe lay in ruins? It can only be because the power of money, which the Resistance fought against so hard, has never been as great and selfish and shameless as it is now, with its servants in the very highest circles of government.[25]

Hessel urged resistance in the face of "the current dictatorship of global financial markets that threatens democracy and peace" and issued a call for a "peaceful insurrection" against a world of mass consumption and collective amnesia.[26] Released to little fanfare with a small publishing house from Montpellier, the thirty-two page manifesto — of which only eight thousand copies were initially printed — exploded unexpectedly into a global phenomenon, selling four million copies and being translated into thirty-four languages.[27] The impact was undeniable.

Propelled by the three-euro cost and the unique stature of the author, Hessel's perfectly timed polemic crowned the rising crescendo of scholarly alarm, which travelled from the ivory towers down to the streets to ignite a populist phenomenon. Hessel's cries had ruptured a vein.

The 2008 financial collapse and resulting global recession, sparked largely by the irresponsible practices of banks that had been deregulated in the late 1970s, pummelled Europe's economies, with youth often hit especially hard.[28] In Portugal, where half of the country's unemployed were under thirty-five, a pop group called Deolinda sparked a spontaneous awakening with the release of a hit entitled "*Que parva sou eu*" ("How Stupid I Am"), whose lyrics condemned a "stupid world where you have to study first to become a slave."[29] Moved to action by the song's channelling of their frustrations, four young professionals launched a call over social media for a "Protest for the Generation in Trouble." Within days, the Facebook page had garnered tens of thousands of "likes," and on March 12, 2011, hundreds of thousands marched nationwide in the largest protests since the Carnation Revolution that toppled the dictatorship in 1974.[30] Inspired by Hessel, the protesters called themselves the Indignados and defined their movement as non-partisan, nonviolent and bottom-up.[31]

No one expects the #spanishrevolution: Spain's youth and the fight for real democracy

In Spain, where the situation known simply as "the crisis" put a brutal stop to decades of prosperity, similar conditions were manifested in what was termed the "*ni-ni*" generation — neither working, nor studying, in a country where nearly half of those under twenty-four were unemployed. The massive housing bubble had burst and left over a fifth of the population out of work, as eleven million people were at risk of falling into poverty, and hundreds of thousands of families had been evicted from their homes.[32] Panicked at the thought of following Greece's 2008 collapse and subsequent vassalage to international lending institutions, the Socialist government of José Luis Zapatero, ceding to pressure from the International Monetary Fund (IMF), abruptly reversed longstanding party policies and enacted wide-ranging austerity measures to stem the rising debt. With the imposed surrender of the governing left as backdrop, the legitimacy of the system then took its final hit: Amidst the belt-tightening and the worst economic crisis in decades, Spain's bankers made off with princely bonuses after the government issued bank bailouts to the tune of $70 billion U.S.[33]

Soon, an independent and decentralized coalition of over two hundred civil society organizations arose under the banner of Democracia Real Ya ("Real Democracy Now"). Fronted by the slogan "We are not goods in the hands of bankers and politicians," the organization's online campaign mobilized 130,000 citizens into the streets on May 15, 2011, giving birth to the movement known in

Spain as "15-M," or the Spanish Indignados. Inspired by the power of leaderless and social media-driven protests both in Portugal and in Cairo's Tahrir Square, a few dozen protesters occupied Madrid's Puerta del Sol that evening and summoned reinforcements over Twitter. The hashtag they launched then, #spanishrevolution, went viral as the "Acampada Sol" grew to 150 members. As young eyes were turning to Sol, a heavy-handed police crackdown dislodged the protesters at dawn on May 17 and incited a fateful transmission that would echo out across text messages and social media to announce the protesters' return in force: *toma la plaza,* take the square. And so that evening, they did.

The days that followed witnessed the eruption of a truly historic popular uprising and the laying of seeds that the winds would transport to fertile soil at the four corners of the globe. Tens of thousands of citizens occupied squares in 166 cities across Spain and brought protesters out cloaked in the Guy Fawkes masks popularized by the 2006 film version of the revolutionary *V for Vendetta.* Image, however, was only the surface: The occupiers dug in their heels, as they set to crafting assembly-based models of participative and horizontal democracy that drew on decades-long Spanish traditions of *autogestión* (leaderless self-management) — and that, after spreading eastward to Athens, later travelled across the Atlantic to be carefully recreated in New York's Zucotti Park.[34]

At a conference held in June 2011 at Birkbeck, University of London, Spanish sociologist Carlos Frade summed up the underlying sentiment of the 15 M movement with the popular rallying cry, *¡No nos representan!* ("They don't represent us!").[35] And indeed, a canvassing of the slogans recited at Spain's protests revealed a strikingly recurrent theme: "This is not a crisis. It's fraud"; "We are not anti-system, the system is anti-us"; "Democracy is our fight"; "We will not pay for this crisis"; "Democracy is a two-party dictatorship"; and on it went. Spanish journalist Elena García Quevedo explains the rage of Spanish youth by saying that "Spain's democracy does not seem real to them [...]. They are more prepared than the generation that preceded theirs; they are better educated, speak more languages, are more well-rounded. They have so much to offer, but their country has nothing to offer them."[36] And indeed the refrain being echoed by other protesters in Spain will likely come as little surprise to youth in Western democracies. "We have alternation [of political parties] without alternatives," was the succinct conclusion of twenty-six-year-old Olga Arnaiz. One journalism student, Sabina Ortega, channelled the same sentiment: "You name it. Nothing works [...]. It's against a two-party system. And my goal is to feel represented. I want politicians to know they are not listening."[37]

The list of demands adopted at the nightly assemblies fit neatly within the narrative. Of the broad array of youth concerns raised by the participants, *The Nation's* Andy Robinson reported that the most widely supported were the ones centred on democratic reform.[38] The movement's manifesto, written, debated and voted on by the general assembly and diffused via the 15-M website, is abundantly clear on this. It asserts that the economic troubles plaguing Spain are primarily due to the corruption of the system — of the "government, bankers and businessmen alike."[39] Other observers readily noted as much in the discourse of 15-M. New York University professor Gianpaolo Baiocchi and Spanish sociologist Ernesto Ganuza have written that "Although [Democracia Real Ya] targeted unemployment and mortgage reforms, the main message was not about the economic crisis but about the breakdown of political accountability and representation."[40] In short, while the economic crisis was the catalyst to the protests, it served largely to unleash a wider generational anger directed at the hijacking of Spain's democracy.[41]

Only part of 15-M's message was contained within its opposition, however. The rest, and most telling component, was embedded within its innovations that channelled the maturing world view of a generation that is today entering into mounting conflict with prevailing structures and values. On this, the 15-M manifesto left no room for ambiguity: "We're organising around assemblies, reaching decisions openly, democratically and horizontally. We have no leaders or hierarchy." Significantly for 15-M, horizontality meant not only no leaders, but a rejection of the very principle of representative democracy. Remaining fiercely independent of all organized groups and parties, Spain's young protesters sought to bring people together "as equal citizens, not as representatives of particular interests or bearers of particular identities."[42] This radical egalitarianism clashed head on with the top-down structures and competing interest groups against which they sought to define their new civic society. And it was a dream, diffused far and wide through the media networks of their generation, that soon resonated across cultures and continents.[43]

Athens is burning: Outrage in the cradle of democracy

The economic situation in Greece was even more dire than in Spain, and the intensity and duration of protests there attested to the fact. Populist unrest had been simmering in Greece since at least December of 2008, when the country exploded into large-scale rioting after a police officer shot and killed fifteen-year-old Alexandros Grigoropoulos. Almost immediately, the media and political parties were speaking of the "students' revolt" or "childrens' democracy," as Greece's young protesters channelled the rage of a generation beset by a debilitating sense of political disenfranchisement.[44] Spurred suddenly to rebellion, they demanded nothing less, writes Greek youth sociologist Yannis Pechtelidis, than the immediate "democratization of the state and society."[45] Through Pechtelidis' lens, we see the striking similarities with Spain immediately rise to the surface: "Young people's protest wasn't solely about the financial crisis or the bleak forecast for the near future," he writes; "it also concerned the violation of social, individual and political rights. It was a democratic struggle around citizens' rights and citizenship."[46] The Greeks' protest in fact seemed to foreshadow the orientation of Spain's Indignados two years later, evoking a maturing system-wide critique that evolved in tandem with their peers in other countries. Much as elsewhere, writes Pechtelidis, "Young people in Greece criticised both neoliberal capitalism and the hierarchical organisation of the traditional Left." The scale of the contestation was historic and amounted to nothing short of a wholesale rejection of the current political order.[47]

The December 2008 revolt marked the onset of a troubling and often violent phase of upheaval in the country.[48] On May 5, 2010, as hundreds of thousands of furious citizens massed outside the parliament, Greek legislators approved drastic spending cuts in exchange for accepting the eurozone's first IMF bailout to the tune of 110 billion euros.[49] In the wake of Spain's 15-M movement a year later, Greek protesters rebranded themselves in the guise of the Indignados, pushing the violent protests to the side as they adopted the Hellenized moniker of the Aganaktismenoi ("The Outraged") and launched a website called Real Democracy (real-democracy. gr).[50] Yet as each subsequent round of the draconian austerity measures cut deeper into Greek society, the democratic crisis grew ever more grave. In an op-ed piece published in the *Guardian*, renowned Greek legal scholar and director of the University of London's Birkbeck Institute for the Humanities Costas Douzinas was scathing in his assessment:

> In the Greek case, manifesto promises of the government before the last elections were comprehensively broken. No consent has been sought or given to the various measures that are destroying the post-war social bond. These measures have led to the surrender of national sovereignty to a motley crew of international bankers and deluded Eurocrats and the demotion of parliament to the position of a multinational company's local branch executing the orders of the headquarters. In all these senses, Greece is in a state of emergency ruled by the diktat of foreign powers.[51]

With the same target but decidedly more rage than the Spaniards, the crowds at Syntagma Square hurled anathema at the Royal Palace that houses their legislature, with the favoured chants of "Thieves!" and "Burn this brothel of a parliament!" routinely erupting from the angry citizenry.[52] The Greek protesters laid the blame squarely at the feet of the corrupt political élites who have ruled the country for the last thirty years.[53]

Following in the footsteps of 15-M, the Aganaktismenoi therefore embodied the same horizontalist ethos as articulated at Acampada Sol, bearing neither hierarchies nor leaders and remaining rigorously unaffiliated with any organization or party. At #Syntagma, the occupiers constructed an elaborate and autonomous city-within-a-city that channelled the thirst for a new republic for the twenty-first century. And inspired by their ancestors who inhabited Athens millennia ago, they erected the contemporary vision of a direct democracy that may rise from the ashes of the one they saw smouldering in ruins beneath their feet.[54]

Revolt at the heart of empire: #OccupyWallStreet

Government responses to the 2008 economic crisis in the United States laid the grounds for a similar narrative to take root west of the Atlantic. Fearing a collapse of its financial sector in the wake of a housing market crash, Washington poured trillions of dollars into rescuing America's "too big to fail" banks, as citizens struggling to make ends meet were being routinely evicted from their homes. America was poised for a Spanish-style awakening, and beneath the eyes of the media, the frantic sowing of networks was already under way.

Kalle Lasn and Micah White, editors of the popular Canadian anticonsumerist magazine *Adbusters,* began sending out emails to subscribers in early June 2011 to respond to the anger they felt bubbling up among their American base. Inspired by events in Spain and Egypt, the two sensed a unique moment at hand and wrote to their followers to plant the seed of a thought: "America needs its own Tahrir." The missive marked the onset of preparations, and the website OccupyWallStreet. org (AcampadaWallStreet.org was also floated, but rejected by the duo) was registered by Vancouver-based Lasn on June ninth.[55] Invoking the "worldwide shift in revolutionary tactics" embodied by the horizontal, decentralized and networked structures of the young Egyptian and Spanish protesters, the *Adbusters* website published a call on July 13 in the form of a brazen question: "Are you ready for a Tahrir moment?" *Adbusters* demanded the ouster of the American "corporatocracy" and evoked the "radical democracy of the future" as their ultimate objective: "On Sept 17, flood into lower Manhattan, set up tents, kitchens, peaceful barricades." Together they would storm the "financial Gomorrah of America," because it was time, they proclaimed, to "#OCCUPYWALLSTREET."

With the glossy zine's characteristic flair of hyper-aestheticism, the graphic artists at "Culture Jammers HQ" produced posters that cast the image of a ballerina rising serenely from out of a tear-gas-choked mob, balanced effortlessly on the back of the Wall Street bull. Instantly, groups from across society (Anonymous perhaps being the most well-known) seized on the call as it snowballed out across activist networks and social media.[56] The Debordian sign subverters at *Adbusters* had tapped into something far deeper than they had ever imagined. Overwhelmed by the massive response, their website soon pumped out excited updates addressed to all the "rebels, radicals and utopian dreamers out there," along with more of their signature culture-jamming imagery to tempt the thirst for revolt as the fateful day approached. One potent meme showed the New York Stock Exchange in the background with the façade's monumental American flag spangled with corporate logos in the place of stars (a recurrent *Adbusters* meme), while in the foreground, shoes were held high in revolt from an angry Arab mob. Along the bottom ran the trigger line: "September 17th. Is America ripe for a Tahrir moment?" The response, as we know, arrived to Wall Street with a thunder on that clear fall day and rippled out across the world in the weeks that followed to reignite the Indignados encampments across Europe.

The revolt, said Indian author and activist Arundhati Roy in the *Guardian*, had attained "the heart of empire."[57]

The linkages between 15-M and Occupy were more than simply ideational. They were organizational in a most explicit sense. Following outreach in July by *Adbusters'* White, activists from New York and around the world met in the city throughout August to lay the grounds for the September actions.[58] Among the crowds, reported journalist Andy Kroll, were Egyptians, Spaniards, Japanese and Greeks, many of whom had been actively involved in the protests across Europe and in Cairo's Tahrir Square.[59] The nightly assemblies, working groups, voting procedures and other components of ows's internal organization energetically mirrored the structures built by the Indignados and which were laid out in step-by-step manuals translated into different languages and published in English on one of 15-M's websites, takethesquare.net. In a section of the website later renamed "How to #Occupy" — an explicit sign of the synergy that emerged between 15-M and ows once the latter had formed in late 2011 — the areas covered included communication strategies, group dynamics, facilitating assembly debates, health and safety procedures and even organizational charts and tables for those wishing to set up their own encampments.[60]

The occupiers of Wall Street thus benefitted immensely from the months of experience gained by their Spanish peers, which facilitated the swift profession-alization of the North American camps. When the protest movement arrived in the U.S., Americans, like the Greeks before them, adopted the modes and model of the Spanish Indignados. In the words of Michael Hardt and Antonio Negri in *Foreign Affairs*, Occupy Wall Street "sprung up from outside and from beneath the political establishment" and mirrored the populist and anti-system messaging of its European cousins. Both were linked through a "defining affect" of indignation that was aimed not only at the panoply of social and economic troubles, but more fundamentally at the underlying failure of a "political system incapable of addressing these issues."[61]

Building on the successes of 15-M, ows brilliantly distilled an expansive critique of the United States' political and economic structures into one potent mantra: "We are the 99%." Their famous rallying cry — and the attendant epithet it created of the loathed "One Percent" — succeeded in sharply delineating a democratic crisis that has seen an "unelected dictatorship of money" seize control of "both the nation's major political parties and so much more."[62] Rising up from the grassroots that the system had tried to shut out, ows's attack on the founda-tions of the corporatized establishment took the fight against austerity out from the stale confines of left versus right and exposed a deeper crisis of representation produced by a subversion of the country's democratic institutions by the economic élite. Indeed despite efforts at co-optation from Democratic Party officials, ows vigorously defended its orientation as an independent, non-partisan and leaderless movement beyond the control of the political establishment.[63] In the image of the Spanish and the Greeks, ows steadfastly refused to endorse candidates from either party, condemning both as agents and symptoms of the same virus that has corrupted American democracy.

The mirroring by ows of the forms adopted by protests overseas was profoundly significant and bespoke a shared set of political values emerging among the globalized network generation that launched them. For this youth, the perennial disconnect between citizens and their democratic institutions seems an endemic and even essential component of the concentrated and top-down nature of representative power — less a system felled by corruption than a system that *is* the corruption itself. In his aptly entitled article "Occupy Wall Street: From Representation to Post-Representation," political theorist Simon Tormey engages incisively with this central premise of Occupy's message:

> ows [...] offers further evidence that the paradigm of representative politics, the politics of political parties, elections and voting is on the wane[...]. It tells us that no form of representative politics, no political party, can change the basic coordinates of the liberal-democratic capitalist system[...]. "Not in my Name" is an emblematic expression of this winding back of the representative paradigm. It says that I will not be annexed for a larger purpose. I must myself speak to and embody the changes we need in order to address inequality.[64]

With Tormey's observations, the abstention of youth from traditional modes of political interaction (voting, political party membership, etc.) emerges in a new light, as the recent explosion of youth activism across continents becomes reconciled with the supposed apathy ascribed to them by others. Indeed, the bewilderment with which establishments greeted the eruptions of revolt perhaps spoke only to the political assumptions of those it caught off guard. The tea leaves, however, were there for all to read: The same generation that has increasingly rejected the political structures bestowed on them by their parents is now taking to the streets and online, where they are slowly crafting new models that aim to rebuild democracy from the ground up. And far from being a contradiction, the question engenders its own response.[65]

Sap rising in the trees: The CLASSE takes up the torch

The year 2011 was a veritable watershed for popular resistance movements that arose around the world to condemn the subversion of political establishments by market powers. Spreading to over one thousand cities in more than eighty countries, the protests reached Montréal on October 15 when the Occupy encampent arrived in the heart of the city's Quartier International business district.[66]

Much of the American and English-Canadian media establishments paid scant attention to Occupy's global antecedents. The networking linkages between activists in different countries thus likely remained unknown to many North Americans. Yet for Quebecers, who share a linguistic and cultural sphere with France, both Hessel's call to action and the movements that it sparked across Europe, including France, were well known. A significant number of Quebecers keep one finger on the pulse of political happenings in that country, aided by the mainstream media's interest in French affairs and the free-flow of the Internet, as well as the massive influx of French expatriates to Montréal in recent years. It was telling that Québec's French-language press often preferred the French designation "les Indignés" to refer to the hundreds camped out in Square Victoria, which was renamed "Place du Peuple" by the Occupiers. Likewise for the French press, "Occupy" was simply the North American designation for the movement of the Indignés, as confirmed by the "Global Day of Indignation" that marked Occupy's expansion across the world on October 15. In sum, Québec's cultural location at the crossroads of Europe and North America placed it at the locus of two waves of a timely and potent tide: that of Occupy Wall Street travelling from six hours south and that of the Indignés, which lapped faintly at our shores from across the Atlantic.

There were no bailouts or fears of financial collapse in Canada's more regulated banking sector, and when held up against the crises afflicting its American and European counterparts, Québec indeed seemed an island of relative calm amidst the storm. Yet the distinction, ultimately, was one of degree (which I'll discuss at length in Chapter 4). For now though, it's important to know that years of corporate and income tax cuts by both governing parties in Québec — including the governing Liberals' 2007 abolition of the 0.7 percent capital tax on business and financial transactions — had emptied the public purse of nearly $10 billion since 2000 alone; yet in 2010, the Liberals imposed $3.5 billion in flat user fees on health care and other essential services by arguing that the state was too poor to fund them.[67] Not poor enough, it seemed, for the Liberals soon uncovered up to $70 billion in state largesse to flaunt to foreign mining giants in a bid at spurring massive resource exploitation under the twenty-five-year Plan Nord[68] — and at the same time, they turned to debt-strapped students, whose interest fees directly profit the banks, and demanded they dig deeper to pay their "fair share."[69] That share, estimated by the government at $265 million, could have been wholly funded by reinstating less than one third of the capital tax; reinstating it all could abolish tuition entirely.[70] But this, to the Liberals, was beside the point. The Charest government, its legitimacy already tarnished by a flood of corruption allegations (discussed in Chapter 4), refused to negotiate the issue with students. In the March 2011 budget, Charest simply decreed an increase of 75 percent over five years. With finance minister Raymond Bachand boldly proclaiming the launch of a "cultural revolution" to definitively do away with Québec's collectivist mentalities, students didn't take long to connect the proverbial dots. It was time, they felt, for a little indignation.

In Québec, the ASSÉ was the actor best placed to channel the mounting challenge to the One Percent. Indeed while the broader agenda and interests at play in

Charest's tuition increase in 2012 were ignored entirely by the FEUQ and FECQ, the CLASSE stood alone in linking its challenge to the wider crisis of representation. In many ways, the student association was actually one of the world's numerous precursors to the Indignados and Occupy movements.[71] We'll recall that both the ASSÉ and the World Social Forum were founded in 2001, only two years after the alter-globalization movement had broken into the mainstream with the Battle in Seattle around the WTO summit. Both enunciated a bottom-up counter vision to corporate-led globalization that was structured around decentralized networks and based on principles of direct democracy, pluralism and social justice. This distinctively twenty-first-century paradigm of horizontalism became the model for the social movements of 2011 and 2012 (and after).

For the ASSÉ, the explosion of Occupy Wall Street six hours south of Montréal thus landed as an untold gift from out of the blue, or a four-star general come late to the battle bearing an army of reinforcements. Seeing the impressive percolation of OWS's narrative among the student base, the ASSÉ moved swiftly to seize on the historic moment. Its manifesto, released in the summer of 2012, tied together the arguments and ideals that motivated their struggle throughout the spring. In *Nous sommes avenir* (suggesting both "We are future" and "We are to come"), the CLASSE lauds the young marchers for awakening what they term "a far deeper malaise" in society that extends far beyond the issue of tuition fees, or even the domain of education. The "collective political problem" that motivated the mobilization, they write, is at root a problem of democracy. The CLASSE drew the battle lines sharply:

> Our vision is one of a direct democracy that is experienced in every instant of every day. It is one of a "We" that expresses itself in the assemblies: at school, at work and in our neighbourhoods. Our vision is one of a permanent appropriation of politics by the population — the foundation of political legitimacy. It's the possibility of heeding those whose voices are never heard.[72]

The CLASSE's diagnosis of a grave democratic crisis echoed the rejection of representative politics embodied by OWS and the Indignados and joins with the voices of its global cousins to move beyond a conventional left-right critique to challenge the legitimacy of the system at its roots. The CLASSE accuses:

> Their vision, their democracy, they call it representative: we ask exactly whom it represents. It lives but once every four years and serves too often to merely change faces. Election after election, the decisions remain the same and serve the same interests, preferring the soft murmurs of lobbies to the chorus of the *casseroles*.[73]

Much as elsewhere, youth anger in Québec was directed at an old guard that embodied the twentieth century's closed and top-down structures of élite power:

here, the Liberal-Péquiste establishment, which has controlled the province since the sixties and has since the 1980s grown increasingly homogenous in its embrace of marketizing policies. Yet in Québec, the genesis and core of the revolt within the student population, and the messaging cohesion lent by the CLASSE, served to bind together the vast indignation that inspired the movement's precedents and to crystallize the generational challenge to the structures and values of the ruling class.

From post-politics to post-representation: A new world beckons

Whether in the streets of Madrid, Athens, New York or Montréal, one can no longer ignore the stunning convergence of voices that are rising to declare their democracies in peril. The young chorus betrays no confusion as to the culprits in their crosshairs. The globalized financial and economic oligarchy has for decades deployed its unprecedented hegemony to manipulate our public debate, commandeer our institutions and divert our common resources to serve their private ends. But now they are facing a historic challenge from the generation whose media are eluding their grip. From the protest cries of "They don't represent us!" heard in the streets of Spain, to the iconic "We are the 99%" of Occupy, their timely and incisive refusal has raised the contours of this moment into sharp relief — and triumphed in tracing an arc that ran from Europe to America to around the world, and finally found echo in Montréal.

From the squares of the Middle East, to Europe and North America, each movement's models became the next segment of a planetary conversation taking place among those now readying to inherit the world. Indeed, in an age where the daunting litany of crises before us has never required a more global response, the next generation of leaders, raised in the decentralized, participatory and horizontal currents of the Web, are slowly forging new systems that may rise to the unprecedented challenges ahead. Parallel to the establishment's pillars of media, cultural, political and economic control, new instruments and practices are emerging to circumvent the dominant structures and begin to turn the tide. If on the surface the façade of inertia remains unfazed, signs from ground level — and from the online underground — hint at a fresh breeze blowing in. And beyond premature judgments over the short-term gains of these movements are the outlines, now coming into focus, of a new generation's dream of democracy on the rise.

4

JEAN CHAREST

Of Corruption, Élite Rule and the Winter of Representation

"The paternalism of power taught that we had to erase social
differences and unite the great Québec family behind the single banner
of the language. This sugary unreality devoid of all sense has been
shattered to pieces."[1]
— Patrick Tillard and Jasmin Miville-Allard, *"Une clarté qui
envahit"* (my translation)

In recent years, Québec's political narrative has been dominated by issues of corruption and abuse of power that have turned a floodlight on the unsavoury proximity between the state and moneyed élites. In seeking to grasp why Québec became a battleground in the global fight to restore collective and democratic rights, the government of Jean Charest is thus a fitting point of departure. A former leader of the centre-right Progressive Conservative party in Ottawa, Charest had arrived to power in 2003 on a pro-business platform that promised to "reinvent Québec" by slashing taxes and reducing the size of government.[2] Much as elsewhere, the neoliberal discourse that had been gaining sway in prior decades became hegemonic over the nine years of Charest's rule, as Québec's social-democratic heritage, traditionally drawn on from both the left and right, was targeted by right-wing reformers for whom "modernization" meant dragging the province into line with "an imagined North American standard."[3] Québec in these years saw the emergence of neoliberal think tanks and university research centres, as well as the growing presence of neoliberal pundits and columnists in the corporate press.[4]

Who speaks for society?

Despite the overwhelming hold of neoliberal ideas over the élites, a profoundly rooted attachment remained to the communitarian conception of Québec society bestowed by the Quiet Revolution, echoes of which persisted in the political class. In Québec's more neo-corporatist political culture — where society is viewed more as an agglomeration of interest groups than individuals — premiers generally sought out a degree of consensus among social partners before engaging significant reforms. High-profile summits, such as those surrounding the Bouchard government's *"déficit zéro,"* were convened to rally civil society to collective efforts

50

whenever possible, with each group (labour, business and the social economic, or "third," sector) represented by their delegates gathered around a common table.[5]

Charest's view of society broke sharply with this framework and embraced the neoliberal vision that recognized the individual's as the sole legitimate political voice, to be expressed, in his view, through the ballot box alone.[6] Charest thus abandoned the consensus-building summits of his predecessors and consistently rejected dialogue with labour unions, community organizations and other social groups who traditionally entertained cordial relations with the state.[7] To talk with them would have been to acknowledge the representative legitimacy of social entities, which Charest was determined to discredit.[8] Quebecers, he argued, had through the expression of the ballot box approved the entirety of his electoral program and chosen him over "corporatist interests."[9] The collectivities that had long been viewed as the building blocks of Québec society were thus reduced in one foul swipe to private interest groups to be bulldozed over and disdained. "There is no such thing as society," said Margaret Thatcher famously. "There are individual men and women and there are families." Following in the truest Thatcherite traditions then, Charest's ultimate aim, cloaked in a vow to reengineer the state, was to break the back of social forces and whittle away the cultural currency of collectivism, entrenching in its stead the neoliberal (non)society populated by families and individuals alone. This rupture in the province's political discourse was where the campaign would begin.

In its governance style, the Charest government thus broke significantly with the traditions of the province, yet only in a way that took to its logical extreme the province's transformation of recent decades: Democracy too would be brought in line with the new Anglo-Saxon standard whereby each citizen speaks alone, and only once every few years. The neoliberal crusaders across North America and Britain had fought hard to reframe labour unions, environmental organizations and other citizen associations as obstacles to prosperity and illegitimate private forces who selfishly block the way to reforms "approved" by the electorate.[10] Thatcher's infamous quip was nothing if not tactically astute: The more these social groups are weakened, the stronger the leader's hand in imposing her or his agenda on a divided collectivity, with the purely individualist and electoralist idea of democracy serving as the adequate legitimation. Within its historic context, Québec's lurch toward autocracy thus appeared as the audacious next step on the decades-long road to the erosion of once-mighty social forces, and all to the benefit of an ever more powerful economic élite.

The "democracy" that breeds autocrats

This acceleration of the neoliberal revolution must also be viewed within the continuity of twentieth-century top-down structures of power, as Charest's combative unilateralism was effectively the product of the fusion of the two. Even the neo-corporatist model, after all, is in practice a system anchored to the hierarchies within each group, where those at the top are the ones invited to the table. This elitist democratic culture has long been the rule in Québec, and in 2012 it found itself at the centre of the *carrés rouges'* challenge to the establishment's power. The province's traditional penchant for social-group oriented approaches only softened this basic tendency toward authoritarian governance; it did little to alter its fundamental parameters. Make no mistake: All efforts at consensus-building aside, at the end of the day there has always been but one *Chef.*

In Québec's modern history, premiers have exhibited little patience in having their authority challenged outside of elections: In 1972, Liberal Premier Robert Bourassa brought down the hammer of emergency back-to-work legislation only ten days into a general strike launched by the 210,000-strong Front commun inter-syndical in response to failed labour contract negotiations between the government and public sector workers. The three national union leaders were jailed for a year for urging members to defy the injunction, inciting massive demonstrations across the province and launching a full-blown social crisis, which ultimately tipped in favour of labour.[11] In 1982, PQ Premier René Lévesque, who is widely considered the most democratic premier the province has known, suppressed a fourth action in a decade by the Front commun in response to his government's public sector pay cuts. Yet this time, the strike action was easily stifled, when the PQ passed emergency back-to-work legislation, decreed 20 percent salary cuts and levelled steep fines at labour leaders for inciting civil disobedience.[12]

Charest, in this light, fit the mould of a leader within Québec's élite-representative framework: Confronted by a mass contestation in a province prone to shows of force from the street, he responded with autocratic muscle aimed at reasserting his government's authority. In this old world, the legitimacy to wield power derives largely from the transaction of voting, with the complex and evolving realities of public opinion cast aside in favour of fixed "mandates" interpreted freely by the victors. The votes cast for the opposition parties, however, even when the majority, are often ignored. In short, the relation between the institution of voting and democratic decision-making is tenuous at best, a fact that is accepted for one reason: that our nineteenth- and twentieth-century system of representative democracy is based first and foremost on the maintenance of order, not consensus. That is why under our electoral system, electoral minorities are translated into parliamentary majorities as a matter of design, with the outcome in every case a perversion of the popular will, and even more so with abstention rates considered. But of course, all electoral systems become divorced from the popular will the second after the freeze-frame is captured, if indeed they ever channel it at all: Within the forced simplicity of partisan politics, the sacrosanct Ballot Box is a choice between sealed boxes, where voters can't select elements from among different candidates and yet are disenfranchised for years after providing carte blanche to their choice.

In less delicate terms, this idea of democracy may be called the theory of the elected dictatorship. Such an adversarial dynamic is of course not unique to

Québec but is especially endemic to Westminster parliamentary regimes where a first-past-the-post (FPTP) electoral system rewards minorities with power that is undivided and absolute. The winner-take-all Westminster model, which fails most spectacularly in multipartite environments, thus calls for high-minded leaders capable of exercising a good deal of decency and restraint. Such statesmanship is vital to respecting the fundamental tenet of the consent of the governed, which at a bare minimum demands engaging and working *with* opposition parties who almost invariably represent the majority of voters in FPTP systems. Yet in practice, the politicians bred by our structures of representative governance have been precisely the opposite and have not hesitated to wield the full weight of the power we entrust so naïvely in their hands.

Charest's interpretation of representative legitimacy may well have been more autocratic than that of his predecessors, who rarely behaved in so consistently heavy-handed a manner. Yet the differences were ultimately of degree, with each authoritarian excess allowed and even encouraged by the laws and institutions in place. In a sense, Charest's governance then at least had the benefit of crystallizing the essential juxtaposition between old and new ideas of democracy. Thus during the student crisis, the government's intransigence belied a bunker mentality that saw Charest consistently reducing the struggle to a binary choice, with the order of "democracy" (read: the irrevocable authority of electoral rules) on one side and the chaos of "the street" (which challenged this authority) on the other. In the eyes of the Liberal premier, the hundreds of thousands of citizens in the streets embodied not the voice of the people, but the dangerous and destabilizing threat of mob rule.[13] To him, the premier and her or his handpicked ministers were to be the sole defenders of Quebecers' democratic rights and the lone bulwark that would protect them from themselves. *La démocratie, c'est moi.*

The pyromaniac premier

Charest's decade-long tenure was marked by a seemingly unending string of provocations and a governance style that frequently met opposition with denial and derision. The Liberals had barely been elected in 2003 when he sparked the first crisis by loosening protections in the Labour Code pertaining to subcontractors. The move raised the ire of labour unions and incited a large province-wide mobilization that launched a phase of persistent hostilities with civil society. The premier's very liberal understanding of the mandate conferred to him even angered many who had supported his party: Within nine months of Charest coming to office, the opposition PQ was already comfortably ahead in the polls, and dissatisfaction toward his government had soared to a record 72 percent by May 2004.[14] These opinion polls, which remained fairly consistent through his whole time in office, never entered into the equation. Nor did the fact that 63 percent in one poll performed in his first year, including 28 percent of Liberals, felt that

Charest was *not* respecting the mandate accorded him by voters.[15] Duly elected, the premier soldiered onward.

Acrimonious protests were a regular feature of the landscape through the Liberals' first term, with critics reproaching the "pyromaniac premier" of dogmatic manners that consistently stoked anger and social unrest.[16] Whether the imposition of a natural gas plant outside the town of Beauharnois or the partial privatization of Mont-Orford National Park to build condos at its summit, vociferous opposition, both from locals and from within his own government (environment minister Tom Mulcair, now leader of the New Democratic Party, resigned over the Mont-Orford issue), too often failed to slow the Liberal bulldozer. In the face of overwhelming opposition on Mont-Orford, the government invoked parliamentary closure to force a bill through the Assemblée nationale in 2006, thereby paving the way for promoters by removing the area in question from the national park. The penalty for showing such contempt for his opposition was steep, however, as Quebecers showed little desire to go along with Charest's designs: In the 2007 election, the Liberal government suffered a historic setback when it was reduced to minority status, the first in Québec since 1878.[17]

It took this stinging rebuke to push the government to halt the sale of lands in Mont-Orford and maintain their public character. (After years of delays, the Charest government finally reintegrated the 459 hectares into the park in 2010.) Yet such was the pattern under Charest, where retreats came rarely and only as a reluctant last resort. In the same vein, we'll recall that it took the student movement over a year of protesting and a (then) historic record of seven weeks of striking in 2005 to force the government into partially reinstating $103 million a year that was cut from student grants (and only with the last-minute help of the federal government). The $500 per semester increase to fees that followed the Liberals' re-election in 2007 did indeed keep with a campaign promise. Yet it was one that was endorsed, in the most generous interpretation, by a mere 33 percent of voters — the lowest ratio to support the party since the Canadian federation was born in 1867.[18] With polls in fact showing more than 60 percent opposition to the measure, the hike came without so much as a debate in the Assemblée nationale and was imposed unilaterally through a modification to the Ministère de l'éducation's internal budget regulations.[19]

Many other instances abounded in the same direction, namely from the top down. Time and again, Charest waged war against central actors of Québec society who presented a resistance to his agenda of commodifying the public good. And time and again, the unprecedented degree of popular opposition it stoked brought his government to the precipice of defeat, only to be re-elected by a public with a bitter lack of credible alternatives. Perhaps nothing was more emblematic of the Charest government's autocratic culture than its cavalier abuse of closure, a parliamentary tactic that cuts off debate and circumvents the opposition parties by forcing legislation through the Assemblée nationale on the strength of the government's artificial majority of seats. Charest passed no fewer than thirteen (often highly unpopular) bills in this way.[20] Yet while Charest certainly pushed the envelope further than past premiers, it's also important not to overstate the extent to which Charest departed from Québec's democratic norms: Charest's predecessors, after all, were far from shy in their invocation of the same tactics. Indeed, in the context of an electoral system that rewards minorities with absolute power, the very existence of so undemocratic a tool resounds as a stinging condemnation of our representative system. Its foundations, the vestiges of another time, were built first and foremost not to support democracy, but authority — its opposite. And in this light, Charest is far from an anomaly of our representative system. In truth, he was perhaps its purest creation.

Austerity overdrive:
The cultural revolution of the capitalist class

In the face of massive popular opposition during his first term, Charest was forced to moderate his ambitions of "reinventing" a society that showed little interest in being reinvented. Charest learned an important lesson, writes sociologist Éric Pineault: that in a society whose identity since the sixties has been shaped by "progressive nationalism and social-democratic exceptionalism," it was "politically untenable" to impose "the complete commodification of public services" — without the legitimating factor of "a major fiscal shock or crisis."[21] That crisis arrived in 2008. In the wake of a new wave of austerity measures launched across the United States and Europe to respond to the "Great Recession," the chance to press the government's foot on the neoliberalizing accelerator was not one the Liberal leader would lightly pass up.[22]

Starting in 2008, government-commissioned reports began to take aim at what they termed Québec's "free-lunch culture,"[23] a deeply ideological bit of sloganeering that could only be read as a frontal assault on Québec's social programs. Immediately, it became apparent that those expecting a sober and thoughtful analysis of Québec's finances were looking to the wrong government. The Montmarquette task force formed in 2008 was to serve as a public relations tool, directed by its narrow mandate to elaborate a "new user fee policy" that the government was *a priori* determined to implement.[24] The fact that the authors, including economist Claude Montmarquette and former PQ minister Joseph Facal, were high-profile members of the "Lucides" group, which advocates for the commodification of public services, only amplified the inevitability of its recommendations. This was no study at all, but a legitimation campaign, Phase One.

The second phase of the exercise would be launched less than two years later, when another government-commissioned report — in which Montmarquette again participated along with three other economists, almost all associated with the neoliberal think tank CIRANO headed by Montmarquette — reinforced the push toward flat fees on all public services.[25] Yet even more notable than the renewed audacity of the austerity drive was the disingenuous and manipulative framing of the "problem": the culture of the "free lunch"? No public service has ever been *free*, as the authors rightly point out in their guise.[26] As a fundamental principle of social justice, rather — one common to all Western welfare states established after the Great Depression — services are funded through income taxes so as to account for each citizen's ability to pay. It's a fairly simple and widely nurtured principle, and yet there it was in black on white in the 2008 report: The "perception that a service provided by the government must be free of charge," the task force wrote, is a "myth" that they were determined to deconstruct. Citizens, in their view, were "not informed about the real cost of the public services they use" and were therefore prone to engage in abuses.[27]

It's hard to find flaw with their diagnosis of a civic knowledge deficit in contemporary democracies. Their prescription, on the other hand, instantly gave the game up. In line with the government's ideological objectives, the task force's mandate was not to reflect on the serious educational reform needed to rebuild the civic values that have been eroded by the consumerist "me" society — a long-overdue initiative if ever there were one. No, the authors were not hired by the minister of education but of finance, and with one aim: to legitimize a paternalistic policy that simply smacks citizens with enough fees until they get the message. The stepped up Liberal agenda post-2008 thereby announced a radical transformation. Yet politics obliging, the question was never phrased as a clear choice between progressive and regressive taxation, and no debate was ever had on the fair share that could be expected of corporations or the rich. The straightjacket of neoliberalism not only prevented any discussion of raising income or corporate taxes; it also shielded successive governments' moves to shower the wealthiest segments of society with ever greater largesse. From 2000 to 2010, PQ and Liberal governments alike ceded $8.9 billion worth of revenues through consecutive cuts to income and corporate tax rates. So much that by 2013, the combined federal-provincial corporate rate had tumbled from 45.6 percent in 2000 to 26.9 percent — thirteen points *lower* than the average in the United States[28] — with the provincial portion accounting for but 11.9 percent.[29] Yet the Charest government's "cultural revolution"[30] announced in the 2010 budget imposed flat user fees totalling $3.5 billion, justified on the pretext that the state lacked the money to fund the essential services.[31]

The Liberal alternative took the form of sharp increases in tuition fees, new health care premiums and per-visit fees, daycare charges, school taxes and increased sales tax and electricity rates, which all shot up under Charest's watch. In the wake of the Liberals' 2010 austerity budget, fifty thousand citizens poured into the streets as dissatisfaction with the government soared to 77 percent, yet the Liberals never flinched nor ever feigned to open a social dialogue.[32] Instead, the 2011 budget pushed ahead with an emboldened agenda of austerity reforms, confirming and specifying the draconian scale of the tuition hike announced in the budget a year earlier. The opposition PQ galloped into a distant lead, yet the Liberals never once paused to acknowledge or address the scale of the opposition.[33] That, after all, would have been to acknowledge the presence of alternatives and to undermine the auras of inevitability that shielded the offensive. Charest took his lessons from the Baroness well: *There is no alternative.* User-pay was simply decreed the new model of the Québec state by dishonest default and sold as a matter of sound financial managerialism neutral of all values or social choices.[34]

It was the classic self-engineered prophecy of the neoliberals' designs. And quite naturally, as the tax burden has shifted from the top of the pyramid toward the bottom, wealth inequalities have soared. Low-income Quebecers with a child in daycare today devote more than 12 percent of their after-tax revenue on public services, while those earning more than $194,500 devote 1.08 percent for the same — and those earning more than $305,000, only 0.68 percent.[35] This is the direct and deliberate effect of services that are charged at the same price for the rich and poor alike and the culmination of a trend initiated at the dawn of the neoliberal age: Between 1976 and 2006, the bottom half of income-earners in Québec saw their revenues decline, while the top 10 percent increased theirs by 24 percent, bringing the gap between rich and poor to its highest level in at least thirty years.[36] And that, says social theorist David Harvey, Éric Pineault and others, is precisely the point. Broad-based economic growth has always been secondary to neoliberal economics, and austerity policies in stagnation-engulfed Europe have even been a "complete disaster" in the judgment of Nobel Prize-winning economist Joseph Stiglitz. "Though facts keep staring them in the face," pro-austerity European leaders "continue to deny reality," he writes.[37] That is because it is not reasoned policy, says Pineault, but a stubborn "ideology of legitimation" deployed to rationalize the restoration of "hegemonic class power by the economic elite."[38] Dogmas seldom like facts that don't fall into line.

Few things could stand as an effective emblem of the new governance regime as well as the resource exploitation plan that was touted as Charest's legacy project and that became cast centre stage in the student struggle of 2012. Much like the government's full-throttle (and highly unpopular) backing of the shale gas industry in its final mandate, the equally controversial Plan Nord — which the Marois government largely maintained in rebranded form and the current Liberal government is set to "relaunch" — was (and is) the expression of a vision that replaces the broad notion of the public good with a narrow form of economic development skewed toward corporations. Charest's twenty-five-year plan foresaw tens of billions of dollars in public funding to the near-exclusive benefit of foreign resource sector giants, yet bearing highly questionable financial and social returns for the province as a whole.[39] Royalties limited to 16 percent were to be calculated based on each mine's profits rather than the volumes extracted, and the public purse was (and is) responsible for post-mine restoration, which already amounted to over $1 billion as of 2012.[40] All of this was unfolding in a context where a 2009 report by the auditor-general of Québec found that fourteen of the twenty-four mining companies then operating in the province had not paid a single cent of royalties for seven years.[41] In sum, this is a mining regime that does more than merely *allow* the private plundering of non-renewable public resources: The government in this system is an active partner in the pillaging and an immoveable ally not of the people, but of the corporate plunderers.

The "democracy" that breeds corruption

Charest's undemocratic governance style was only half the story explaining his unprecedented unpopularity in the province. Beneath the surface of the government's heavy-handed manners and intimate proximity to the business milieu stewed suspicions of unsavoury practices running rampant in the backrooms of power.

The suspicions seldom lacked sources to nourish them. Story after story surfaced in the press portraying apparent instances of collusion between the Liberal Party and firms who paid their way, often illegally, into the government's good books. It should come as little surprise, moreover, that the scandals were in many cases preceded by measures that weakened checks and balances and centralized power in the government's hands. Immediately upon coming to office in 2003, the premier gave cabinet control over the nominations of judges, thereby politicizing a process that for decades had been kept relatively independent of such pressures.[42] Separately, on three occasions, in 2003, 2007 and 2009, Charest loosened regulations governing conflicts of interest involving cabinet ministers and the companies they or their relatives own, including those receiving public contracts from their own ministry.[43] These troubling moves were early signs of a culture of impunity deepening its roots within the Liberal Party, and in retrospect boded nothing well for the sequence of things to come.

Charest's final term saw the storm clouds only darken as they massed relentlessly over the government's head. A string of accusations and revelations by opposition parties, a former Liberal justice minister, journalists and the electoral watchdog all pointed to hundreds of thousands of dollars donated — much of it illegally — to both the Liberals and PQ over the years by engineering and construction firms who were awarded lucrative contracts by the state, often in the absence of a call for tenders.[44] With the government submerged in a swamp of suspicions, another case of abuse was uncovered in December 2011 by the provincial auditor-general that placed the minister of families (and later of education), Michelle Courchesne, at the eye of another storm. After centralizing authority for allocating daycare permits in her office, the minister rejected 3,505 places recommended by civil servants in 2008 while granting 3,700 that they had refused, with a large number of the beneficiaries represented by private promoters who donated nearly $300,000 to the Liberal Party between 2003 and 2008.[45]

With each fresh allegation, Charest and his ministers reacted with vehement denials and at times threats of legal action to protect their sullied reputations.[46] Yet the government's fits of righteous indignation as they lashed out at critics invariably fell on deaf ears. Cynicism toward the Liberals was at an all-time high, and their behaviour in power invited little sympathy from the public. Over the years, three government ministers erroneously affirmed on separate occasions that businesses could legally donate to political parties in Québec, a practice that was banned by the Lévesque government back in 1977.[47] Few things, perhaps, emblematized the government's insouciance for ethics with such utter clarity.

With public trust in the government unravelling at the seams, the premier's personal credibility underwent several onslaughts from which he would never recover. It wasn't helped when in March 2010, former justice minister Marc Bellemare accused Charest of "lying like he breathes" when the premier denied knowing about illegal financing and trafficking of influence at the Liberal Party. Bellemare insisted he possessed evidence of having broached the subject with the premier numerous times while he was in government in 2003 and 2004.[48] Nor was it improved in May of 2011, when Charest's former environment minister, Tom Mulcair, told the press that Charest vetoed an environmental protection law because it would have angered Laval Mayor Gilles Vaillancourt by protecting valuable land from development. The Liberals needed Vaillancourt for the elections, Charest reportedly told Mulcair. This is the same mayor, often nicknamed the "king of Laval," whose quasi-unchallenged twenty-three-year reign came crashing down in a spectacular heap when he became the first mayor in Canada to be arrested in office for "gangsterism." The former mayor is accused of being at the head of criminal stratagems involving corruption and collusion dating back to 1996.[49]

Most damaging to the government's credibility, however, was its tone-deaf response to the public outrage that rose in tandem with each new scandal. Faced with quasi-unanimous calls for a full public inquiry into the construction industry, Charest twice gambled on half-measures aimed at appeasing public opinion. In February 2010, the government named former Montréal police chief Jacques Duchesneau to head a new anti-collusion taskforce within the Ministère des transports (MTQ) that was initially provided with no mandate to produce a report, nor any police powers or devoted resources — not even a computer or a vehicle (months later, its resources and mandate were expanded).[50] In the interim, however, calls for a full public inquiry only grew louder, including from Duchesneau himself, who upon his appointment insisted that the creation of the Unité anticollusion (UAC) did nothing to diminish the necessity of a full inquiry.[51] So in February 2011, the government again deflected such calls by creating a new "super-unit" under the Ministère de la sécurité publique, which absorbed the UAC and drew from a wide array of ministries and existing structures. This time, the special unit was invested with broad powers of investigation and recommendation, as well as a permanent budget and a staff of nearly two hundred. In parallel, the ministries of justice and public security announced the joint creation of a special bureau of thirty prosecutors devoted to combatting corruption and malfeasance.[52]

The creation of the Unité permanente anticorruption (UPAC) would prove a major step in the fight against corruption, as their high-profile visits, searches, seizures and arrests regularly fuelled the headlines of media outlets across Québec. Yet far from neutralizing the issue politically, the troubles for Charest were only beginning. In September of 2011, an Earthquake shook the grounds beneath the political establishment when the report of the MTQ's Unité anticollusion was leaked to Radio-Canada by Duchesneau himself, who after meeting with transportation minister Sam Hamad feared the government would shelve the report.[53] The Duchesneau Report's shockwaves rippled out to the furthest reaches of the province, offering a sinister portrait of corruption that had found a comfortable seat at the highest echelons of power.

Indeed, to Québec's viewers and readers sitting at home, the facts, as laid down in the report, proved more compelling, and far more unsettling, than fiction. The Duchesneau task force uncovered a system of an "unsuspected scale" that had seen organized crime massively infiltrate the industry, diverting public funds to line the pockets of criminals while producing an explosion in the costs of public infrastructure works.[54] In this sordid state of business-as-usual, many construction companies and engineering consultancy firms maintained regular relations with organized crime. In certain domains, criminal organizations achieved a stranglehold, with one Hells Angels insider testifying that "everything asphalt in Montréal and around it, we have it all."[55] Shocking passages of that sort filled the pages of the Duchesneau Report, which drew from testimony from a wide range of actors in its rigorous outline of the clandestine system's inner workings. "Everyone is scared," confided one anonymous source in describing the climate of fear and intimidation that reigned. And with the mafia and biker gangs everywhere, said the witness, you're wise "to mind your own business."[56] It was all enough to send an icy shiver down Québec's collective spine.

Among the key findings, engineering consultancy firms were said to be deeply implicated in the organized deception, engaging in the routine inflation of cost estimates to make room for the inevitable kickbacks down the line, known as "extras" in the parlance of the milieu. The practice is so commonplace that many firms had taken to employing "specialists in extras" on their permanent staff, who took a 10 percent cut of the amount they wrested from the government.[57] Even those construction companies without ties to organized crime were described by the report as functioning like cartels themselves, manoeuvring aggressively and colluding among themselves to eliminate the competition.[58] With ten entrepreneurs responsible for 39 percent of road works in the province and 68 percent of all contracts for professional services being claimed by ten firms alone, the shadowy causes of the overwhelming concentration in the industry suddenly stepped into daylight.[59]

Most damaging for the government, however, was the report's findings that targeted the political class, which was far from spared the shrapnel from the explosive revelations — quite the contrary. A former political advisor testified that the province's political parties were massively funded by construction companies and engineering consultancy firms, who gained privileged access to decision-makers in return and royal treatment to match.[60] The decades-old ban on political donations from businesses was thus frequently circumvented by the widespread stratagem known as *"prête-noms"* (name-lending), which had long been among the worst kept secrets in Québec political circles. The report's findings fit perfectly with what police captain Éric Martin of the anti-corruption Escouade Marteau told *La Presse* in February 2011:

> To advance construction projects or for them to be authorized, [the firms] have to finance political parties. They will ask collaborators or employees to commit fraud by deceit, falsehood or other means. They will fabricate false invoices or charge for services never rendered.[61]

According to the testimony garnered by the Unité anticorruption, political parties were far from victims in the game, nor even hesitant partners in the trafficking of influence: party bagmen routinely went knocking on the doors of engineering consultancy firms and construction companies, actively nourishing the rot at the core of our democratic structures.[62] In 2013, *La Presse* even uncovered Charest's agendas from his time as Liberal opposition leader in 2001, which depict a leader engaged first-hand in the door-knocking targeting firms and offices in Montréal. Charest's spokesperson of course insisted all donations were legal, but the specific targeting of engineering and other firms leaves ample room to doubt that individuals were the ones whose wallets the Liberal leader had in his sights.[63]

Separate from political parties, the official government apparatus was far from impermeable. The employees at the Ministère des transports, along with those in the engineering consultancy firms, often leaked privileged information to select entrepreneurs so as to favour them in calls for tenders.[64] The ministry's lack of vigilance and expertise, which has been hollowed out by years of outsourcing to the private sector, effectively provided free rein to engineering consultancy firms to exploit and manipulate the MTQ and allowed for corruption to flourish right under its nose. Even when the MTQ would opt to challenge the claims of entrepreneurs, they bully the government by launching civil lawsuits, knowing that the ministry had the practice of reaching settlements out of court. In short, the government's main point of contact with the industry had been gradually defanged and left at the mercy of criminal elements with far greater resources, skill and resolve.[65]

The depth and breadth of the systemic corruption shocked even the seasoned Duchesneau, and the ominous conclusions he drew seemed aimed at preempting any doubts as to the urgency of the situation. "If there were to be an intensification of influence-trafficking in the political sphere," he warned, "then we would no longer be simply talking about criminal activities on a marginal or even a parallel scale: We could suspect instead an infiltration and even a takeover of certain functions of the state or municipalities [by organized crime]."[66] As one may imagine, the wave of public indignation that rose up to meet the release of the report was matched only by the volume of the alarm it had raised.

The Duchesneau task force was intended as a preventative tool and lacked the authority to publish names of companies and individuals in the report. To this day, no one has yet been convicted of any crime, though many big names in the construction and political worlds have been arrested and charged. Yet the court of public opinion had seen and heard quite enough: When Angus Reid asked Quebecers in February 2013 whether they suspected nine of the province's post-Duplessis premiers of being involved in corruption, Charest sat alone in his unenviable corner with 76 percent answering in the affirmative. Robert Bourassa, Jacques Parizeau and Pauline Marois all hovered around fifty percent, while René Lévesque fared best at 33 percent.[67] In matters of trust, it rarely gets worse for a government than this, and in the case of Charest, his behaviour did little to reassure. Faced with overwhelming public pressure and unanimous calls from the opposition to call a public inquiry into the construction industry, Charest, true to type, stonewalled inexplicably for two years. The government finally ceded to pressure one month later, but it was only after the first iteration was panned for lacking teeth that Charest reversed course days later and invested the new Charbonneau Commission with full powers of subpoena.[68] The Commission adjourned in November 2014 and has until April 19, 2015, to submit its final report.

Servants of money: Power in a Potemkin democracy

With cynicism and voter abstention at all-time highs, it's time the ritual head-shaking made way for hard and honest conclusions: Our élite-based structures have bred corruption in all its forms. For indeed when we understand the term most fully as the diversion of our public institutions and resources for private gain, the phenomenon emerges as a ubiquitous and even integral component of our democracies; its illegal expressions are then but one side of the ugly coin. This is not meant to evoke a caricature of shadowy élites guffawing as they gather around in their VIP lounges to plot against the people. That would be too easy. Yet it is an earnest suggestion: that humans possess an uncanny ability to rationalize that which benefits them and their friends, and even to convince themselves that their own objectives serve the good of the many.

In Québec, scandals alleging various forms of abuse flowed invariably from measures that concentrated power in the government's hands. Yet while efforts to increase checks and balances and expand transparency may momentarily blunt the system's natural tendencies, ultimately, they may always prove cosmetic and illusory, for they go against the grain of a model that is by nature hierarchical and closed to grassroots involvement — such is the meaning of the authority vested in our "representatives." In 2012 the students of Québec, aided by the Indignados and Occupiers before them, gathered the plot. They no longer condemned corruption as a virus that's infiltrated the political organism, no longer viewed it as an external impurity eating away at otherwise sound foundations. To the CLASSE and its backers, the widening chasm between the people and their democratic institutions had laid bare nothing less than the failures of a twentieth-century idea of democracy that owes more to élite paternalism than any true notion of citizen empowerment.

Whether one agrees with this mounting rejection of the representative paradigm is secondary to acknowledging the underlying reality it reveals: that a generation is fast losing hope that the broken democracy of their parents is reformable and that the chances of restoring its legitimacy grows dimmer with every year. This does not mean that their hope and civic engagement aren't harboured elsewhere, however, and if anything, the historic events of recent years have forcefully laid such notions to rest. But more, they have painted a historic possibility: for on the centuries-long road to the democratization of Western societies, the present is doubtless a chapter more promising than the last — but may yet, with the dreams of this awakening generation, be remembered as a period darker than the one to come.

PART TWO

THE AWAKENING

PREPARING THE SOIL
In the Corridors of the Movement

We were born with the disillusions of an autumn
and grew up with the despair of a winter.
We are the children of a world asleep
beneath the snows of cynicism, of bitterness
and of individualism.

They called us land that bore little fertility, a generation laying fallow,
deficient soil, in short,
quite a meagre harvest...[1]

— Sébastien Moses, *"De ventôse à germinal"* (my translation)

The student movement was the heir to the Quiet Revolution's democratic dream of Québec and the keepers of the commons, who embodied one of the last remnants of a time when social forces had the power to sway governments.[2] In the Liberals' push to accelerate the shift away from that legacy and toward a commercialist society, education was thus a central plank. The students lived these years on the perpetual defensive. So when government reports and comments by finance minister Raymond Bachand presaged the arrival of a new "cultural revolution" to Québec, they began to fear the worst was finally arriving.[3] In the corridors, rumours circulated among the activist core that foresaw "a defining struggle for the survival of public and accessible education, and for the future of the student movement itself."[4] The rush to a war footing had begun.

In February 2010, barely three years since the last increase, education minister Michelle Courchesne spoke of a consensus emerging in Québec on the importance of raising tuition fees further — a "consensus" from which she explicitly excluded the students themselves.[5] To the minister of education, it seemed, neither her mandate nor any notion of decency required that the primary ones affected by her policies be involved in the discussion. The stakes were simply too high for such petty concerns: "A tuition hike," explains Éric Pineault, "epitomized the long-term changes sought by the élites: attacking the culture of gratuity and entitlement," challenging Québec's social-democratic exceptionalism and "consolidating a new model of the university as a corporatized research organization."[6] As goes education, so would go Québec: toward a landscape of consumers and investors, all competing for materialist advantage in the forums of the ultimate market society.

The establishment within: The student movement's divided currents

The ASSÉ saw the government's long game immediately and launched a meticulous two-year process in preparation for an eventual general strike.[7] The student federations, the FEUQ and FECQ, began their own campaigns by launching a petition on the site of the Assemblée nationale in the fall of 2010 that was submitted on December 9. It garnered thirty thousand signatures, representing a (then) record number for an official online petition in Québec.[8] It made no difference. Two years before the $500 five-year increase decreed in 2007 had fully entered into effect, the Charest government convened a *Rencontre des partenaires en éducation* in which the Conférence des recteurs et des principaux des universités (CREPUQ) requested yet another, much sharper, round of hikes — and the premier quickly acquiesced.[9] The labour unions and student federations, joined by the smaller Table de concertation étudiante du Québec (TACEQ), which had recently formed,[10] responded by walking out in protest, leaving only business leaders, the government and the CREPUQ to discuss the modalities of the hike amongst themselves.[11] The ASSÉ, for its part, had boycotted what it decried as a public relations stunt aimed at legitimating a fait accompli, and organized a one-day strike to protest outside the meeting, which drew an estimated sixty thousand students.[12] The 2010–2011 school year announced growing turbulence, as dozens of small student protests followed one after the next, cumulating in a large demonstration days before the release of the March 2011 budget. Fifty thousand citizens from across a wide swath of civil society poured into the streets that day, rallying around a simple message that channelled the hardening rebuke of the government's there-is-no-alternative (TINA) rationale: "An equitable budget: a question of choice."[13]

The different approaches of Québec's national student associations revealed the conflicting currents within the student movement. On the one side, the FEUQ and FECQ operated from within the establishment and were the outflow of the same élite-based culture that produced the governing parties, and in particular the PQ. Transparency and information-sharing are more highly valued by the ASSÉ's culture, which explains in large part the relative lack of indepth information currently available on the behind-the-scenes organizational and mobilization campaigns of the federations, and the resulting imbalance in the information offered here (Martine Desjardins is said to be publishing a book shortly, which we can hope will shine further light). What we do know at present is that in the 2012 campaign, the presidents and executives of the FEUQ and FECQ focused their strategies on person-to-person contacts within government and the opposition, and prioritized lobbying and participation in official negotiations over pressure tactics (although they engaged in both). While the government closed all communications channels with the associations at the start of the conflict in February, before and during the crisis the FEUQ and FECQ entertained regular contact with the opposition parties, and especially intimate relations with the leadership of the PQ. The Official Opposition became the eyes and ears of the federations in the corridors of power, providing intelligence on the advent of any tensions within Liberal ranks that were otherwise hidden from public view. The Opposition also served as their direct channel into the Assemblée nationale. The education critic for the PQ, Marie Malavoy, coordinated her questions in the assembly with the FEUQ, and both kept each other abreast of developments that could impact the debate.[14]

By sharp contrast, the ASSÉ (widened to become the CLASSE in December 2011) vigorously defended its independence from all political parties and positioned itself solidly outside and beneath the establishment in the same vein as Occupy Wall Street and the Indignados. The association's culture of direct democracy leads it to a deep mistrust of the institutions of representative power and to a wariness of being co-opted, deceived or instrumentalized for partisan purposes.[15] Instead, the horizontalist organization is built on a highly decentralized structure that empowers the local associations, and the ASSÉ invests its resources heavily in educating, engaging and training its base. While not always refusing negotiation (any more than the federations shy away from protests), their strategies favoured grassroots engagement and the mass mobilization of its members to apply pressure on the government from below.

The CLASSE's contestational character became the focal point for tensions on numerous occasions during the conflict. They came to the fore at the end of Martine Desjardins' term as president of the FEUQ in 2013, when she accused the CLASSE of having hurt the cause by encouraging violence and vandalism.[16] This criticism, while facile and frequent, has always been incorrect. The diversity of tactics model defended by the CLASSE/ASSÉ, with its roots in the alter-globalization movement, upholds the legitimacy of a wide array of protest actions, which includes both economic disturbances (such as bridge blockades) and direct action (such as occupations of campuses or ministers' offices). Yet pointedly, the CLASSE/ASSÉ draws its red line at violence perpetrated against individuals. They have no blanket position to either support or condemn acts of vandalism, but generally refrain from condemning such actions that, for example, target the property of multinational banks and corporations.[17] Never did the CLASSE directly or indirectly encourage vandalism or violence during the spring of 2012. They were pilloried, rather, for not rushing to show revulsion at the minor collateral damage that is the inevitable outflow of a deepening social crisis.

This was in fact the triumph of government strategy: Every minute the media lights were aimed at the CLASSE's position on violence was one that spared the government questions on the *causes* for the rising anger in the streets. Every microphone in Gabriel Nadeau-Dubois's face was one far away from Jean Charest's, sparing him scrutiny of the government's responsibility for having let the conflict envenom for months. Prodded incessantly by the mainstream media, which sheepishly took up the government line, the CLASSE reacted with genuine disgust: For as its spokespeople were being tried publicly for not condemning a handful of broken windows — which they neither directed, nor encouraged, nor ever had the power to control — real physical violence was being meted out daily against unarmed protesters and with the wholehearted complicity of the political and economic establishment. The FEUQ and FECQ played the government's game in consenting to the moral equivalency between violence against humans and property. Yet the CLASSE called the question the deflection that it was and tried to turn the spotlight back on the government's sanctioning of force against civilians.

Frustrations over the CLASSE's tactics were exhibited both during and after the strike by Bureau-Blouin and Desjardins, then presidents of the FECQ and FEUQ, respectively. Yet in hindsight, we can say that the former presidents doth protest too much. For when all is said and done, the unlikely complementarity between the CLASSE's campaign and that of the federations produced the most important mass mobilization in Québec history.

The first student common front

By May of 2011, the ASSÉ's campaign was well under way, and despite the important differences that opposed them to the federations, they were determined to prevent a repeat of the divisions that undermined the student mobilization in 2005. At the ASSÉ's initiative, therefore, all student associations were invited to a *Rassemblement national étudiant* held in May 2011 at the Université Laval in Québec City. In an effort at devising a solidarity pact between the national (i.e., Québec) associations, the ASSÉ proposed an *"entente minimale,"* which included the following three deceptively simple yet astute clauses: that all national student associations refuse to negotiate if the government excludes one from the negotiating table; that the national executives commit to not recommending any entente to their members, instead allowing the local assemblies the first and final word; and that all national and local associations refrain from denouncing to the media the actions of other national and local associations.[18]

Renaud Poirier St-Pierre, who was the CLASSE's press attaché during the strike, and Philippe Ethier, a member of the executive at the time, explain that the intention of the pact was to bring the FEUQ and FECQ closer in line with the more robust democratic practices of the ASSÉ. Most crucially, the second (or "non-recommendation") clause sought to prevent the executives of either federation from announcing an entente before the local assemblies had a chance to consider it, as the FEUQ had done in 2005 much to the anger of its base. The pact caused an enormous amount of consternation in the ranks of the federations, and ultimately the FECQ ratified it while the FEUQ balked. In practice, however, it appeared the exact inverse: It was the FECQ's Bureau-Blouin who ultimately criticized the CLASSE publicly for not condemning violence during the 2012 strike, and even offered to sit down with the government without them present on the pretext that they had thereby excluded themselves.[19]

Most important is that the significant tensions that existed within the student movement were ultimately confined to the corridors, owing to two young leaders with an uncommon sense of duty. The *entente minimale* had planted the seeds of a fragile common front, the first of its kind in the history of the student movement. Yet it was the student leaders themselves who would ultimately be charged with nurturing or neglecting the pact, and throughout the duration of the crisis, they who would be sorely put to the test. Independent of personal or ideological sentiments, thirty-year-old Martine Desjardins and twenty-one-year-old Gabriel Nadeau-Dubois, of the FEUQ and CLASSE respectively, demonstrated a shrewd and unwavering grasp of the political necessity of maintaining a united front. The result, which prevented the movement from fracturing, was a Léo Bureau-Blouin of the FECQ who, despite numerous attempts to break ranks, ultimately found himself too isolated to go it alone.[20] In spite of plentiful backroom dramas, the events of spring 2012 therefore publicly exhibited a student movement united in common cause for the first time since the schisms of the 1980s. The importance of this triumph for the success of the movement was enormous, as Charest discovered much to his dismay.

Indignation's in the air this year

Following from the *Rassemblement national étudiant*, protest actions were stepped up by all three organizations, each in line with its particular character. On the side of the FEUQ and FECQ joint sit-ins were organized every weekend throughout the summer of 2011 in front of the offices of the Ministère de l'éducation.[21] On November 10, 2011, a demonstration organized jointly by the FEUQ, FECQ and ASSÉ drew a crowd of between twenty thousand and thirty thousand students in Montréal despite the rain, marking the second largest student protest in Québec history after the rally in 2005.[22] More than 200,000 students were on strike throughout Québec that day.[23] Yet the response from the government was swift and clear: "The hike will be maintained at all costs."[24] It was around this time that the ASSÉ began to talk publicly of the potential for an unlimited general strike for winter 2011.

From the perspective of St-Pierre and Ethier, this moment also marked a turning point in the campaign. Before, many of the ASSÉ's local affiliate associations were virtually moribund, having been inactive for so long that even the most traditionally politicized members had trouble achieving a quorum at their assemblies.[25] But an important shift was suddenly under way, and it was coming from beyond Québec's borders: In the spring of 2011, massive student revolts had erupted in London against the tripling of tuition fees by the British government. In Chile that year too — where Pinochet, freed of democratic confines, had imposed one of the world's purest iterations of the free-market educational model[26] — the students mounted a historic mass mobilization to restore the democratic and civic nature of the system through demands for free and universal post-secondary education.[27] All of this was happening as the Indignados were in the streets and occupying squares across Europe with their networked and leaderless movements inspired by Spain's Democracia Real Ya. By autumn, the protests had travelled across the Atlantic in the form of Occupy Wall Street, which cascaded across North America and to Montréal where hundreds occupied Square Victoria (or "Place du Peuple") in the heart of the city's business district. Against this backdrop of worldwide struggles to reclaim the public good from powerful private actors, the organizers with the ASSÉ noted a surge in students' attendance at general assemblies near the end of 2011. Suddenly, the assemblies were packed to breaking point.[28] Something historic was under way, as the potent convergence of global currents was laying fertile ground for what would become the Printemps érable.

The ASSÉ, positioning itself as the natural heir to the Occupiers and Indignados, eagerly seized on the moment. Reviving a strategy from 2005, they formed the Coalition large de l'ASSÉ (CLASSE) in December of 2011, inviting in all CEGEP and university student associations (whether unaffiliated or already affiliated with one of the federations) who had voted a strike mandate, were governed democratically via general assembly and shared their longer-term goal of free university education.[29] Contrary to the FEUQ and FECQ's lengthy and bureaucratic processes of affiliation (and disaffiliation), the CLASSE was able to quickly widen its reach and influence, and initiate new local associations into its culture and structures of direct democracy. Much to the annoyance of the FEUQ and FECQ, who ardently opposed the CLASSE's luring of their members (to the point even of refusing to accept the disaffiliation votes of local assemblies), the youngest of the national associations thereby became the undisputed motor of the 2012 mobilization.

The CLASSE's structures simply extended those of the ASSÉ to encompass the new members. The national congress was held almost weekly during the strike and actively oversaw the actions of the executive to ensure close adherence to the decisions adopted democratically.[30] The limited manoeuvring room of Gabriel Nadeau-Dubois and Jeanne Reynolds was reflective of their mandates during the strike as spokespersons rather than presidents. In his book *Tenir Tête*, awarded the Governor General's Literary Award in 2014 (and soon to be released in English as *In Defiance*), Nadeau-Dubois explains how the distinction, to which the conventional media had evident trouble adapting, was far from merely nominal. In fact, at precisely the same time as Nadeau-Dubois was being lambasted in the press for not exerting "leadership" by condemning all violence, those within the CLASSE were actually taking him to task for taking *too many* liberties in his public stances, to the point of even placing his mandate into question.[31] The distinction between the horizontal and hierarchical student associations was one of substance and quite patently, one of consequence.

A discourse of weakness, a discourse of revolt

At the moment the tuition increase was officially announced in the March 2011 budget, many of the ASSÉ's affiliated associations were in need of rebuilding from the ground up. The national executive sent representatives onto campuses to find members to lead class-by-class tours aimed at introducing the local associations to students and to organize general assemblies to elect executives and approve action plans for the coming year. As St-Pierre and Ethier stress, the amount of organizational and educational work required was tremendous, and the ASSÉ was determined this time not to be caught off guard. Once the local associations were placed on a solid footing, they could move on to the crucial task of raising awareness and rallying the base through a rigorous line of argumentation. The main thrust of the CLASSE's rhetorical offensive was to undercut the government's TINA-esque insistence on the hike's financial necessity by highlighting the government's priorities. It was thus that the policy's ideological underpinnings would be exposed. Throughout, the CLASSE's discourse around this *"choix de société"* was heavily imbued with the language of Occupy Wall Street, and their anti-austerity protest that was fuelled by indignation at the control exerted by "the One Percent" over the democratic process.[32]

Following in this line, the daily class visits cast Charest's multibillion-dollar Plan Nord centre stage to illustrate the government's guiding values, and most especially its partiality to foreign resource-sector giants that came at the direct expense of its commitment to Québec's students.[33] Visits emphasized recent government decisions that removed billions of dollars from the public purse, ranging from years of corporate and income tax cuts to the rich, to the specific $1.9 billion decision in 2007 to abolish the capital tax on business and financial transactions.[34] Representatives further pointed out that even if *only* the part applicable to banks were reversed, the resulting revenue would cover the full cost of free university education for every Quebecer.[35] The issue of tuition fees was thus inscribed within the Liberals' broader shift from progressive taxation toward flat user fees across all public services, with the direct result of deepening economic inequalities. In the wake of the Duchesneau Report in 2011, the stench of corruption overhanging the government served handily in the CLASSE's campaign as well, and aided in completing the portrait of an illegitimate and self-serving élite — now challenged by the CLASSE in the name of "the 99%."[36]

It was a sharp contrast from the economistic discourse of the two student federations, which limited itself to condemning the steepness of the hike for its impacts on educational accessibility and the budgets of "middle-class families."[37] From the release of the provincial budget, the FEUQ and FECQ adopted the government's language to challenge the tuition hike from within the boundaries demarcated by the capitalist class. Their arguments accepted the basic premise of tuition fees as the mark of students' contributions and objected only that students were struggling to make ends meet after having "already done their share"[38] following from the 2007 increases. Yet according to all evidence, the progressive mantle they claimed in defending the living standards of students was the cannibalized and commercialized "social democracy" of the present-day PQ: The student federations argued for the importance of educational accessibility within a globalized knowledge economy where an educated workforce is seen as the key to attracting foreign investment.[39]

In its effort to combat the governmental premise of insufficient public funds, the FEUQ rightly targeted the mismanagement within the university network, most notably by spotlighting the exorbitant salaries of university presidents.[40] The low-hanging fruit of waste and inefficiency seemed a bid at positioning the federations as reasonable in the eyes of a monetarist establishment. Yet targeting the academy's own internal One Percent may amount to attacking the symptoms while neglecting the disease, and ultimately prove highly inadequate. Martine Desjardins has written, with reason, that the tuition hike was a betrayal of the legacy of the Quiet Revolution.[41] Yet the discourse of the FEUQ and FECQ wholeheartedly endorsed the commercialist paradigm used to rationalize such hikes and accepted the necessity of the tuition fees that the same Quiet Revolution had promised to abolish. The casting of their arguments within the establishment's language may well have been designed to attract the sympathies of the public at large, which skews toward the older generations. In any case, it certainly succeeded quite naturally at garnering them the label of "moderates" awarded by the corporate press.

From the grassroots to the horizon:
Building a twenty-first-century movement

The CLASSE's campaign, by contrast, took direct aim at the market logic on which a tuition increase depends, and turned to the emerging tactics of social media-era movements to expand the mobilization as broadly as possible. Their robust argumentation and demands at the ready, outreach followed with the creation of an Internet site and with class-by-class visits, face-to-face mobilization and the massive production and distribution of informational material that included flyers, pamphlets, buttons and online videos.[42] Petitions were used primarily as a mobilization and outreach tool by the CLASSE to build a preliminary database of supporters; only once significant numbers adhered to a petition could the true organizational work commence, and the CLASSE took pains to ensure that no step was initiated before students exhibited a readiness to proceed.[43] Significantly — for it is indicative of the new era in Québec — the "question nationale" was evacuated from the discourse of all national associations, with the CLASSE consciously avoiding sovereignist (which is not to say nationalist) language for fear of alienating anglophone and federalist sympathizers.[44]

The escalation and diversity of tactics model embraced by the CLASSE was central to efforts at gradually amassing a wider and wider base.[45] Beginning with petitions, it graduates to symbolic actions, then small-scale demonstrations, and then escalates to include limited strikes, direct action and economic disturbances. If all other measures should fail to sway the government, the final step is an unlimited general strike whose crescendo effect is achieved by freeing up students' time and resources to mobilize en masse. The students, however, were not the only target of the CLASSE's outreach strategies: Building networks and synergies outward was equally instrumental and was facilitated by the breadth of the CLASSE's discourse, which invited solidarity across civil society.

The student federations, for their part, had also engaged in alliance-building, forming the Alliance social, which encompassed seven union federations, namely the Fédération des travailleurs et travailleuses du Québec (FTQ), Confédération des syndicats nationaux (CSN), Centrale des syndicats du Québec (CSQ), Centrale des syndicats démocratiques (CSD), Syndicat de la fonction publique et parapublique du Québec (CFPQ), Alliance du personnel professionnel et technique de la santé et des services sociaux (APTS) and Syndicat de professionnelles et professionnels du gouvernement du Québec (SPGQ).[46] Where the conventional federations built ties to the union leaderships, however, the CLASSE — whose relations with the latter have often been frosty, since their defence of their members' narrowly defined interests has served to undermine student mobilizations in the past — instead sought support from the labour grassroots, in a bid at exerting pressure on the leaderships from below.[47] Outreach was also initiated with community, feminist, environmental and other groups in a bid at sharing best practices and nurturing networks of solidarity (feminism is one of the ASSÉ's core orientations and was front and centre in their campaign owing to the disproportionate impacts of fee increases on women). Among the most important of the CLASSE's allies was the Coalition opposée à la tarification et la privatisation des services publics, a decentralized coalition of eighty-five civil society organizations formed in 2010 to challenge the government's austerity budget that year. The CLASSE was able to rely on the Coalition's support on numerous occasions, both on the organizational front as well as with communications.[48]

The CLASSE executive envisaged a strike lasting approximately eight weeks (then a record in Québec) and circled the week of February 20, 2012, for its launch. The campaign necessitated an enormous degree of intelligence work, research and ground-level political organization. Specialized committees were created and together counted fifty members (and over a hundred volunteers) at the height of the struggle, including legal, communications and training teams, among others. The Comité pour le maintien et l'élargissement de la grève (for the maintenance and widening of the strike) occupied a particularly crucial role, sending more than twenty people every day to campuses across Québec to aid in the organization of strike mandates and to keep the troops motivated and mobilized through speeches to the general assemblies.[49] The scale of the mobilization committee's work was nothing short of tremendous, with one member alone travelling 60,000 kilometres in his car in the space of a few months — one and a half times the circumference of the Earth.[50] One of the committee's principal tasks was the construction of a database listing every vote result from every affiliate association, most of which held weekly assemblies to either reaffirm or revoke the strike mandates.[51] The CLASSE was thereby able to keep its finger on the pulse of the membership and anticipate trouble brewing weeks in advance, allowing the executive to prioritize its support accordingly.[52] The CLASSE's contestational campaign was in marked contrast to the strategies of the federations, which favoured less obstructive and symbolic fixed-term strikes in the place of unlimited strike mandates, which encourage an escalating mobilization.[53] This explains why the strike's peak arrived on March 22 when it attained 304,242 students during a national day of action launched by the federations, but why CLASSE affiliates demonstrated far greater resilience over time. For most of the spring, the CLASSE represented approximately three times the average number of striking students represented by the FEUQ and over five times the number represented by the FECQ.[54] Despite the frames of the mainstream media, CLASSE affiliates were thus the overwhelming heart and muscle of the student revolt.

Courage to cast the dream: The messaging of the CLASSE

On the level of branding too, the ASSÉ had learned the lessons of 2005. The polysemic acronym for its coalition this time around, CLASSE, cleverly evoked the class-based interests behind the government's austerity agenda, as well as their campaign for the right to education. It was a positive contrast to the maladroit selection of CASSÉÉ in 2005, which played to government attacks in evoking *casseurs*, the derogative French term for vandals or rioters.[55] The red square was proposed as the emblem of the contestation by the ASSÉ as early as fall 2011 and was adopted by all national associations to highlight that students are "*carrément dans le rouge.*" This was another play on words invoking *carrément*'s dual meaning of "squarely" (literally) and "completely" (in colloquial usage) to signify a population that is "in the red," or in debt.[56] While substance was always the heart of the CLASSE's messaging, they knew too well the power of image for their generation, and employed it astutely to strike the imagination and brand their cause with force.

The CLASSE's mass media strategy was another area where the lessons of 2005 were instrumental.[57] The contestational nature of the organization renders it naturally hostile to mass media (and vice versa), who are considered inherently conservative social actors by the CLASSE: too attached to and dependent upon the establishment and too prone to personalizing conflicts by attaching leaders to broad-based movements.[58] In the particularly hostile environment of Canada's corporate media oligopoly, this wariness was all the more entrenched. In 2005, this ambivalence prevented the CASSÉÉ from dealing with the media effectively, but by 2012 the lesson had been fully absorbed. Well before the strike was launched in fact, the CLASSE set to developing a sophisticated and innovative *modus operandi* for the media, which sought to turn the tables and place the students in control of their messaging. Where the conventional federations directed their media interventions at the broad swath of public opinion, the CLASSE decided to use mass media to mobilize five to ten percent of their most devoted sympathizers first and aim for the general public second.[59] The strategy is one that stresses the importance of coherence and sincerity to an organization's messaging, if even at the expense of being perceived as radical. Rather than fearing criticism, the CLASSE thereby invited it, and confidently embraced the full range of public debate that would follow. This also enabled the CLASSE to stay loyal to its stances and principles — a further aid to keeping a base motivated — without the need to cater toward a mushy middle or elusive majority of public opinion.[60]

In sum, the CLASSE made the highly strategic decision to play the game, but on their own terms. Press attachés (three at the height of the crisis) were made available twenty-four hours a day to respond to up-to-the-minute events and requests and maintain constructive contacts with the press. The strategy would at times call for intelligent manipulation of coverage as well, for instance by providing "exclusive" information to select outlets so as to guarantee front-page coverage. Frequent press releases, briefings and the entirety of the political milieu's professional communications strategies were deployed to combat the governmental campaign and keep the spokespersons abreast of anything that could affect the movement.[61] Students they may have been, but these Net Geners were no media amateurs.

On top of traditional media strategies, the CLASSE's manipulation of mass

Demonstrators strip down for a maNUfestation on June 7, 2012, at Place du Canada in Montréal.

media's cinematic and photographic qualities — especially its affinity for the clip, soundbyte and image — revealed a shrewdly sophisticated grasp of the affective power of symbols and spectacle in inspiring and casting a movement. Members of the CLASSE often engaged in symbolic protests and those known as the "pseudo-event" in a bid at harnessing the qualities of mass media to construct a potent political imaginary. Some examples were the Kraft Dinner *eat-ins* to highlight student poverty, or more famously, the many *maNUfestations* where protesters stripped down to highlight the Charest government's lack of transparency, evoke humans' fundamental equality and contrast the heavily armed riot police with their own pacifism and vulnerability.[62] Often, the CLASSE would issue a call-out to graphic design students, most notably at UQÀM's École de la montagne rouge, to stamp the movement with a twenty-first-century revolutionary aesthetic.[63] These were the apt pupils of Guy Debord, raised in a hypermediated age where representation had become its own reality. And more than just playing the media game, the CLASSE often seemed a few steps ahead of it.

The revolution will be networked: The CLASSE's social media campaign

The CLASSE's mastery of contemporary communications tools shines through with even greater force when we turn to their social media strategies. Activists within the ASSÉ early on expressed reservations in relying on corporate-owned social media platforms, particularly flowing from privacy concerns. Yet having witnessed the power of Web 2.0 mobilizations with the Arab Spring, Spanish Indignados and Occupy Wall Street movements, they quickly recognized the enormous potential of social media's unmediated sharing of content and information and its capacity to bestow autonomy to the grassroots of a movement.[64] Reflections on the use of social media during strikes thus began as early as the summer of 2011, and by September of that year a member of the ASSÉ's executive submitted a plan to the congress on a strategy for the coming campaign.[65]

Here as with other areas, the CLASSE, through a four-person dedicated social media team, demonstrated a keen grasp of the medium employed: More than broadcasting the organization's own messages and information over Twitter, the team of tweeters engaged in constant debate with users online, posting articles and multimedia content related to the movement and creating the hashtag #GGI (*grève générale illimitée*, or unlimited general strike) to serve as the principal wire through which people could tap in to the movement.[66] The CLASSE account was also a steady source of up-to-the-minute information, from assembly vote results to live press conferences, updates on government negotiations, media articles, images, videos and more.[67]

Significantly, the CLASSE knew to harness Twitter's potential in nourishing synergies with sympathizers by engaging with them and retweeting their posts, thereby favouring reciprocity and solidarity between them. Rather than the unidirectional flow common to traditional political parties and media, the CLASSE understood social media's distinctive character to serve as a forum and facilitator of networks.[68] The results were clear and concrete: The CLASSE's online presence in social media during the spring eclipsed that of all political parties, mainstream media and the student federations.[69] The CLASSE's broader approach to the Internet followed the same line too, with their website, Bloquonslahausse.com ("stop the hike" conjugated in the collective imperative) hosting an open calendar where members could freely post actions and activities organized in their campuses and communities. The CLASSE's Web strategy thus fell squarely in line with their organizational, outreach and communications campaigns, which all came together to form a single and spirited thrust: to empower the base and favour the cause's appropriation by the grassroots. It was felt that such a networked and horizontal movement — diffused and decentralized, self-reinforcing and self-propelled — would by its nature and structure be that much more motivated and that much harder to divide, discourage or defeat.[70]

Fuelling the dreamers, framing the debate

Many have criticized social media politics for producing what some call "cyber-balkanization," where citizens "glue themselves into electronic enclaves" and find confirmation of their beliefs, thereby hardening and radicalizing into camps as a result.[71] Yet in a context of acute media concentration like Canada's, where the corporate press is often an echo chamber for the opposite side, social media can also become a crucial counterweight. In 2012, the autonomous space of the Twittersphere, its population heavily dominated by youth, became such a base of the pro-student left, serving to deepen and inform the convictions of those at the core.[72] And by virtue of quite literally incarnating the future, the young *carrés rouges* were even permitted to believe, all hubris aside, that they fought on the side of history.

Such passion, when sincere and cogently defended with substance, can surprise with its force of persuasion. The more that Quebecers came to view the depth of what this struggle meant for the youth, the more those sitting on the sidelines were invited to reflect and choose their camp. Beyond the inevitable polarization that followed, the heart and fire that fuelled a generation's protest brought a truly remarkable and more consequential triumph: In an age of debilitating cynicism, where the space for democratic debate is being persistently narrowed by market "imperatives," Québec, for six long and intense months, came face to face with its image in the mirror. And for the first time in decades, the people were forced to question the most fundamental values on which society ought to rest.

If nothing else remained of the Printemps érable, this, alone, will have been worth the whole fight.

WE ARE THIRSTY
The Voices of the Printemps Érable

> To dive. They are afraid of drowning, but we want to drink. Life is drying out and the cities are becoming deserted of souls. Your numbers have populated everything, even our well-thinking heads. Your numbers have eaten life and our ideas cry famine.[1]
>
> — Catherine-Alexandre Briand, "*Ça sent la poussière*" (my translation)

Hysteria seized much of the corporate media during the strike, as populist commentators erupted with uncommon vitriol at the young barbarians they imagined at the gates. Patently, the students had struck a nerve: "vandals," "anarcho-communists," "true savages," "drunken ideologues," "armed and masked goons," "budding terrorists." No invective seemed off limits to the most ardent defenders of the capitalist creed, not even the spectors of North Korea and Cuba.[2] Threatened by the daily disruptions and the increasingly ambitious aims of the *carrés rouges*, the pitch of the media's panic was matched only by the paternalism of their interventions. And indeed in the lead-up to the tuition increase, the dubious hegemony of those in favour of tuition increases within the establishment press was beyond qualification: Of 143 editorials and opinion pieces published in Montréal's three francophone newspapers between 2005 and 2010 (the anglophone Postmedia-owned *Gazette* would certainly prove no outlier), only four opposed increasing tuition fees.[3] Even *Le Devoir*, the province's only independent and most respected newspaper, tilted heavily against students, with the bulk of its editorialists and columnists backing increases, even while its news reporting was deemed more fair-minded by the study conducted by IRIS's Simon Tremblay-Pépin.[4]

As the strike sparked a society-wide debate during the spring of 2012, however, the students' defenders emerged increasingly from the woodwork: *Le Devoir* redeemed itself by opening its pages wide to the hike's opponents, and shone as a bastion both of democratic debate and of Québec's dwindling humanist and social-democratic traditions. A few of *La Presse*'s columnists also bucked the trend and backed the students. And contrary to its mostly anti-student English-language equivalent CBC, the public broadcaster Radio-Canada was more balanced in its coverage, frequently engaging in in-depth analyses that did much to contextualize the students' struggle both historically and globally. Yet with such few exceptions, the corporate-controlled media served largely as the zealous defenders of the neoliberal establishment, with none more rabidly anti-student than Pierre-Karl Péladeau's Québécor outlets that account for 40 percent of Québec's media.[5] Freed of the shaming of the provincial press council — Québécor withdrew from the non-binding body in 2010 — its journalists often had few reserves in distorting or inventing the facts to better suit their youth-bashing ends.[6]

Yet outside the walls that house the media élites, a profound shift was under way. A few weeks after the strike was launched in February, support for the students began pouring in that presaged the historic scale of the movement. The CLASSE's calls were reverberating far beyond the student base. For indeed, with scarce exceptions, when we listen to the voices that rallied to the students' struggle, we don't hear the echo of the establishment federations' apology for neoliberalism. Their defence of educational accessibility was universally supported, but the bulk of the non-student actors who leapt into the fray were spurred by far greater aspirations. What we hear in fact, through the words of the students' myriad supporters, are the overwhelming and unmistakable sounds of a society rising to challenge its élites and to rattle the foundations of their political order.

The most radical of the student associations had thus proved more attuned to the popular mood than any student association in Québec in decades. For in the public debate as in the on-the-ground mobilization, the influence of the establishment federations peaked near the end of March, when the unlimited general strike was still largely just a strike. But as the movement expanded and mutated in degrees to a full-blown social revolt, the FEUQ and FECQ often seemed like witless passengers caught in the march, surpassed by the events pushing them ineluctably toward a horizon they couldn't see.

A new political imaginary signed in rouge: Progressive Québec rises

The first expressions of support for the students arrived in the days leading up to the first Québec national march planned for March 22, 2012, and at first, it followed the well-worn pattern of mobilizations past. Québec's three largest labour union federations, the CSN, CSQ and FTQ, came to the students' defence on March 13, when CSQ president Réjéan Parent declared that "the struggle of Québec's students is the struggle of all the citizens of Québec."[7] And indeed, while not "all" the citizens were to see it with quite the same eye, Parent's profession of solidarity, ordinary on the surface, did ultimately presage the magnitude of the wave to come. For the rest of the spring, political and corporatist considerations led the union leaderships to remain prudently aloof of the student mobilization in public. Yet behind the scenes, the rallying of organized labour to the cause was without question and even reached far beyond the province's borders: Unions from across Québec and

Canada funnelled tens of thousands of dollars to the three main national student associations, along with enormous logistical and organizational support.[8] Before the mobilization had truly taken flight, there were signs that Québec's students had ignited a movement that progressives across Canada, where tuition levels are often multiples greater, felt a personal stake in.

The next day's round of support was less ordinary, and traced the outlines of the public debate that would dominate the spring and summer. On March 14, the academic community closed ranks around the youth in a spectacular and excited display of solidarity, when more than 1,600 university and CEGEP professors[9] — the figure would eventually climb to 2,400[10] — issued a rousing declaration that warmly embraced and encouraged the protesters. Arriving as a veritable rush of wind at the students' backs, their letter, timely and instructive in its language, went on to define the substance and tenor of much subsequent support. In "We are all students! The Manifesto of the Professeurs contre la hausse,"[11] the academics boomed that they were lining up behind the "youth that is standing up" in their "democratic defence of university accessibility and in their justified opposition to the commercialization of education."[12] Yet most telling, perhaps, were the words reserved for the pocketbook discourse of the traditional student federations. The professors urged the FEUQ and FECQ, whose stance limited to cancelling the hike obviously failed to impress, to go "beyond [these] legitimate demands." This movement, they stressed, was infinitely greater: "It's the future of education and of Québec society that is at stake[...]. This strike represents the extension of numerous contestations that have emerged over the last few years in response to the subordination of the public good by private interests."[13]

These "numerous contestations," of course, were a clear reference to the Indignados, Aganaktismenoi and Occupiers; to the students of Chile, and of Britain as well. Largely overlooked by the corporate media, these social movements were a steady source of inspiration for many of Québec's *carrés rouges*, perhaps few more than to the Professeurs contre la hausse whose own decentralized coalition was a mirror of the rising twenty-first century paradigm. It is their well-developed critiques that the academics draw from in the remainder of their letter to deplore Québec's new status quo: the hegemony of financial and business interests and their class-based austerity agenda; the commercialist mutation of education and its undermining of the academy's fundamental mission; the legitimacy of demands for free university education; and the humanist and civilizational vocation of the university. Inflated by the students' "resistance," the professors launched a full-throated endorsement of their revolutionary appeals to forge "a new political imaginary."[14] In rallying to the movement, the professors left no doubt as to what moved them to action: The CLASSE had declared the battle for the commons open, and Québec's restless academics threw themselves headlong into the fray.

The parade of reinforcements continued two days later, when the pages of *Le Devoir* announced the formation of another group on March 16, this time at the initiative of parents. A Facebook group accompanied the formation of the Parents contre la hausse that counted 230 members on the day of its announcement.[15] The header on the group's website took up the cause of "a high-quality, democratic and accessible education system that genuinely contributes to the development of individuals and society."[16] The "call to parents" then continues, leaving little uncertainty as to the group's values and goals: "Without prior debate worthy of the name, the government is thus imposing a *choix de société*: They are modelling us on the North American system, which rests on the equal payment of taxes and fees for all, thereby obviously impacting the less fortunate."[17] The parents propose instead the European model of "quasi-tuition-free education" and demand that "the state fund education *as well as other public services* based on citizens' and businesses' means."[18] In going far beyond concerns over accessibility and the financial precarity of students, the Parents contre la hausse thereby aligned themselves fully with the CLASSE's call for a broader return to values of collectivism, humanism and social democracy. A week later, as high school students voted to walk out of classes and join the March 22 day of action, the parents were joined by the Commission scolaire de Montréal (CSDM), which publicly expressed its backing of the student cause.[19]

A month later, an exceptionally large crowd of thousands was marking May Day with a march against capitalism in Montréal.[20] In 2012, the spirit of anti-capitalist revolt was in the air. Against this backdrop, Québec's wider civil society stepped forward to announce its wholehearted solidarity with the students, with over two hundred prominent public figures signing a declaration under the title "We are with the students. We are together." The open letter, published in the weekly *Voir*, drew from a wide array of Québec's cultural, professional and intellectual communities, from artists, musicians, actors and film directors to academics, environmentalists, doctors, lawyers and economists.[21] Sociologist Éric Pineault, one of the letter's authors, echoed the professors' admiration for the youth — tinged with his own latent riposte to Thatcherite TINAism — when he lauded the students for having "revived Québec's economic imagination."[22] The letter itself was no less wide-eyed in its estimation of what the students had already accomplished: "This cry of the youth, which pushes us to break with our *immobilisme* [social and political paralysis], to recover our collective capacity to act and to work for the common good, we hear it," answered the authors.[23] Like those of the professors before them, their words were heavy with hope and awe, as if rushing to seize on a chance they once thought so distant, yet now had suddenly surfaced before their incredulous eyes: to strike at the neoliberals in a moment of weakness and at last begin to beat back the tide. It was evident that their impassioned leap into the melee was inspired not by the federations' campaigns for more generous grants or the status quo in tuition fees, but by their shared dream of another, more just and democratic Québec. Indeed in their eyes, the Printemps érable had nothing to envy of Occupy Wall Street:

The questions raised are fundamental; they pertain to social governance. The students in the street are but the tip of the iceberg of a much larger movement that seeks to counter rising inequalities and social insecurity, the growing indebtedness of households, the poverty of those solitary people neglected by government policy and the environmental degradation engendered by an anachronistic model of development.[24]

Whether in the commercialization of post-secondary education, the privatization of health care services or the corporate exploitation of our natural resources embodied by the Plan Nord, this model, which "sabotages our public services" say the authors, is the regressive model of the neoliberal élites. Faced with this system that sees individuals charged "excessive fees in violation of the principles that helped build a modern Québec based on equality of opportunity," the public figures answer together:

> We want none of it[...]. We want no more of it.[...] And we are launching a pressing call to the associations, to the political parties, to the unions, to the professional bodies and to the citizens: In uniting our forces, we believe it's possible to make the winds of the Québécois spring blow stronger still.[25]

Their words were heard. In the following days and weeks, many groups of different sizes and under various banners would form to answer the call: Infirmières (nurses) contre la hausse, Chomeuses et chomeurs (the unemployed) contre la hausse, Travailleurs (workers) contre la hausse, Écrivains (writers) contre la hausse, Mères en colère et solidaires (mothers), Têtes blanches, carré rouge (seniors) and on it went.[26] The tuition hike itself had become almost secondary to the fire it lit in the hearts of Québec's progressives. This was now their battle, inspired by a collective dream and the newly ignited hope of the possible.

In between these large-scale outpourings of solidarity from influential (and less influential) segments of society, prominent intellectuals and former politicians lined up in the pages of Le Devoir to outline similar arguments."We have a hard time understanding how the current government can consider dismantling one of the major gains of Québec's modernization," deplored Jacques-Yvan Morin on March 22, who served as René Lévesque's first education minister from 1976–1981.[27] He was later joined by Jean Garon, Jacques Parizeau's education minister in 1994, who also lent his support to the students on April 17 by endorsing the CLASSE's campaign for free university education.[28] Former premier (and one-time student leader) Bernard Landry completed the triad of PQ stalwarts when he followed suit on May 15 and also proposed free undergraduate education in the interests of resolving the crisis.[29]

Professors emeritus Guy Rocher and George Leroux, the former a member of the Parent Commission in the 1960s and one of the report's co-authors, along with professors Christian Nadeau and Yvan Perrier, all signed letters expanding on the arguments from the manifesto of the Professeurs contre la hausse. They variously aimed at questioning the values underlying the government's view of students' "fair share," at rekindling the long-time aspiration (and demonstrating the feasibility) of free university education, at highlighting the inherently regressive nature of tuition fees and at pilfering the mounting trend toward the commercialization of public services. Echoing the CLASSE's invocation of the Plan Nord as the sign of a wider shift in governance paradigms, Guy Rocher sounded incredulous before the government's priorities: "How can we provide such gifts to companies who exploit our natural resources and at the same time refuse students the investment needed to ensure their future at university?"[30] Indeed, Rocher's was a question that imposed itself repeatedly throughout the student crisis. The government had built the entire rationale for the hike on the assertion that the state lacked the sufficient resources to fund education, and yet two words, "Plan Nord," sufficed in easily washing away the façade. Beneath it we saw the image of an élite that was growing ever more emboldened in its race to sell off the commons to powerful private actors. To the Rochers, Lerouxs, Nadeaus and Perriers, it was eminently clear that the students' struggle was at heart a struggle over the very future of Québec.[31]

The force and fire with which others took up the baton spoke to the pulsing vein that the students had ruptured, but more, to the surging hope that suddenly inflated the hearts of so many. On May 30, a rousing appeal entitled "We are immense" appeared in the pages of Le Devoir, in which actor and stage director Philippe Ducros composed a moving paean to the young citizens in the streets. To Ducros's eyes, the events of the Printemps érable were "historic" and the students, "visionary."

> For over one hundred days ... Little by little, step by step, in spite of the decadent cynicism and outrageous condescension on the part of our leaders, Québec rises, calls for solidarity, and proclaims its absolute refusal ("ras-le-bol") of economic fundamentalism. What is happening here is historic, as the struggle reaches far beyond our borders and stakes its positions on issues far larger than tuition fees.
>
> For over one hundred days ...
>
> In spite of the tear gas, in spite of the truncheons and mass arrests, we are redefining the world. Instead of once more suffering the neoliberal enslavement, we are forcing History, little by little, to take the next step, to cross the barricades of an unbridled and sacrosanct capitalism's preconceived ideas.
>
> The mirage no longer holds. We are thirsty.
>
> This commercialization of education and the rerouting of our places of knowledge toward corporate interests are inscribed within an ideology that envelops all the spheres of our lives, from the industrialization of art

to the privatization of health care, from the deforestation of the Amazon, to the gutting of Africa by the mining industry.

The students of Québec are visionary. They have opened the way. We are now a new buoy in the dangerous channel of the changing global paradigm. After the Jasmine Revolution and the Arab Spring, after the Indignados of Spain, the Occupy movement, the insurrections of London and the strikes of Athens, here we are, the bearers of the torch. All around the world, people are rising up, indignant. We have taken up the reins. We speak now in the name of a global population in search of justice, solidarity, equity.

What we carry surpasses us. [...]

We are giants. And it takes giants to force History to take the next step.[32]

Other allies came before Ducros and others came after, all marching almost invariably along the path prepared by the CLASSE. Whereas polls throughout the spring consistently suggested a public heavily divided (though slanted against the students), it was clear that the broad call to revolt launched by the radical current of the movement had tapped into a deep-seated thirst among Québec's seas of restless progressives, tracing an arc that ran from Europe, to Wall Street and finally to Montréal. Indeed, the CLASSE's themes overtook the arguments of the federations to become what Pineault calls the "hegemonic discourse" of the movement.[33] For it was their shared dream that rallied civil society and triggered a broad-based social struggle whose origins long lay simmering, awaiting a spark — when the youth of Québec at last arose to strike the match.

Voices of the underground: The Twittersphere speaks

In Québec, the student spring saw the CLASSE emerge as the children of the social media revolution, with their campaigns demonstrating an unrivalled grasp of the Web 2.0's inner architecture and potential. Indeed as CLASSE activists Renaud Poirier St-Pierre and Phillippe Ethier recall, in the early days of the strike movement the *carrés rouges* seemed to exert a virtual monopoly over the social media debate, which was later slightly attenuated but never successfully challenged by their opponents.[34] Yet as astute as the CLASSE's social media strategies were, the preponderance of the pro-student camp in the Twittersphere also spoke to something deeper and more portentous: namely, the chasm in social and political values between the Net generation and their elders. Indeed according to self-disclosed age in a recent sample study of 36 million Twitter users worldwide, youth aged 18–25 may represent upwards of 73.7 percent of the Twitter community.[35] And while these numbers may admittedly be exaggerated — younger users are presumed to be less hesitant in disclosing age — there are ample studies, most notably a 2012 report by Pew Research as well as another by Sysomos Inc., that corroborate the overwhelming youth bias in the use of social media.[36] Simply put, social media is the phenomenon of a generation.

It was perhaps inevitable then that Twitter would become *the* core instrument of the student struggle, serving as an online agora for civic debates, a decentralized infrastructure of organization and coordination and an unfiltered and up-to-the-second news, image and video feed for all things related to the movement. Videos of widely varying budgets were diffused through social media, produced by individuals and organizations ranging from leftist think-tank IRIS, to OWS offshoot 99% Québec, to many artists, filmmakers, activists and others.[37] As an important sign of the growing role of the anglophone community in Québécois social movements, Concordia University's CUTV community broadcaster became a central pillar of the mobilization, and the movement's unofficial video feed. Where the mainstream media wouldn't tread, the CUTV team was on the ground to provide uninterrupted, real-time and bilingual reporting from within every protest (whose openly pro-student bias, interestingly, was defended for exposing the opposite bias of the establishment press). Facilitated by its hand-held video equipment, its coverage was broadcast live on its website and complemented with constant updates over Twitter, despite frequent on-air attacks by the Service de Police de la Ville de Montréal (SPVM), who twice destroyed the student network's equipment.[38]

Olivier Beauschene is a private sector data analyst who performed in-depth analyses of Twitter use during the Printemps érable, designing graphs that grouped and visualized the content of tweets sent, as well as the structures of influence within the Twitter community.[39] Beauchesne's studies, published in *Le Devoir*, collected more than 500,000 tweets sent from mid-February to June 27, 2012, identified by a series of hashtags linked to the student contestation, of which 320,000 were marked by the most ubiquitous, #GGI.[40] He then used an algorithm to group tweets according to subject and vocabulary, and graphed them in constellations whereby similar topics appear clustered together. Finally, he listed the principal hashtags used and recipients of the tweets. In the lead, the SPVM figured prominently, followed distantly by *La Presse*, the ASSÉ, Gabriel Nadeau-Dubois, *Le Devoir*, leftist MNA Amir Khadir and then CUTV News.[41]

In a second graph current to June 1, more significant to identifying the most influential voices online, Beauschene analyzed and visualized the structures of the Twitter exchanges as identified by the @ sign, which directs a user's publicly visible message to its recipient (for example, @ SPVM). Based on 21,000 distinct individuals engaging in 235,000 conversations (including more than 400,000 tweets over all), Beauschene was able to construct a graph (see Figure 1) where the size of circles illustrates users' degrees of influence, as measured by the total volume of retweets (and thus scope of diffusion) received by their messages.[42] The data he gathered show the CLASSE, Nadeau-Dubois and their allies (like Josée Legault from the weekly *Voir*) clearly dominating the Twitter community, with the FEUQ, FECQ and their respective leaderships confined to virtual irrelevance — in the company of establishment media and political parties (with the lone exceptions being former journalists and PQ MNAs Bernard Drainville and Pierre Duchesne). Revealingly, the only Twitter user with greater online influence than the CLASSE during the strike was one located south of the border: Occupy Wall Street, which actively followed and supported the revolt raging across their northern frontier.[43] In fact, Québec had never been so active on Twitter, with St-Pierre and Ethier even claiming that "before the strike, for the majority of young Quebecers [...] Twitter

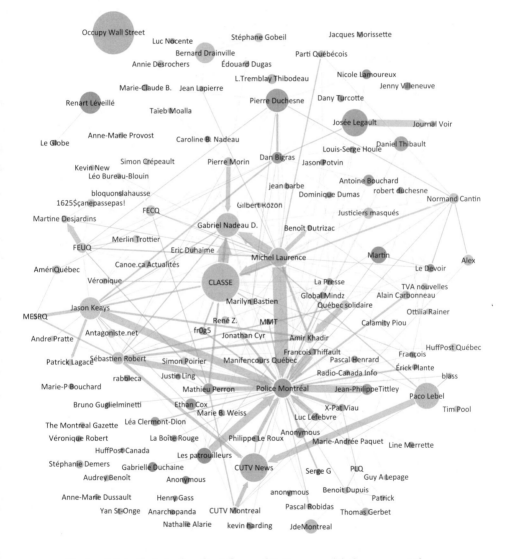

The size of circles illustrates the online influence of Twitter users, while the arrows map the interactions. Image credit: Olivier Beauschene.

simply didn't exist."[44] If they are correct, then the student spring truly propelled our youth into the social media age: For one week in the spring of 2012, Québec's #GGI became one of the top five tweeted subjects on the planet.[45]

Strike a match: The time of the Québecois spring

In 2012, the CLASSE rallied Québec's progressives around their democratic struggle to rescue the commons from the rapaciousness of the élites. Nothing in their success was foretold, and indeed, the impact of the CLASSE could well have stayed confined to the activist core of the student population, as was the case with the ASSÉ's prior mobilizations. But this time, it didn't. It should go without saying that success or failure in campaigns can only rely on effective organization to a point. Strike as hard or as persistently as you may, without a deeper resonance of the cause in society, all the well-placed tinder in the world will remain moist and unwilling to catch.

But evidently, the days we are living are no ordinary times. The CLASSE rode the wave of Occupy Wall Street to lead a broad-based challenge to the political order of Québec's One Percent. And in spite of government and media attempts to sideline them as marginals, the overwhelming pull exerted by their discourse on society's ground level told a different tale. Letter upon letter (and tweet upon tweet) booming excited encouragement were the unmistakable sign that their finger had been placed directly on the pulse of the progressive electorate and six long and intensely charged months, the sign that their struggle had ruptured a vein in a frantic search for an outlet. The words of the students' backers confirm an intuition: that the hundreds of thousands of citizens were not in the streets all that time only to challenge a tuition hike. Indeed, the thousands of professors would perhaps not have found themselves so eagerly by their sides but for that — and certainly not the artists, actors and film directors, nor the environmentalists, economists, doctors, nurses, seniors and lawyers. Yet in the streets and by the students' sides they all were, with their small patch of red felt displayed proudly — not for what it signified to others, but for what it signified to them. *Ceci n'est pas une grève étudiante.* This was not a student strike, but a spring awakening — though summer, as so often in Québec, continues to wait.

*Students march in a demonstration called by the student associations
of the Université de Montréal on March 27, 2012.*

Young protesters take part in a CLASSE *demonstration on April 4, 2012, in Montréal.*

Red and green converge in Montréal as 250,000 mark a historic rally "for the common good" on Earth Day, April 22, 2012.

Students lighten the mood with a protest celebration in Montréal on May 11, 2012.

A musical parade of carrés rouges *brings Montréal's streets to life.*

The carrés rouges *make a statement after the* CEGEP *de Valleyfield ordered classes to resume in April in spite of strike mandates.*

Students occupy UQÀM *on May 16 in response to court injunctions ordering the resumption of courses. Along the floor is scrawled the message: "Occupy our neighbourhoods."*

Anarchopanda looks on as riot police prepare to brutally dislodge student picketers at the CEGEP de Rosemont on May 14, 2012.

A demonstrator captures his generation's attitude toward authority at a maNUfestation on May 16, 2012.

For months, the police helicopter became a regular feature of the Montréal sky.

*A lawyer addresses a crowd gathered at Place Émilie-Gamelin during
a demonstration against Bill 78 on May 28, 2012.*

Protesters bang pots and pans (and channel Guy Fawkes) to protest Bill 78 in a casseroles march on May 30, 2012, in Montréal.

A maNUfestation on June 7, 2012, takes on the feel of a carnival.

Swarms of heavily armed SQ officers were deployed in Montréal to guard the F1 Grand Prix from protesters in June 2012.

Protesters flood Montréal's streets for a national march against neoliberalism on July 22, 2012.

YOU CAN'T STOP THE SPRING

The Irrepressible Force of a Twenty-First-Century Revolt

We will have to bear witness to the moments etched into our retinas, that leave us breathless, that impose a silence. Like that man, with the greying beard, who grabs the paintbrush and draws red clouds on the dirty asphalt. Like the hundreds, the thousands of students, two fingers raised to the sky, their mouths closed, mute, in a long contained cry, the silence more violent than the batons [...].

Like the grandmothers who skip on the sidewalks. Like the people in the apartment towers who spontaneously brandish red fabric and clothing above the melee. Like the man who cuts through the human tide and announces that we are more than 250,000 comrades united in the streets.

And I dreamed of this astonishing we that would rouse the crowds. I saw it deploy against the prevailing cynicism. I saw it respond to contempt. To those who gamble with loaded dice on the future of a people.[1]

— Amélie Faubert, "*Éclaircies*" (my translation)

The spring of 2012 finally arrived, as two worlds were racing toward a fateful collision: the state was the disciplinary father, the students the offspring come of age and the streets, the stage for a high-stakes drama the likes of which Québec had rarely seen. In its bewildering intransigence and contempt for the students, the government response was to pull relentlessly at the rips that were tearing society in two. Yet in fuelling the movement's expansion and resolve, the Liberals' ineptitude also laid bare a brutal and most fundamental disconnect. Clearly, this was a movement unlike anything the Liberals ever experienced or expected to, and this was a generation whose language they could neither decipher, nor speak. And alas, perhaps Charest never could grasp the source or soul of the revolt that would be his undoing: The two camps were of different centuries, and the canyon between them seemed too wide for a twentieth-century bridge to cross.

On a meme and a dream:
The artivist imaginary of the Printemps érable

On February 13, the day the first students were launching the strike, the École de la montagne rouge, inspired by the workshops of France's Mai 68 and the Black Mountain College of the Depression-era United States, was formed in the studios of the graphic design department at UQÀM. The artists' collective would emerge as the movement's unofficial creative and semiotic factory, arming students with a potent repertoire of symbols and slogans and casting it with a distinctly 2.0 visual stamp. In an early glimpse of the mobilization's bottom-up form, some of their slogans would later be taken up by the CLASSE in its messaging, most notably "*Le combat est avenir*," a play on words suggesting both "The future is our fight" and "The struggle is to come." Yet the most important was without a doubt its iconic print of a square clenched fist above "Printemps érable," a nudge-and-wink *détournement* of the French term for the Arab Spring, which struck the popular imagination and was quickly embraced by many as the movement's unofficial moniker.[2] The École de la montagne rouge was but the most influential of many artist groups that formed during the strike.

From the minute the *carrés rouges* burst onto the landscape, their movement bore the likes of nothing Québec had ever seen. The "artisticopolitical fervour of Mai 68" seemed reborn Montréalais, broadcasting the aesthetic stamp of a twenty-first-century cultural metropolis renowned globally for the vibrancy of its design and digital arts communities.[3] Given both Montréal's nature as a hub for contemporary arts and the hypermediated age in which this generation came of age, it's of little surprise the movement exhibited an intensely multimedia quality from the start.[4] From the street art and projections that washed over the city's walls, to the photographic testaments that immortalized the movement, the creative effervescence that infused the revolt may yet prove one of its most enduring legacies. The omnipresent and frontline role of artists in the Printemps érable cannot be understated: They lent the movement its language, its iconography and its name.

In the same mould as groups like Profs contre la hausse, the artists who took up the fight were decentralized and autonomous in the image of the mobilization. Citizen videos appeared on YouTube that drew on the richness of Québec's symbols and history, such as "Speak Red," inspired by Michèle Lalonde's 1968 nationalist poem "Speak White." Others, like the "*Lipdub rouge*" or Jon Lajoie's "Song for the Students," met with equally massive success online, with the latter ultimately attracting over 500,000 views.[5] Internet memes that delighted in lampooning the government added humour and pithy rejoinders to the students' arsenal and often went viral, such as one exploiting revelations of Line Beauchamp having breakfasted with a member of the mafia — who pays his "fair share" to the Liberals.[6] And the movement even had its unofficial mascots in Québec City (Banane rebelle) and Montréal (Anarchopanda), where in the latter case a philosophy prof in a giant panda suit turned the image of anarchists on its head through his unsolicited hugs of riot police and protestors.[7] All in all, the number of groups and actions that appeared was incalculable, as a continuous festival of artivist happenings probed and prodded at the preconceived notions of the cultural mainstream.

There were the writers and poets of the journal *Fermaille,* founded in February but never distributed commercially, where alternately rousing and irreverent verses embodied and inspired the dreams of the movement.[8] There were Les oiseaux rouges, Brass band du grève, La boîte rouge, La chorale des grévistes, Le fil rouge, Danse ta grève and countless more, all sprouting up spontaneously for the time of a struggle and wielding their diverse mediums in the service of a common dream.[9] Artists and existing artivist collectives like Nous sommes tous art joined the fray and made the walls of the city their living canvases for street art and projections, while Artung, a collective against the commercialization of public space, replaced three hundred ads across the city with art inspired by the symbol of the red square.[10]

As cultural symbols met culture jammers, Montrealers were engulfed in a semiotic war that laid raw the revolutionary thirsts within the movement, and confronted consumerist complacency with ever more intrusive invasions of the everyday. The power of the artists' arsenal should not be casually dismissed. If indeed the artivists and sign subverters of the Printemps érable were central to the struggle, it is because they took seriously the extent to which neoliberal capitalism

The École de la montagne rouge runs a print-making station at a demonstration on June 22, 2012. The image on the T-shirt is the iconic fist of the Printemps érable.

has colonized our cultural conceptions and assumptions. Such was precisely what lay behind *Adbusters'* campaign when they launched Occupy Wall Street. In exposing and exploding these cultural symbols, they sought to strip them of their sanctity and erode the airs of inevitability that protect the mythologies they represent.

The gauntlet of Jean Charest: War is declared

It was January 27, 2012, and students were still in their classes. A protest organized by the CLASSE had wound its way to outside the Montréal offices of the Ministère de l'éducation, where two hundred demonstrators stood in a cordon behind their banner. In the midst of the peaceful protest, an SPVM officer was caught on tape punching a protester and throwing another woman to the ground, later claiming it was because they were blocking access to the police vehicles (a weak excuse in any case, and which students denied).[11] The episode quickly exploded across social media, and snowballed into a scandal in the mainstream press that forced the police to announce an internal inquiry. The strike hadn't yet begun when the brutishness of the police force emitted shockwaves that rippled out through the movement. The police had declared war, and the CLASSE needed no further invitations to create a Defence Fund to aid anyone arrested in the coming conflict.[12]

The government, meanwhile, had launched its own war, this one in the semantic and ideological realm: That which in nearly sixty years of Québec history had always been a "student strike"[13] — despite the lack of explicit legal recognition — was to be no longer. The democratically organized walkout of hundreds of thousands was now, in the government's insistence, a "boycott" — not the action of a social group asserting its rights, but a mere agglomeration of individual consumers choosing to refuse provision of a service.[14] "Strike" became the Word-We-Dare-Not-Utter, and the campaign it referred to was not to be recognized or responded to for fear of granting a collective action the slightest shred of legitimacy. The corporate press and university administrations needed no further convincing to embrace the government's Newspeak and leap onto the bandwagon that plowed through more than a half-century of history.[15]

Yet acknowledged or not by the powers that be, the student strike took off. On February 13, CLASSE affiliates representing ten thousand students at UQÀM and at Québec City's Université Laval voted unlimited strike mandates, thereby launching the 2012 unlimited general strike. The train had left the station, and 84,500 students were already on strike when on March 2, twenty-year-old Léo Bureau-Blouin, the calm and measured president of the FECQ, hesitantly called on its eighty thousand members to follow suit, lamenting that Charest's intransigence had rendered the call "inevitable."[16] Both federations had traditionally been recalcitrant toward calling for strike mandates. Martine Desjardins, the headstrong thirty-year-old doctoral candidate who served as the FEUQ's president at the time, spoke openly of aiming for a majority of their 125,000 members on strike, and yet the organization nonetheless took a rather hands-off approach to the internal debates of its members.[17] Throughout February and into March, rolling general assemblies and some referenda were held by student associations across the province, with one after the next voting to rally to the strike in function of each's democratic structures.[18]

As the results of the first strike votes were rolling in, Charest hastily threw down the gauntlet: Missives were sent out by the government to university administrations inviting teachers to force their way through picket lines.[19] After the police, it was now the government's turn to confirm the tone. Throughout February and March, university administrations responded to the student movement's traditional tactic of occupations by summoning riot police and private security agents to brutally eject protesters, in turn sparking violent clashes, injuries and arrests on campuses and paving the way for wider confrontations to follow.[20] The unprecedented government offensive took on a variety of forms aimed at denying and delegitimizing students' historic right to strike.[21] In the media, ministers incessantly parroted the line accusing striking students of "violence and intimidation" and tried to discredit the votes by accusing the pro-strike camp of resorting to strongarm tactics targeting dissenters in the student assemblies.

The leaders of the Liberal Party's youth wing began organizing student opponents of the strike into the Mouvement des étudiants socialement responsables du Québec (MESRQ), which launched a Facebook page and adopted the green square as its emblem. Numerically and organizationally insignificant as they were, the carrés verts nonetheless enjoyed the full protection and backing of all levers of power, from the premier down to the university administrations.[22] Acting as the government's long arm on campuses, every hint of hostility directed at strike opponents was exploited by the group and magnified by the mainstream media, as these self-styled martyrs were cast front and centre in the government smear campaign. These students were essentially libertarians and hyper-individualists who objected to the decisions of their local assemblies, despite in certain cases failing to even attend the deliberations.[23] Losing the democratic battle, they launched legal challenges demanding the resumption of courses so that they — read: I, I and I — could attend their classes in the midst of the greatest student mobilization Québec had ever known.[24]

(G)rève générale illimitée: The #GGI takes flight

As the number of associations on strike snowballed out at a dizzying rate, the frenetic momentum of the mobilization left the most wide-eyed expectations lingering in the dust. Barely three weeks after the first students walked out of their classes, the cap of 100,000 students was reached on March 1, and by March 8, 125,000 students were on strike.[25] The force of the strike mandates was just as impressive. At the CEGEP de l'Outaouais, 65 percent of students voted in favour of an unlimited strike mandate with a participation rate of 78 percent. At the CEGEP de Saint-Jérome, 61 percent voted to strike with a participation rate of over 75 percent, while the strike mandate voted by St-Jean-sur-Richelieu rested on an 81 percent participation rate. At institutions where general assemblies were held, such as Matane, Mont-Laurier and St-Félicien, participation rates hovered between 66 and 75 percent, and the yes votes in all cases were just as strong. Convinced by the government line that the pro-strike students were but an activist minority, the administration at the CEGEP André-Laurendeau in Montréal organized a campus-wide electronic vote in April in a bid at ending the strike. Yet the student body instead reconfirmed the initial mandate of the general assembly, and with a participation rate of 83 percent.[26] The realities just kept on slicing their way through the veil of the government's propaganda. Whether via general assembly, referendum or electronic vote, the strength of the majorities varied little. The truth was that the Liberals could only dream of such enthusiasm for them at the ballot box.

Never had Québec seen a student strike take off this fast. The numbers skyrocketed to a peak of 304,242 by March 22, representing a historic crest of 72 percent of Québec's post-secondary students in 2012.[27] Anglophone CEGEPs were barely touched, but for the first time in the history of the student movement, faculties and departments at Québec's anglophone universities, Concordia and McGill, joined the mobilization, with over 60 percent of English-speaking university students going on strike at some point during the spring.[28] The motor of the revolt did remain concentrated within the francophone student body, but the tidal change was historic: Québec's anglophone youth, the bilingual generation of Bill 101, were slowly leaving behind the cultural insularity and divisions of their parents' days to join their francophone friends in defending the Quiet Revolution's shared dream of a just and democratic Québec.[29] In the political life of this nation-within-Canada, this was an important moment indeed.

As the strike mandates added up and the number of students freed of their course obligations soared, the *carrés rouges* fanned out into the streets to unleash a flurry of protest activities that were impossible to ignore. Striking students picketed in front of CEGEPs and universities and launched temporary occupations of campuses and offices of Liberal MNAs. In *la vieille capitale* of Québec City, a Valentine's Day "die-in" was held in front of the Assemblée nationale, while in Montréal a symbolic marriage was performed between students and financial aid to "unite by the sacred bonds of debt."[30] Variously creative and often theatrical forms of protest dotted the landscape with ubiquitous apparitions of red: Students practiced "yoga in red" in the park or adorned red to hold public readings at the library, while a string of red-clad UQÀM theatre students formed La ligne rouge and took to the metro for weeks to raise awareness among passengers.[31] They would line the platforms so that passengers on board saw a blurred red line as the cars left the station.

Meanwhile, CLASSE members targeted economic symbols, briefly blocking access to the Montréal stock exchange on the morning of February 16 before being dislodged by police.[32] Confronting the silence and indifference of the government, Nadeau-Dubois explained that the CLASSE would engage the Liberals in the only language they seemed to understand: money.[33] On February 26, therefore, a few hundred CLASSE activists mounted a rush-hour blockade of the Jacques-Cartier bridge that paralyzed the main entry onto the island of Montréal, at once inciting the ire of thousands of suburban commuters, the hyperventilation of the establishment press and the brutality of the SPVM riot squad sent in to clear the structure.[34] Yet the students weren't bowed. Blockades and other instances of direct action multiplied across Montréal in the weeks that followed, including two simultaneous yet uncoordinated blockades of the Champlain and Jacques-Cartier bridges that sent the SPVM scattering to opposite ends of the city.[35]

More than the political repression, the heavy-handed police response stunned many students who, raised in a Québec they thought peaceful and democratic, had never before borne the brunt of the state's violence. The first jolt arrived early in the spring, and the awakening was brutal. On March 7, a group of five hundred to six hundred students blocked access to the Loto-Québec building in downtown Montréal where the offices of the Conférence des recteurs et des principaux des universités du Québec (CREPUQ) are housed.[36] Approximately two hundred of them, some of them masked, gained entry into the building, while shouts of "We're staying peaceful!" sought to reassure those working inside and helped prevent confrontations — until, that is, the rapid arrival of the riot police.[37] They dislodged the unarmed protesters from the building with generous deployments of baton strikes, tear gas, pepper spray and sound grenades, resulting in clashes that ended with four protesters and one police officer being hospitalized.[38] There was at least one young man there who will remember that day for the rest of his life: The face of CEGEP student Francis Grenier was maimed when police launched a sound grenade that erupted close to his face. Grenier will never again see out of his right eye.[39]

The premier responded later that day by defending the police without a hint of qualification and by opting to blame the students for the tragedy that had robbed a young man of half his vision. "Invading a public building, scaring everyone, obviously this has consequences," intoned Charest.[40] Students were in shock and organized a candlelight vigil that evening to denounce the police's brutality, as well as the premier's callous response. But what unfolded next was nothing short of surreal. One demonstrator, Fannie Poirier, captured the scene in a letter entitled "I saw my police state," written to local weekly *Voir*.

> That night I saw a cohort of thirty anti-riot police, shields and batons out, charge my friends and comrades as we were pressed together side by side with our candles in silence. I saw them disembark, an entire pack, and descend on us without the slightest hesitation. Not a single moment to judge the situation, to evaluate the necessity or the sense of their actions. There was a gnawing energy in my legs, that for-real kind of fear that grabs you by the guts. The police pushed me further away. [...] I heard people screaming. One guy, from behind his candle, dared

to ask the policeman in front of him if he could explain what they were doing wrong. The only answer he got was spat out of a canister of pepper spray directly in his face.[41]

This was the sinister backdrop. And against it, the Québec political and media establishments, to their eternal disgrace, became the apologists for such mindless brutality unleashed to pacify an unruly youth, and the dutiful parrots of the government talking points that tarred students as the perpetrators of "violence and intimidation."[42] The Grenier episode came as a wake-up call to students, who were abruptly stripped of any illusion their government would treat them as full citizens with rights protected by the Québec and Canadian Charters. Instantly, they had become enemies of the state. Yet far from ceding to the violence, the movement turned en masse to the one media sphere they dominated, social media, in an effort to combat and circumvent the official media frame.[43] A week later, on March 15, the annual march against police brutality in Montréal became the largest since the event began in 1997, attracting four thousand people and the official backing of the CLASSE congress after a large majority voted in favour in a vote held three days after the Grenier incident. Eighteen minutes after the march began, the police charged and dispersed the crowd, provoking a riot in the evening that ended in 226 arrests.[44]

This degree of repression was unknown to many students, as in the past a "relative tolerance" of strike actions prevailed that reflected the respect of the élites for the movement that many of them had once been part of.[45] But then, this is the apex of the neoliberal age, and "the economy" was now to be guarded at all costs. Much as elsewhere, police management of demonstrations became increasingly authoritarian from the mid-1990s in Québec, with the 2001 Summit of the Americas in Québec City marking a fateful milestone in the criminalization of dissent. Years after the SPVM and other police forces were severely reprimanded by the U.N.'s Human Rights Council for their repression of alter-globalization protests[46] — and after Ottawa was issued recommendations by the U.N. body that federal Liberal and Conservative governments both pointedly ignored[47] — mass arrests have become increasingly common in Canada, and police activities, increasingly political. Left-wing organizations have become the focus of expanding police resources in Montréal, with so-called "marginal and anarchist movements" targeted by the SPVM's Guet des activités des mouvements marginaux et anarchistes (GAMMA) squad created in 2009. "Radical" groups (read: that threaten powerful business interests) have become subject to mounting pressures by the Canadian Security Intelligence Service (CSIS), while the Conservative government in Ottawa brands environmentalists as terrorists.[48]

Where police had long reserved their contempt and discrimination for the homeless, indigenous and young immigrants, the student strike of 2012 shook Québec's middle-class youth awake with the brutal realities of society's underclasses, as they were stripped of their "citizen immunity" by police who directed the same disdain at "anyone causing the slightest disorder in the streets."[49] Throughout the spring, it became increasingly clear that in today's Québec, the police force's imperative "to serve and protect" applies only to obedient workers and consumers who thereby gain the badge of good citizenship. Those who disrupt the economic flow place themselves in the crosshairs of the economy's tyranny, where the police don't prevent riots. They cause them.

#22mars: From cyberworld to sunlight, the movement hits the streets

With the warming temperature announcing the early coming of spring, Québec seemed to burst into a bloom of red squares that preceded the budding of the trees. The ubiquitous emblem sprouted on surfaces and people across the province, dotting the landscape with splashes of crimson that struck the public imagination and inflated the movement's aspirations. From organized phone-ins to MNAs to "musical marathons," from silent marches and choreographed funeral processions to singing, dancing and occupations of public space, small-scale actions proliferated at a frenetic pace throughout Québec, as from Victoriaville to Rimouski, protesters dogged government ministers at every turn.[50] In the streets and metros of Montréal, the small felt squares proliferated on the lapels, backpacks and clothing of citizens, and before long members of the Official Opposition PQ had joined the parade.

March 22 was fast approaching, and with it the moment when the mobilization strategies of the federations were set to reach their end, and according to plans, their climax. The class walkouts were racing toward a crescendo as they passed the 300,000 mark, and the FEUQ and FECQ had gambled on a thunderous procession of *carrés rouges* to at last force the premier to acknowledge the scale of the contestation and accept to negotiate. Launched by the federations and actively promoted and diffused by the CLASSE, the Facebook event page for the March 22 national march — so called because students were to converge on Montréal from all corners of Québec — ultimately sent out 130,000 invitations.[51] Yet nothing could have prepared anyone for the sight they were about to behold and that those there that day will certainly never forget. On March 22, 2012, a human tide estimated at 200,000 people swept through the streets of downtown Montréal, washing away all doubts as to the movement's resonance.[52] All precedents in Canadian history had instantly fallen into irrelevance, as the movement of Québec's *carrés rouges* emerged with full force into the light of day to become aware of its own strength and scope. Amidst the sea of handcrafted slogans, memes and the carnivalesque costumes and makeup of the masses clad in red, two thousand silkscreened placards signed by the École de la montagne rouge held up a square clenched fist, above the call for a "Printemps érable."[53]

Suddenly, all but the most cynical or rigid of thinking were forced to acknowledge the historic scale of a generational revolt unfolding before their eyes. "May

68 is the past," declared Léo Bureau-Blouin, "from this point on, we'll talk about March 2012!"[54] And indeed even the mainstream press gushed with astonishment at the unexpected show of force. In a column whose simple title, "Impressive," spoke volumes, *La Presse*'s Patrick Lagacé penned a prescient warning to the government:

> The students played the game. They held an intelligent, disciplined and festive demonstration […] that resulted in no material damage or arrests. […] If the government stubbornly persists in its paternalistic silence, it will at least have to share in the responsibility for the broken windows. If it insists on not talking over the course of the next few days, it will be sending this message: that being nice, being playful, gets us nowhere.[55]

The (non) response:
Pay no attention to the man behind the curtain

Before the marchers had even gone home, the premier glanced down his nose at the seas of restless commoners massing below and stretched wide his mouth to let go a protracted yawn. "Unfortunately," chided Charest, "they chose to boycott the discussion" when they walked out of the (preordained) *Rencontre des partenaires* in December 2010.[56] Repeating the government's talking points on the state's inability to adequately fund its universities, Charest affirmed that the hike was inevitable and rejected any and all dialogue with student representatives.[57] Indeed, "even the Iranians and Americans have diplomatic 'back channels'," Lagacé had quipped, and yet not a single channel of communication existed between the government and Québec's national student associations. It had been decided by the people's elected representatives, argued the Liberals, and students must simply accept it and go home.[58]

The government was nothing if not disciplined in its messaging. From the moment the tuition hike was announced, it was carefully presented not as the result of choices conditioned by sets of values and assumptions, but as the outflow of cold economic truths merely observed and responded to by impartial managers. The government's "studious silence denied even the political nature of the object of the conflict," says the anonymous citizens' collective, the Collectif de débrayage (the "walkout" collective). Their magisterial work, *On s'en câlisse: Histoire profane de la grève printemps 2012*, eloquently captures the story and soul of the Printemps érable. "The tuition increase was presented as a natural phenomenon," they write, "a spontaneous adjustment of the economy upon itself, determined by internal imperatives."[59] And so, rather than engaging in a conversation that would have admitted the presence of alternatives — which would, in short, have acknowledged the possibility of a *debate* — the government stuck meticulously close to its script and then upped the ante by accusing protesters of hurting Québec's workers and, of course, the economy.[60]

In the days following the March 22 march, the FEUQ and FECQ's members fell off to bring the number of students on unlimited general strike to around 190,000 (almost half the post-secondary student population), where it hovered for the rest of the spring. The CLASSE represented more than half of them.

Rouse from your coma: Capitalists versus the carnival

Faced with the government's refusal to even acknowledge the strike, a flurry of protests engulfed Quebecers in what seemed like an unstoppable explosion. The CLASSE's economic disturbances intensified as small-scale actions erupted every morning at new locations across the province, while Montréal became ground zero where the *carrés rouges'* diffuse offensives clustered and converged.[61] On March 29, *La grande mascarade* gave the launch signal to a wave of satirical protest-performances that plunged the streets into an atmosphere of carnivalesque hilarity and defiance.[62] With a bylaw change being debated at City Hall designed to ban masks in protests and make preauthorized routes obligatory, costumed youth departed in thematized marches from four locations across the city, with each colour-coded as a metro line (such as one denouncing the violence of the government, another mocking the manipulation of the *carrés verts* strike-busters and so on). In the same absurdist and irreverent vein as a march that days later decided its itinerary by "spinning a bottle at each intersection,"[63] the roving masquerade balls wound their way through the streets in random processions that made them "practically uncontrollable by the police."[64]

Citing theorist Mikhail Bakhtine, authors Stéphanie Lemoine and Samira Ouardi have written that

> revolution and the carnival have identical goals: to turn the world upside down with a joyous abandon and to celebrate our indestructible thirst for life — a thirst that capitalism strives adamantly to destroy with its monotonous round of work and consumption.[65]

And indeed as a freshness and even magic invaded the streets, every day stood apart with its spontaneous eruptions and shock-apparitions that broke the monotony of the daily treadmill. Employees at the Ministère de l'éducation, du loisir et du sport (MELS) arrived at work on April Fools' Day to find their building painted red, the same day as a protest in the form of theatrical parody lampooned the *carrés verts* (or MESRQ) as the "Mouvement des étudiants super-riches du Québec."[66] One night, a massive red banner appeared on Montréal's landmark Jacques-Cartier bridge; on another, one appeared on the city's iconic illuminated cross that overlooks the city from atop Mont-Royal's summit; and all along, public art interventions by collectives that backed the students increasingly intruded on the everyday.[67]

The black robes of the power: Judges for repression

With political and police repression already in full swing, the judiciary — appointed largely by the Liberals after Charest politicized the appointments process[68] — then rained down a dramatic triple pressure on the student mobilization. Presented with students arrested for the first time, judges imposed draconian conditions for release pending their trials, with bail at times set as high as $15,000 and often between $2,000 to $3,000, along with the threat of steeply augmenting penalties for subsequent offences.[69] Bans on participating in peaceful demonstrations or even on being found in certain neighbourhoods or cities (like Montréal) were also imposed.[70] Quite possibly unconstitutional according to legal experts Lucie Lemonde, Andrée Bourbeau and Véronique Fortin, the conditions far surpassed any public danger posed by the students and likely served but one overriding goal: to intimidate and neutralize activists.[71] Judicial repression is far more "insidious" than police brutality, they explain, as its "repercussions are more diffuse: the financial burden of the defence, the psychological stress, the conditions of release that break apart social networks, the obligation to relive painful moments during the testimony, the fear of being incarcerated, the perverse effects of having a criminal record, etc."[72] Indeed, the broader impacts of these measures could not have been unknown to judges, and yet these were only one strain of the conservative judiciary's mobilization against the students.

The first injunctions requested by the *carrés verts* were handed down by the courts on March 30 and ordered administrations to resume classes so as to provide the student-clients the "service" they had paid for. It's important here to remember that the 1983 *Act respecting the accreditation and financing of students' associations*, modelled on the Labour Code's Rand Formula, expressly encouraged students to group together to defend their interests to the state by granting associations a monopoly of representation.[73] Yet in one terrifying swipe the judges circumvented its spirit and erased over forty years of history during which student strikes had never been known as anything but. Suddenly in 2012, the judiciary embraced Charest's lexicon "word for word"[74] and denied the collective and democratic foundations of the strike by debasing the movement to the level of a "boycott."[75] The judges, however, had greatly overestimated their moral authority over students, and rather than leading the youth down the consumerist path they pointed to, they had instead only sabotaged themselves. To an important segment of the population, the perception of the justice system's impartiality had been gravely undermined, as judges became eagerly instrumentalized in a political offensive aimed directly at the collective mobilization of a generation.[76] While some judges did refuse to grant injunctions on the (correct) basis of not wanting to interfere in a political debate, the majority rallied dutifully to the government line, with the minute number of student dissenters winning fifty injunctions up to May 18.[77] Yet Québec's youth were neither fooled nor deterred.

The politicization of the judiciary outraged students and professors alike and fuelled a sharp rise in violence on campuses as picketers refused to accept the injunctions' legitimacy. No direction was required from the national associations — and in fact, Léo Bureau-Blouin even urged the FECQ's members to respect the decisions of the courts. To no avail.[78] A province-wide network of solidarity was organized to bus in reinforcements to defend the picket lines, aided by professors who were now joining the front lines in ever growing numbers. Provincial police at times responded by detaining entire busloads of students "preventively," before escorting them to police stations to examine "their intentions and identities."[79] Some institutions simply abandoned the idea of forcing the resumption of classes in the face of such resistance, while the most bellicose administrations hired private security agents and summoned riot police to dislodge the protesters. Campuses were transformed into war zones, as phalanxes of police unleashed an indiscriminate storm of batons and tear gas on rows of unarmed students, professors — and in one case, mothers — as they stood side by side in solidarity with the besieged students.[80]

In the end, the fierce resistance rendered the injunctions effectively inoperable, as the *carrés verts* were forced to accept that it's simply not possible "for a teacher to teach in clothes drenched in pepper spray," or their own blood.[81] The battles were energetically invoked by the government as the supposed sign of strikers' contempt for the law. And indeed, the government's politicization of the courts *had* pushed the movement into a zone of illegality. Yet far from being to the Liberals' benefit, Charest's machinations had only stripped the state's institutions of their airs of untouchability and delivered youth an enduring lesson on the hidden structures behind élite power. Ironically, the government sought throughout the spring to discredit the democratic basis of the strike and to ascribe the "boycotts" to a vocal minority. Yet neither Charest's own contempt for the independence of the courts, nor for the democratic processes of the students' local associations, ever concerned the government a whit — no more, anyway, than the untold violence that tore through campuses as a result.

Of depravity and deaf ears:
A government that beats its youth

On April 5, nearly two weeks after the historic demonstration on March 22, the government finally delivered its first offer to students, in which it proposed the addition of $21 million into the loans program, along with the creation of an option for an income-dependent post-graduate tax.[82] To summarize: After a historic show of opposition that saw nearly three quarters of Québec's post-secondary students walk out of their classes and 200,000 citizens fill the streets, the government judged it appropriate to respond by creating avenues for youth to amass more debt. Predictably, the national associations angrily rejected the offer as an insult, as all signs were pointing toward a fairly avoidable escalation.

Conciliation and compromise were never part of Charest's strategy, however. A week later, the Liberals' bombast aimed at tarring the students as violent began to take on the appearance of a highly concerted and vicious propaganda campaign. While on an overseas trip to São Paolo on April 11, Charest launched a blistering attack on student democracy by comparing campaigns for affirmative strike votes in the assemblies to union intimidation in the construction industry (and considering the conclusions of the Duchesneau Report, that particular analogy indeed took some gall). Manning the home front, education minister and deputy premier Line Beauchamp fired her own rounds in issuing a call urging all university and CEGEP administrations to take "all necessary measures for courses to take place."[83] The sabre-rattling enraged the student leaders, who were already witness to rising tensions on campuses in the wake of the government's bellicose provocations.[84] But the students weren't the only ones aghast at the government's chest-thumping: With the national associations warning that Charest was encouraging violence, over a thousand professors signed a petition demanding the government respect student democracy and calling for the immediate resignation of Line Beauchamp.[85]

The government belligerence was not without its enlightening contrast: The very same day as Charest and Beauchamp fired their cannons, the FECQ and FEUQ released proposals aimed at keeping tuition fees frozen by reducing the salaries of university presidents and freezing expenditures unrelated to teaching and research.[86] It was perhaps at this point, outflanked by a youth whose poise and maturity in the midst of an unprecedented onslaught highlighted the infantility of the government's comportment, that the Liberals began to worry, if somewhat belatedly, about their image. On April 15, after the strike had attained a historic record of eight weeks, Beauchamp finally offered to sit down with the federations. It seemed the Liberals weren't quite worried enough. After two months of an unprecedented mass mobilization, the secondary issue of university management was the only one the government was willing to discuss. The core issue of tuition fees, the Liberals decreed, was off the table, and the CLASSE, by far the most important actor in the strike, was pointedly excluded from the talks.[87] Léo Bureau-Blouin of the FECQ responded positively to the government's invitation, which briefly threatened to derail the students' common front. Yet the decisive opposition from the FEUQ's Desjardins, more politically savvy than her younger counterpart, preempted the splintering of the student camp and forced Bureau-Blouin to fall back into line. Desjardins adamantly refused on account of both of Beauchamp's exclusions, and offered to cede two seats from her own delegation to the CLASSE — with or without the minister's consent.[88]

In the streets, emotions inflamed further as protesters were being regularly subjected to liberal deployments of tear gas, pepper spray and batons.[89] Yet in the Assemblée nationale and through the media, the premier and his ministers were unfazed by the youth being beaten in the streets. They were more concerned, obsessively even, by the minor but growing incidents of material damage that were dominating the headlines. Despite ample warnings, which were faithfully borne out in fact, the government seemed either incapable or unwilling to acknowledge any link at all between their contemptuous approach to students and the raw emotions spilling over in the streets. Charest and his ministers seemed only to take encouragement from the trend and to exploit it to escalate their rhetoric accusing the students of violence and intimidation. The single-mindedness that characterized the government's leap into the vicious cycle was so bewildering as to stoke suspicions of a Machiavellian strategy aimed at nourishing the conditions for violence so as to better discredit the movement. Yet whether the government strategy flowed from manipulation, dogmatism or ordinary incompetence, the consequences on the ground changed little, and Charest's responsibility for them will cling to his skin all the same.

FOR THE FUTURE, FOR US ALL
A Generation's Struggle to Rescue the Commons

you don't want to sleep anymore
the visions have seized you
sufficiently

you dreamed of a dazzling world
and you returned to us
blind and collapsed

lend your ear
our steps call to you from the possibilities
of a shared insomnia[1]

— Zéa Beaulieu-April, *"Entre l'amorce et la suite"* (my translation)

With the student mobilization fast exploding into a full-blown social crisis, Jean Charest organized a "job fair" in the heart of downtown Montréal to promote his Plan Nord. The temeritous move painted a massive bull's eye on the Palais des Congrès where the event was being held. Three separate protests targeted the event, where a growing throng of angry demonstrators massed outside as indigenous activists, anarchists, organized labour and members of the CLASSE converged to soon outnumber the ill-equipped police that were guarding the site.[2] Before long, a group had penetrated inside the underground parking lot, as protesters smelled their rare advantage outside and rained stones down on the police contingent to beat them into retreat. For four hours straight, the riot at the *Salon du Plan Nord* rattled many with the intensity and resolve of demonstrators that was unlike anything Montréal had ever known.[3] As the fierce street battle raged outside and protesters were poised to gain entry into the building, Charest, standing before a room full of white-collar executives and corporate investors, ventured a light-hearted jab at the violent unrest that their gathering had so thoughtlessly sparked: The meeting, quipped Charest, was so popular that "people are running from all sides to get in." And indeed, pursued the premier, it was a good occasion for job-seekers and students in particular, who may find opportunities — "in the North, as much as possible."[4]

Instantly, the premier's indelicate Gulag-esque evocation sparked a firestorm in the press, in social media and among the opposition parties, who were all utterly incredulous at his aggressive lack of decency and judgment.[5] The Radio-Canada clip of Charest's joke went viral to become one of the most watched YouTube videos of the strike, and had been viewed over 411,000 times by March of 2014.[6] Fuel had been thrown once more onto the flames with what seemed like such gleeful, and inexplicable, abandon, as the street chanted back its irreverent retort: *"Charest, dehors! On va t' trouver une job dans l'nord!"* ("Charest, out! We're going to find you a job in the North!") Fortunate enough for the *carrés rouges,* Charest's sense of timing proved nearly as astute as his sense of humour.

#22avril: For the common good

Simmering beneath the surface of the contestation from the start, Charest's controversial Plan Nord had invited itself forcefully into the crisis mere days before the arrival of the second national march on April 22 — Earth Day, 2012. With the student crisis at its height and the Liberals' fire sale of Québec's natural resources now front and centre, the released torrents of unrest converged on Montréal as the Printemps érable grew outwards to fully assume its lofty moniker. Sixteen red maple trees were planted that morning at the base of Mont-Royal by the École de la montagne rouge. Once grown, they will form a perfect square that will endure as a natural imprint of the spring of 2012.[7] The force of the symbolism punctuated the historic moment. That day, a seemingly endless throng of 250,000 to 300,000 citizens flooded the city streets. They converged on the mountain, as the ubiquity of red rivalled the green slogans of the traditionally small Earth Day processions to announce that the protesters were one and the same.[8] The people marched for public education, for the Earth and then for more: They marched, in the words of the protest theme, "for the common good."[9] On that Earth Day of a spring awash in red, the sea of colourful and creative slogans spoke eloquently and imaginatively to the thread of a unifying narrative: *"Le combat est avenir,"* proclaimed the newest set of placards signed by the École de la montagne rouge. Not for us but for the future, and the real fight is still to come.

Faced with a second outcry from the streets that surpassed the prior shattering of all precedents only a month before, the government at last conceded it could remain silent no more. The following day, as Amnesty International issued a pointed plea for Charest to cease all violations of the rights to free expression and peaceful protest, Line Beauchamp announced the imminent launch of negotiations with student representatives and the inclusion of all topics — and all actors.[10] The crisis had just entered its tenth week.

The democrats at the generals' table

The show of humility was fleeting, however, as the government's obsession with stratagems resurfaced almost instantly: The student associations would be allowed at the table only after condemning the protesters' "violence," and they would have to observe a forty-eight-hour truce on all "economic and social disturbance" activities or else risk being excluded. "Obviously, the envisaged truce is unilateral: Never will there be any question of withdrawing the police from the streets."[11] The federation heads, with their full decisional authority independent of their base, immediately agreed to the government ultimatum. The glare of the spotlight was aimed directly at the CLASSE, as their members debated for hours in a special meeting convened to decide on a response. Eventually, the CLASSE congress voted a "classically humanist" compromise that pointedly rejected the equivalency between material property and human life, denouncing only violence directed against individuals except in cases of legitimate self-defence.[12] Yet on the public relations front the government had won the day, exploiting the slowness of their ultra-democratic procedures to again present the CLASSE as violent radicals and its spokespeople as lacking in leadership. The autocracy of the status quo is admittedly more efficient.

Succumbing to enormous pressure, the CLASSE executive went against its own nature in trying to suspend its members' actions, but to no avail.[13] To all evidence, the movement no longer belonged to them, if indeed it ever did. It belonged to the youth. By mid April, the great majority of protest actions and economic disturbances had in fact become entirely autonomous from the student leaderships, as Nadeau-Dubois relates in his book *Tenir Tête*. With many of them anonymous, even to the CLASSE, it became "impossible — as much for the police, the media, the CLASSE and its spokespersons — to know who is responsible for which action and what is the target."[14] In short, this social media-era mobilization had little to do with the world imagined by the Charest government. And as the Collectif de débrayage relates so eloquently, the Liberals' demands only served to shine a piercing light into the political culture of another age.

> With this idea of a truce, we're transported suddenly to the era of the civilized wars, where we agreed in advance on the time of the battle and the weapons allowed; where peace was negotiated between generals around a cup of tea and biscuits.[...] Its transposition to a strike context, in the face of an adversary like the CLASSE, amounts to conceiving of the levers of resistance to power through the same model as that power itself; to consider it as a competing sovereign, disciplining its troops, directing their aspirations and launching their actions by a pyramidal network of authority.[...] Yet the movement that's emerged at present is by all accounts without a head.[15]

Pushed to mould itself to the frames of a top-down political culture that didn't fit, the CLASSE's membership fiercely rebuffed the affront to their autonomy. "Never were we consulted about the ridiculous truce proposed by a desperate minister," fumed one group that launched a call on Facebook for an "*ostie de grosse manif de soir*" (loosely: "a fucking huge night demo"). That call drew twelve thousand angry protesters into the streets on April 24.[16] "Will the injunctions also hold a truce, will the administrations suspend their courses, will the police stop their investigations and their repression that are dragging our comrades through the courts? WE ARE WINNING. No time to stop."[17] The government saw the protest call posted online to an unmoderated open-source calendar hosted by the CLASSE, yet that bore no tie to the national executive.[18] Beauchamp wasted no time in seizing on the apparent violation as a premise to expel the CLASSE from the talks. Whether the minister genuinely failed to grasp the grassroots and autonomous nature of the movement — and of the Internet — or whether she merely used the protest as a cover to keep the wheels of Charest's divide-and-conquer tactics turning, is open to conjecture. Less so, however, was what would come of aborting the first glimmer of hope to surface in more than ten weeks of escalating unrest, and how the street, already ready to burst, would respond to a spit in the face of their primary spokesperson.

In a fury, the FEUQ and FECQ immediately broke off talks and closed ranks around the CLASSE. "That's enough," boomed an exasperated Martine Desjardins. "We're not in a classroom. The minister has to stop playing school headmistress and assigning consequences and punishments to everyone. She has to sit down and negotiate with us in good faith, because we've seen no clear openness from the minister, who's been there for one hour out of the last forty. It's unacceptable."[19] Gabriel Nadeau-Dubois (GND) added that Beauchamp's exclusion of the CLASSE, which then represented more than half of students on strike throughout the province, was a simple pretext that hid her unwillingness to even discuss the tuition hike.[20] Yet Beauchamp, warned GND, had "just thrown oil on the fire"[21] — and the response from the fire was immediate. That night, April 25, thousands responded to a protest call issued by the law and political science association of UQÀM, as the students' rage boiled over into the streets.[22] Corporate media outlets (including Liberal-friendly *La Presse* and Québécor-owned TVA) were physically and verbally attacked by protesters, as banks, cars and shop windows were vandalized.[23] In the face of such unceasing disdain and dismissals, the students' untiring resolve to stare the premier down grew ever more unshakeable: "*Chaque soir! Jusqu'à la victoire!*" they promised to march — every night until victory.[24] And with that defiant vow from the street, the crisis entered its tensest, and most violent, phase.

#manifencours: The streets are ours for yelling

With the advent of the nightly marches, any remaining illusions that the student representatives controlled anything at all were washed away to reveal a leaderless and autonomous movement of the twenty-first century. As the marches ebbed and flowed in size from hundreds to thousands in intimate relation with the day's events, the nightly processions dominated morning headlines and became a finger placed on the pulse of the student base.[25] The street had taken over, and Twitter moved into the front seat of the mobilization.[26] Trending almost constantly in Montréal for months, the hashtag #manifencours ("demo in progress") became an open window into the movement's collective brain. Every evening at eight o'clock, without organizers, itineraries or prior confirmation of any kind, people converged at Place Émilie-Gamelin downtown before winding their way through the city streets for hours on end. The SPVM had its well-stocked arsenal, but the students had their own: Tracking the crowds' movements on Twitter, protesters met up with the marches en route as they inflated and decreased in mass, splintering and reconverging in a game of cat-and-mouse with police that often stretched well past midnight. As the exhausted security forces were worn thinner by the around-the-clock protests, their brutality escalated to match their anger and fatigue. In response, protesters armed with smartphones continuously monitored the actions of the riot squads and converted all records of their repression into fuel to further the movement's expansion and resolve. The police couldn't win.

Pursued for over 130 nights straight, the marches would come to form a core pillar of the student spring, and provided the setting for the daily reinforcement of its values and goals. More than a simple vow of defiance or a pressure tactic, the regular occupation of public space was also an essential outflow of the movement's collectivist riposte. In this deeper sense, Québec's students picked up the baton from the citizens who occupied public spaces under the banners of the Indignados and Occupy — and carried it further. In a talk held in the early days of the Occupy movement, Judith Butler attempted to capture the common thread of these interventions.

> Bodies congregate, they move and speak together and they lay claim to a certain space as public space.[...] Collective actions collect the space itself, gather the pavement and animate and organize the architecture. [...] At such a moment, politics is no longer defined as the exclusive business of public sphere distinct from a private one, but it crosses that line again and again, bringing attention to the way that politics is already in the home, or on the street, or in the neighborhood or indeed in those virtual spaces that are unbound by the architecture of the public square.[27]

The regularity of the *carrés rouges*' nightly marches constituted an amplification of this claim to public space, as read against the backdrop of their reimagining as commercial conduits and compartments by neoliberal capitalism; for working and consuming, that is, but not for debating, organizing or launching political demands.[28] The contours of this present-day clash over the nature and ownership of public space was sharply delineated by the unprecedented repressiveness of legal and police tactics employed to crush the 2012 mobilization. In both Montréal and Québec City, municipal bylaws enacted during the crisis imposed a requirement, backed by steep fines, to have protest itineraries approved by authorities in advance, an ordinance justified on the basis of minimizing "disruptions" — read: to the efficient operation of commercial life.[29] Failure to comply resulted in protests being declared illegal, often before they had even begun. Yet in the era of social media, the state's very conception of protests — of organizers and itineraries — was marked by precisely the same model of top-down control that these children of the twenty-first century were revolting against.

Neither police nor the politicians seemed to grasp this essential nature of the movement. No more, anyway, than they understood that in a true democracy, one doesn't require the permission of the state to protest against the state. This first affront against civil liberties then served in turn as a pretext for police to deploy chemical and physical weapons indiscriminately and a degree of violence that was wildly disproportionate to the threat posed by protesters — except, that is, to the unfettered flow of commerce and consumption. Peaceful protesters, bystanders and many established journalists thus found themselves caught in the onslaught, charged at, knocked to the ground, beaten by batons or pepper-sprayed, all by trigger-happy security forces too often devolved into the brutish automatons of state violence and given the enthusiastic and unqualified go-ahead of their political masters.[30] Jacques Nadeau, a photojournalist for Le Devoir for over twenty years, recounted the trauma he suffered at the hands of a police cavalry in his emotional testimony to the Ménard Commission on the Printemps érable, launched by the Marois government.

> There's an arrest. I know that for the police, before …, when there's an arrest, you're not supposed to get too close … because they need to … secure the site. So I start, but the scene there, it was still pretty far away … I'd say about forty metres from me. And so I figured, "Okay, I'll go into the streets to not harm the police so that they don't think I, y'know, want to hurt anyone." And right then, I can tell you, I was almost alone on the sidewalk running and suddenly, I felt a push in the back like I'd never felt. A push … It's not … You don't feel … It's not a hand, it's an enormous mass, that crushes you, and I fell … completely flat, in about … a tenth of a second, the speed I was going at. And what's more, I was running, okay? I have three cameras, I have one across the shoulder hanging in front of my stomach that digs right into my stomach then. […]
>
> Then I found myself underneath the horse, a bit dizzy. I see the hoofs of the horse stepping around my head. It's enormous, it's not a pony, these horses. It's really … It's … They're this big. They stomp on you, and it's over. And then … I'm … I'm completely, I'm totally afraid, I have no idea what's happening, but there are people, the horse continues and in the end, I didn't get … the horse was … was more intelligent, I think, and he … as if … he told me … he spared my life.[31]

One of Nadeau's cameras, worth more than $10,000, was destroyed by the attack and never reimbursed by police.[32] What Nadeau experienced was nothing out of the ordinary for the spring of 2012, however, as police routinely disregarded journalists' repeated identifications as members of the press and even deliberately targeted them — particularly those filming — with intimidation, aggression, arrests, violence and destruction and seizures of equipment.[33] The same treatment, in short, as that experienced by students. Throughout the spring, protesters were often met with kettling and mass arrests by police, despite repeated condemnations from the United Nations in recent years that denounced these practices in Canada as flagrant violations of citizens' rights to peaceful protest and assembly.[34] The legal bases for some of these arrests, moreover, spoke quite eloquently to their underlying goal: namely, safeguarding the myth of the economy's untouchability at the expense of wider social and democratic rights.

The new police model of the corporate age was crystallized in the SPVM's response to the annual May Day march in the spring of 2012. Long devolved into a tired and token parade of labour union activists reciting pre-rehearsed slogans, the student spring transformed the "anticapitalist May 1st" demonstration into an impassioned march attracting three thousand unemployed women and men, students, workers, families, children, anarchists and feminists.[35] With police officers massed imposingly along both sides of the procession from the start, the SPVM decreed the protest illegal barely thirty minutes after it had departed, on the basis of unnamed "offences" that were unremarked by reporters of Le Devoir.[36] The police provocation itself, however, instantly sparked attacks against property that resulted in a barrage of tear gas, sound grenades, pepper spray and batons, which all ended in at least seventy arrests.[37]

The heavy-handed and disproportionate police response is highly typical of the neoliberal order, where the security establishment's overreaction to perceived threats against the economy is directed not only at physical repression, but more importantly, at emotional and psychological intimidation. Thus a week and a half later, a minor incident involving smoke-bombs thrown onto the tracks of the Montréal metro at rush-hour was elevated by media paranoia into a veritable national security crisis. No one was injured, and the smoke was cleared in a matter of minutes; the only tangible harm, in fact, was that employees were delayed in getting to work.[38] Immediately, the media and political establishments erupted with hysteria at the "attack" that caused police to shut down the metro system, leading to a frenetic and high-profile chase to find the culprits of the misdeed. Panicked by the unexpected reaction to their prank, the students turned themselves in to police the next morning. Yet as the Collectif de débrayage observes, "a political act, a symbolic act, demands an equally symbolic response: It requires an exemplary penalty, designed to put an end to the brinksmanship. This last word that the justice system wields carries the sinister name of 'terrorism.'"[39] Indeed, with no threat to public safety to justify it, the three women accused were kept imprisoned for a week pending their court dates, while the fourth accused, a man, was held for two. And with nary a concern for the effects on the futures of the youth in question, the four were charged with the bizarrely contrived offence of "inciting fear of terrorist activities," carrying a sentence of up to five years in prison.[40]

As police interventions multiplied that could not even claim to be motivated by public safety, the benevolent image of police still held by many segments of the population was unmasked as a quaint and fading fantasy. Those arrested were often peaceful by the police's own admission — at times involving journalists, and in one case the leftist legislator and co-spokesperson of Québec Solidaire, Amir Khadir[41] — yet were trapped in kettles (at times for hours), arrested and charged for obstructing traffic (keep the economy moving!), and fined $494 under the provincial highway code.[42] Other instances of mass arrests were on the basis of "illegal assembly" (protesting spontaneously or without submitting your plans for approval), including one that ended in the arrest of 506 individuals at once.[43] Crowning a steady and growing trend toward the criminalization of dissent in neoliberal states, Québec's troubling new status quo was reconfirmed in 2012 as the total number of arrests made between February 16 and September 3 soared to a staggering 3,509, with 83 percent of them the products of mass arrests. To this number of undiscerning detentions, we can add another 1,500 arrested in 2013 following protests linked to the Printemps érable.[44]

"À qui la rue, à nous la rue!"[45] is thus far more than a mischievous police taunt. It is the battle cry, rather, of a protracted social counterattack against the marketization of our city spaces and the narrowing of our human and civic existence to that of mindless consumers and workers on the capitalist treadmill. The police model of preemption exhibited fully during the student spring was the expression, tyrannical in its essence, of what political and cultural theorist Brian Massumi calls neoliberalism's "depoliticisation of life under the mantle of economism."[46] In 2012, the students sought to "collect the pavement," in Butler's memorable phrase, and reconstitute a civic and public realm from the ashes of the streets-cum-commercial-corridors. The act of marching thus represented nothing less than the aggressive reassertion of popular sovereignty over the polis and the revival of the political nature of the community's physical domain.

#Victoriaville wasn't a riot, it was a war

In response to the latest escalation of unrest that was increasingly paralyzing downtown Montréal, the government made a second offer to student representatives on April 27. The Liberals proposed to add $39 million to loans and bursaries, and to replace the $1,625 hike with an increase totalling $1,778, spread over seven years instead of five.[47] Student representatives furiously labelled it yet another insult, and the CLASSE responded a few days later with its own counter-offer: redirect a portion of research funds toward instruction, outlaw spending on advertising by educational institutions, ban the construction of satellite campuses and institute free university education by 2016 by reinstating a 0.7 percent capital tax on banks.[48] The government ignored the proposal, and the demonstrations roared on. Indeed in the fictional board game where Charest played, the pyromaniac premier seemed to be quite enjoying himself. Yet it unfortunately wouldn't be up to the government to pay the price of his frivolity just yet. The next victims came the following week.

Fleeing the unrest that was engulfing Montréal, the Liberal Party moved their congress scheduled for May 4 to Victoriaville, located 140 kilometres northeast of the metropolis. The premier couldn't get far enough away, however, as the name of this small town of 46,000 would soon be marked with a weighty significance for years to come. Summoned by the Coalition opposée à la tarification et à la privatisation des services publics (of which the ASSÉ is a member), two thousand to three thousand protesters converged outside the hotel that housed the congress, which was protected by a metal fence designed to keep the rowdy discontents at bay. No order was given to perturb the event, and the planned march, after a ten minute procession that wound its way through town, ended in front of the hotel.[49] It was around that time that some protesters decided to remove a segment of the fence and throw it toward the Sureté du Québec (SQ) officers guarding the event. Advancing through the breach into the hotel's parking lot, the protesters came face to face with a row of riot police staring them down.[50] And then, all hell broke loose.

Swift and brutal as per their habit, the police unleashed an offensive to shock and awe. An uncommonly potent tear gas was launched into the crowd as plastic bullets were fired at close range, sparking a furious reaction from demonstrators, who pelted the cops with rocks retrieved from a nearby construction site.[51] The riot was of a rare violence and intensity that bespoke a social crisis racing ever closer to the brink. Frontline protesters battled with the provincial police for hours, with many seeking safety far back while others cared for the wounded.[52] A first-hand account conveys the scene so potently that a more abridged version would fail to do it justice.

> I saw the first stones thrown toward the police and wanted to get further back from the front line to escape the coming surge of the crowd toward me. But the first shots of tear gas were immediately launched at the colourful multitude, at the hooded activists and the union members, at the young and old, at the families and their children, and we dispersed in a panic. People were screaming, coughing, and I heard the cries of choking children from afar.[...] Numerous explosions rang out through the grey sky, and I could no longer distinguish the blasts of the fireworks from the detonation of the gaseous bombs.[...]
>
> We approached the combat zone, and a group of demonstrators had suddenly formed behind the front line. And when I was able to see why they were gathering, I saw there was a man unconscious on the ground, blood trickling down his neck, his legs soft; his face had been struck. Around him, some were calling for help while others fumed with rage. They told me he'd received a plastic bullet in the temple.[...] Among the

demonstrators, we asked everyone to create a space to allow an ambulance to arrive. But the police squadron immediately charged the crowd again, and the paramedics struggled to move the man toward a calmer space. They moved many times to avoid the gas, trying in vain to alert the police that they held a gravely wounded man in their arms.[...]

A squadron of police quickly formed a combat line to protect the hotel from the invaders, and we started launching all the projectiles we could get our hands on. We were hundreds, we threw in waves, we surprised ourselves with the power of our strikes. The SQ helicopter was a spectator at the back of the combat scene, a voyeur of the historic rage; and the gawkers looked at the scene from afar, stupefied by the force of the attack.

And it was there, among that epic setting, that the squadron in troubled waters decided to launch a second salvo of plastic bullets. In the middle of the crowd, I first saw a young woman hit in the ankle, leaning on her peers as she fell back from the front. And in the middle of the crowd, a few metres away from where I stood, I then noticed a young man collapse under the impact of another bullet. All around him, some erupted into screams while others sobbed. And when I got closer to the wounded man, I saw the horror of a disfigured face. I heard other shots without being able to localize the wounded in the large crowd, and then I withdrew from the combat zone before the horror of such unspeakable violence.[53]

When the battle at Victoriaville had come to a close, a handful of police officers and upwards of four hundred students (according to certain sources) were injured, including four who were hospitalized, two of whom suffered cranial traumas.[54] One of these, Maxence Valade, permanently lost vision in one eye after a rubber or plastic bullet struck him in the face, and he hovered between life and death while four surgeons laboured over the course of an eight-hour operation. The other, Alexandre Allard, was permanently robbed of hearing in his left ear, which was almost entirely severed, almost certainly by a police projectile. He lay unconscious for days, and also nearly died. A third student who was hospitalized at Victoriaville, Dominique Laliberté-Martineau, suffered a double jawline fracture, lost six teeth and will have to undergo numerous bouts of reconstructive surgery after a police projectile struck her in the mouth.

Arrests that day totalled 106, but the SQ hadn't issued its final word.[55] At around eight o'clock on the night of the riot, two buses full of students were stopped en route back to Montréal and escorted to a police station in Saint-Hyacinthe, where they were detained for questioning. After each being identified, individually photographed and thoroughly searched — a mounting practice that is strictly illegal, but along with the others, highly effective as a means of psychological intimidation[56] — the students were finally released without charge at six o'clock in the morning. They had spent nearly ten hours in detention, deprived entirely of food and water.[57]

Sheep among wolves: The entente that wasn't

At the same time as "bricks are flying" in Victoriaville, "as an eye is lost and lungs are burning in the toxic fog," the national student representatives were locked up in Québec City for a marathon bout of negotiations at the offices of the Ministère de l'éducation.[58] With all sides radicalizing and the talks viewed as the last chance to rescue the school semester, the pressure on the student leaderships was becoming increasingly untenable.[59] The conflict was growing more volatile by the day, and many, the student leaders first among them, began to fear the imminent arrival of a first tragic death. Yet not once did Charest step foot into the room to speak with the students, while Line Beauchamp made "a cameo" of only five minutes, preferring to send professional negotiators and notaries in her place. Labour union representatives were present to act as mediators, or as the Collectif de débrayage suggests, as proxies there to push the students into accepting the first available offer, with the argument that they would "never succeed in getting more."[60] This was not a negotiation, but a high-stakes game of psychological chess that the students had never agreed to play. The government knew very well that the pressure on the student representatives was becoming unbearable, and were determined to exploit their advantage. The students were thus shut up in a twenty-two hour negotiation session with only three hours of rest allowed, while government negotiators overwhelmed them with endless "contradictory paperwork, threats and deceit."[61] The CLASSE, in its naïveté, had taken the meeting seriously enough to come armed with research studies from IRIS illustrating how savings could be made in the education system without the need to raise tuition.[62] Yet facts that fit outside the Liberals' dogmas never concerned the government a whit. Charest's strategy, which the Collectif calls "inspired by the KGB," was to simply wear the students down mentally and physically until they broke.

With the sense of urgency bearing down on them, the student leaders finally accepted a preliminary entente that was concluded on May 5. The tuition increase would be maintained in its entirety, the students announced to the press — the government was utterly immoveable on this point — yet would be compensated for by a decrease in mandatory administrative fees in function of the savings identified by a new provisional committee on universities.[63] "The bill paid by students will not rise,"[64] declared Nadeau-Dubois, as a gust of tepid optimism blew in from all sides of the political spectrum. The excitement in the air at the first signs of hope to surface in almost three months was palpable. Yet unfortunately it also proved premature, as it was not moderated by quite the sufficient dose of cynicism, it seemed. The agreement later presented to student representatives differed from the one they had been read during negotiations. Immediately after, government negotiators had left the room to make "some small last minute corrections," read:

altering anything that could have constituted a gain for the student movement.[65] A war of words immediately erupted in the media that pitted Beauchamp's view of the supposed entente against the leaders and spokespersons of the national associations. In numerous interviews with the press, Beauchamp stated that the total bill paid by students would inevitably rise under the entente, and even went to lengths to reassure Liberals in an email to party members that it was false to presume the increase would be compensated for by decreases to administrative fees.[66] And indeed, the entente modified unilaterally by government negotiators — *after* garnering the signatures of the student representatives — undermined any potential for the committee on universities to identify the required savings. The committee would be composed in large part by business leaders and university presidents and rectors, who would greatly outnumber the student delegates.[67]

The student base fumed, as the student representatives and union leaders of the three largest labour federations accused the government of sabotage.[68] Yet unfortunately for Charest, the student representatives were neither the sovereigns nor generals he took them for, and the true sovereigns, the students themselves, were now eager to have their say. The rolling assemblies held by student associations in the week that followed sounded a virulent condemnation of the government deception. By May 12, 300,000 students — almost three quarters of Québec's student population and far more than those who were still on strike — voted en masse to reject the entente, leaving a scant three of 111 student associations to ratify it.[69] After months of the government dismissing the student protesters as a minority within the student body, the student assemblies thereby launched their most resounding riposte. Yet ensconced within the government's windowless submarine, the Liberals plowed ahead with their tired lines of attack, forever unfazed by the facts laid out before them — or by the aggravating repercussions mounting daily in the streets.

The episode of the *entente de principe* left a putrid taste in the mouths of many, aghast at the depths of treachery to which their government was willing to sink in its senselessly unceasing face-off with Québec's youth. As the soaring costs of the police repression were poised to surpass the amount of the tuition increase, the steely intransigence of the government could only confirm the ideological essence of a move cast in dogmatism, pushed forward with near religious fervour by the reigning priests of the neoliberal creed. The Collectif de débrayage was among those less surprised by the government's comportment. Their cynicism steeled them from the shock.

> To be amazed that a government in power, which manages eight million inhabitants spread out over an immense territory, with its universities and hospitals, could resort to so puerile a fraud, would be to underestimate the scale of the lie that they try to present as the very basis of society: the economy.[70]

They are probably right. For indeed, what is the economy — *oikonomia*, "law of the house" — if not a fiction whose shifting contours are traced by the society that writes the rules? And what use to humanity is an economy that counts anything that produces or consumes as progress, irrespective of the destruction caused; an economy that's severed from all the vital signs that matter to a species — biologically, environmentally, socially or in any way that allows it to survive, to evolve and to flourish? One where the costs are misplaced to the point where nothing has its true value anymore, and to the point, today, of driving humanity off an ecological cliff while those in power avert their eyes from the impending catastrophe announced from all quarters. These are the zealots of our times who will stop at nothing to achieve their "cultural revolution," and the Economy, as defined by the worshippers, is their god that must be appeased — with sacrifices, if we must.

Dear elders, what is this world you've given us?

THE IRON BOOT OF JEAN CHAREST
Crush a Flower, a Thousand Will Bloom

I've never been arrested, but I know: I've been on file for quite some time. I live with the representative of a student association. Every time the members meet at my house, police cars park on my street. Some of my friends have been arrested at their apartments for no reason. Others, at the G20 in Toronto, were imprisoned three days in atrocious conditions. They weren't arrested while demonstrating, but while arriving back at the bus that was supposed to bring them back to Montréal.[...]

I'm afraid, all of the time. And I can no longer control my rage. It's time we opened our eyes.[1]

— Maryse Andraos, "*À bas les masques*, Big Brother"
(my translation)

The spectacular rejection of the entente had shone a light on the government's incompetence and disconnect in managing the worst social crisis to rock Québec in over a half-century.[2] Those who plot from within a bunker, it seems, are the ones most enamoured of their own schemes. Yet Charest had far from played his final card, and the collateral from the Liberals' ideological warfare had yet to be fully tallied. Retreating or compromising on his "cultural revolution" was out of the question, but the situation could not continue like this much longer. The "sovereign authority, the decisive figure of the Father,"[3] was poised to take matters into his own hands.

Victoriaville had rattled the political establishment with the ferocity of the violence, to the point where the Parti Québécois demanded a public inquiry into the Sûreté du Québec's actions that left two students dangling between life and death.[4] The injuries barely fazed the Liberals. In the Assemblée nationale on May 10, public safety minister Robert Dutil rejected the demands from the Opposition, but not without venturing his own constructive proposal: "What police should do is increase the use of force to the necessary level in order to counter the violence while using measures least susceptible to cause injury to protesters."[5] The incoherent and brutally irresponsible comments by the minister — reinforced by Charest's blaming of students for the persistence of the crisis and his bewildering claim of having "made all necessary efforts" to resolve it[6] — presaged a final radicalization of the government offensive. The Liberals had gambled everything on the mobilization fading away from its own exhaustion. Now, their clock had run out.

Suspicions of an impending crackdown began to circulate when deputy premier and education minister Line Beauchamp issued her surprise resignation on May 13. She was "no longer a part of the solution," she said, but her final declarations enlightened as much as her decision shocked. In her departing press conference, Beauchamp lamented, incredulous, that when she asked the student spokespersons if they had confidence in their elected representatives, the answer, swift and unhesitant, was no. This response, so intuitive and even self-evident for many of our generation, was apparently something Beauchamp was incapable of conceiving, and proved so unconscionable as to precipitate an abrupt end to her fourteen-year political career.[7] The next day finance minister Raymond Bachand took to the airwaves on Radio-Canada to warn of "Marxists" and "anti-capitalist" fringe groups (heretics! barbarians!) trying to destabilize Montréal's economy. With such comic hysteria shouting from backstage, Michelle Courchesne took over the reins as education minister and met the student leaders to reopen a dialogue.[8]

Those brief informal encounters were destined to be but a sideshow. The power behind the scenes had other plans brewing; historic plans that would bring the tenacious social crisis to the last brink and spark the final and most spectacular transformation of the Printemps érable. Repeated calls by third parties for mediation, including by respected past Liberal minister Claude Castonguay, had been met with cold refusal by the government since March.[9] Now, rumours filtered out through the press suggesting that Charest was readying a fateful last act that bore the full force of the state's coercive muscle. Addressing the media, Léo Bureau-Blouin urged the premier in his most earnest tones to act as a "good family father" and "speak with his children" rather than "calling the police" to settle their problems.[10] Yet all urgings by student leaders and all pleas by the Official Opposition and the Barreau du Québec (the Québec Bar Association) had fallen on deaf ears.[11] Without having once sat down at the table to discuss the crisis with student representatives, Charest now appeared as "the figure of the paternal authority in its most sombre light: the father that pushes aside the mother Beauchamp to better beat his children."[12]

Bill 78: The tyranny of their economy made law

On May 17, Bill 78, officially entitled *An Act to enable students to receive instruction from the post-secondary institutions they attend,* was submitted to the Assemblée nationale by the Liberal government. Across the province, all eyes were riveted on the legislature as never before. For twenty hours, MNAs clashed late into the night as the PQ spared no indignation at what political scientist Pascale Dufour calls the "most repressive legislative cocktail" seen in Québec since the 1970 October Crisis. Back then, Ottawa invoked the *War Measures Act* after the Front de Libération du

Québec kidnapped a cabinet member and a British diplomat, later murdering the former.[13] No less, it seemed, was required to meet the dire threat posed by Québec's protesting youth. Yet the Opposition was perfectly incapable of doing the slightest thing in the face of the Liberals' parliamentary majority. Panic aired across social media and on the mainstream airwaves, as the democratic gains of one of the most stable polities on Earth seemed to be unravelling so quickly before our eyes. Yet there was nothing anyone could do. The right-wing populists in the Coalition Avenir Québec (CAQ) partnered up with the governing majority, and Bill 78 was passed into law on May 18 to become Law 12.

The "truncheon law," as it was quickly labelled, was utterly without precedent in the history of Québec and engendered wholesale ruptures on a variety of fronts.[14] "Rarely have we seen so flagrant an aggression committed against the fundamental rights that have undergirded social and political action in Québec for decades." This was how dozens of historians denounced the Liberals' move in a joint declaration that was just as rare as the affront that invited it.[15] The title of their open letter said it all: "A rogue law and an infamy."[16] Yet Bill 78's full-barrelled assault on the foundations of the Québec student movement, we now know, had been in preparation from the strike's very onset.[17] In hindsight this knowledge greatly reframes the government's motives, bringing the jagged contours of the Liberals' ideological designs into the light of day. This was no measure of last resort devised in the heat of a crisis, but a sinister bid at reshaping Québec's future by means of opaque schemes and social warfare, and through a deliberate end run around the unpredictable inconveniences of democratic debate. The doctrinaires held so fervently to the righteousness of their ends that the democratic rights and social peace of their people were confined to the margins of consideration — collateral damage, on the path to the promised land.

The Law's reengineering project was nothing if not ambitious. In all past student strikes, part of the course hours lost were considered an inevitable cost of the walkout, which was seen as a learning experience in and of itself that many professors (and politicians) had themselves once participated in.[18] Yet in neoliberal Québec the students were to be punished for robbing the economy of its labour force; education was now "a contracted service that must be rendered once it is paid [by the state.]"[19] To repay the "debt that students owed to society,"[20] they would therefore be made to work: The current semester was suspended and the summer one cancelled, and an immediate summer break was begun, ending between August 17 and 30. The suspended winter semester was to be made up at the end of summer, with the equivalent of twelve weeks of courses condensed into one month at the expense of students' evenings and Saturdays, and the following semester leading directly into Winter 2013. Yet student aid would not be prolonged to account for the changes, leaving many strikers in precarious financial straits.[21] The shortened summer break, suggested Père Charest, should thus be used "to calm the nerves," but also and more importantly, "to work."[22] Students lost one month of their summer vacation and the entire break between the recovered semester and the following one, and their winter break of the following year was shortened as well. Yet the students were not the only ones to be made to repay their "debts." The law ordered "all employees" (mostly professors) to show up for work "as of 7:00 a.m. on 19 May 2012," and to "perform all duties attached to their respective functions, according to the applicable conditions of employment, *without any stoppage, slowdown, reduction or degradation of their normal activities.*"[23] Everything was in place to enforce the resumption of all "normal" activities, as the tyranny of the élites' economy was mobilized with the force of the state's coercive muscle.

These were far from the most incendiary of the law's provisions, nor were they those with the broadest, or most troubling, implications. With the final aim of ending all disturbances in the streets, the government saw fit to suspend the civil liberties of all of Québec's citizens. Law 12, still known colloquially as *loi 78*, was centred on "provisions to maintain peace, order and public security" that barred all gatherings of more than fifty people (changed from ten under pressure from the PQ) where an itinerary had not been approved by police at least eight hours in advance, and gave police forces unilateral authority to modify the venue or route according to their whims.[24] The penalties attached were draconian: Per diem fines were levied on individuals ($1,000–5,000 per offence); representatives of student or employee associations or organizers of an illegal demonstration ($7,000–35,000); and student associations, institutions and associations of employees ($25,000–125,000) found in contravention, with fines doubled for second and subsequent offences.[25] The penalties, however, didn't stop at proven violations. "Anyone who helps or induces a person to commit an offence" was to be deemed to have committed it themselves, as were student representatives and associations who failed to *preempt* offences by organizers of demonstrations in which they participate.[26] All protests were banned within fifty metres of educational institutions, and both the teachers' and students' unions were charged with enforcing the compliance of their members.[27]

Once more, the representatives and spokespersons of an autonomous and grassroots movement were tasked by the Liberals with bringing their "troops" into line, and this time at the risk of their associations being crippled and destroyed under the weight of financial penalties. The wording of the text was left deliberately vague, and the chilling effect desired by the government, abundantly clear: to project the impression, constitutional or not, that "anyone could be incarcerated for being found within the proximity of a demonstration of more than fifty people"[28] — and thus with the help of intimidation, to effectively stamp out all dissent. The government crackdown had begun to take on distinctly Orwellian airs: Questioned in the Assemblée nationale on whether a tweet could constitute an illegal call to assembly under the Law, education minister Michelle Courchesne told the Opposition that she would leave it up to police to decide.[29] With the province providing the cover, Québec City and Montréal then both passed municipal bylaws imposing steep fines (in the former case, up to $1,000) for participating in a protest whose itinerary had not been approved in advance or for wearing masks of any kind during a protest.[30]

In the space of a week, the arbitrary power of the state over its people had expanded by a frightful bound. The Collectif de débrayage writes that the "most pernicious character" of the Law was contained "without any doubt in its rendering equivalent of the act and the omission, repeated at numerous points in the text."[31] This was the authoritarian reflex of a security state on paranoid overdrive, and in that sense at least — as a historical and ideological document — the text of Bill 78 is of high value indeed. For fundamentally, its provisions shone a light of rare forthrightness on the interests and ideals that contemporary power structures are mobilized to defend and on the fears that move them to risk such utter extremes.[32]

In truth, what we term "laws of exception" (*lois d'exception*) have become anything but, as we see with the growing recourse to legislative suspensions of rights since the 1970s in both Québec and Canada.[33] Measures that were once limited to wartime are today deployed as a matter of course against threats of the capitalist élite's power: "From the exterior enemy of the Nazi or Communist, we've transitioned to the interior enemy of the Islamist, anarchist or radical environmentalist through a quasi-natural evolution."[34] Robert Bourassa's crackdown on the unions' Front commun in 1972 and imprisonment of their leaders was an ominous precedent on this path, criminalizing labour disruptions and casting the state as the defender of the economy, and by supposed extension, of the public interest. René Lévesque followed suit in 1983 with his own legislative repression of a labour mobilization, with his Law 111 allowing the dismissal of all teachers who failed to return to work.[35] Between 1982 and 1999 alone, both Liberal and Péquiste governments enacted no fewer than thirteen such "special laws" to crush labour actions and force a return to economic normalcy.[36] Yet in an economic system whose gains are skewed toward the top, the mythical equivalency between the economy and the public good falls away to be replaced by the image of an oligarchy simply safeguarding its dominance. And behind this shield upon which was carved their most central lie, the threats to the ruling class were being marked as the enemies of the neoliberal state, and stamped out.

Ironically for a premier who studiously refused the label "strike," the Law was the first to import into a student conflict many of the same repressive measures used to suppress labour actions of recent decades. In its essence, it was thus the latest expression of the mounting trend toward the criminalization of any and all disruptions to the economic flow.[37] And in drawing the fangs of the Liberals, Bill 78 exposed the open vein that the *carrés rouges* had so ardently struck.

> The target of the special law is [...] clear: anyone who contributes directly
> or indirectly to interrupting the normal course of things. The special law
> takes meticulous care to define the broad spectrum of strike practices. A

striker is anyone who doesn't fulfill their function: every professor that doesn't teach, every student that doesn't study or every janitor that doesn't sweep. But Bill 78 goes even further, since the "slowdown, reduction or degradation" becomes just as reprehensible as the pure and simple stoppage. One must not simply fulfill their function then, but fulfill it with *zeal*, fulfill it to perfection.[38]

Black against white, in the clearest language possible, lay the bald enunciation of contemporary capitalism's most totalitarian ambitions: its remodelling of the citizen, the human, into an obedient soldier in the service of the economy's onward march — or, more accurately, in the service of the class that claims most of the current system's benefits. In retrospect, the very hysteria of the government response can perhaps only be read as the animal instincts of a power whose interests are threatened. Charest's eyes may well have been riveted there, for it becomes difficult to otherwise imagine how so shrewd a politician could not have predicted the scale of the shock his offensive would provoke — if not as a beast who is cornered, their reason clouded by fear.

Dear Leader, we defy you: Québec disobeys

The *loi spéciale* instantly unleashed a torrent in Québec and signalled a watershed in the history of the Printemps érable. Confirming the Liberals' rupture with Québec's historic relationship with the student movement, Charest's law laid bare the smallness of a government whose spiteful bid at destroying the student associations was easily identified just below the Law's surface. Viewed by many as the autocratic excess of a corrupt and increasingly isolated government, the spirited condemnations rained down from all sides: The Barreau du Québec, Canadian Civil Liberties Association and later the Commission des droits de la personne et des droits de la jeunesse, Québec's human rights watchdog, all declared it a violation of fundamental rights guaranteed under the Québec and Canadian charters. Amnesty International and the United Nations also leapt into the fray with statements accusing the government of breaching its international and human rights obligations.

On the side of labour, the rage of the three main union leaders erupted with uncommon vitriol. "Québec must not become a police state," boomed Michel Arsenault of the Fédération des travailleurs et travailleuses du Québec (FTQ), channelling the shock and incredulity of the presidents of the FTQ, CSQ and CSN, who were all beside themselves in decrying *loi 78* as the worst law they'd seen in their lifetimes. "We're not in North Korea, being made to laugh or cry when the premier passes by!"[39] CSN head Louis Roy fumed that the Liberals were a bunch of "impotent old farts (*mon'oncles*)" attacking the generation that will "toss them out," and spat that the Law was "worthy of a banana republic."[40] The CSQ's Réjean Parent said he had "never seen such a perfidious law;" Arsenault chimed in that it was motivated by the "spite, anger and vengeance of the Liberal Party."[41] And the next morning the smaller teachers' union, the Fédération autonome de l'enseignement, purchased a full-page ad in *La Presse* in which a close-up of Charest sat emblazoned above the potent *j'accuse*: "Disgrace has a face."[42]

The presidents of the FEUQ and FECQ were in a state of shock, visibly grasping for the just words to capture and condemn the premier's untoward act of aggression. It wasn't long before their traditionally measured tones gave way to heated declarations of all-out war.[43] "We've just told youth that everything they've done, all they've created as a social movement in the last fourteen weeks, that it will all now be criminal," intoned a stunned and exasperated Martine Desjardins. Bureau-Blouin stood just as aghast at the government's hostility and before an act that he could only read as an attempt "to slowly kill the student associations, but also to silence the voice of the population."[44] Most trenchant of all was Gabriel Nadeau-Dubois, who raised the alarm on the government's slide into authoritarianism. In imposing an emergency law which violated "fundamental liberties" and "recognized constitutional rights," said GND, Charest was "using a state of emergency to apply a special law in the short term, while knowing full well that judicial proceedings are too long to allow us to challenge it. It's an abuse of power." Nadeau-Dubois confides in his book that he "cried of rage" on the night of Bill 78's passage: "I'm convinced that the sense of disgust I felt was shared by hundreds of thousands of people. The bond of trust between a great number of Quebecers and their democratic institutions, already weak, had finished unravelling with this vote."[45] Asked that day by the press whether the CLASSE would respect the Law, Nadeau-Dubois replied curtly: "We'll see."[46]

Charest defended his *loi spéciale* with the need to re-establish social peace; instead, he'd reached for the last drum of gasoline to douse the flames. Immediately after the bill's passage and in the nights that followed, the usual crowd of a couple thousand nightly marchers swelled by thousands upon thousands, as the largest of the spring's nightly demonstrations became the outlets for society's rage against *loi 78*. Police no longer entertained the charade of waiting for (or inciting) a pebble thrown or window broken before attacking the peaceful majority. Newly empowered, the guardians of the power declared them illegal before they began, launching hostilities that provoked intense street battles that played out night after night with a frightful escalation. The rebellion in the streets of Montréal those nights knew no parallel in the city's history. In the Quartier Latin, protesters threw debris onto a bonfire that soared upwards from the centre of Rue St-Denis, almost as if to brush the SQ helicopters whose hums had become etched into the night sky for months. The dancing and singing crowds gathered around the flames to cheer on the havoc, and mounted barricades in the streets to hold back the SPVM riot squads, now reinforced by the provincial SQ, who would soon arrive around any corner. And when they did, it was war.

Shields banging, the phalanxes marched, and anyone caught in the path of their bulldozer was propelled to the pavement, repeatedly at times, with the brutal barrage of their batons. It mattered little that the street was a vibrant nightlife hub lined with busy bars and restaurants, or that peaceful bystanders filled the streets and flanked both sides. As people poured out onto their balconies to watch over and loudly encourage the resistance from above, bars were drowned in tear gas and pepper spray as cops lashed out in a storm of indiscriminate brutality, flailing about at the slightest verbal provocation by indignant patrons.[47] Shop and restaurant owners were detained in their own establishments, and even the elderly and tourists couldn't evade the arbitrary arrests of a police force run rampant, run rabid. Sexual assaults and racist and homophobic slurs from the SPVM attained their apogee, as plastic bullets fired gleefully, "in the ass, my son of a bitch" ("*dans les fesses, mon câlisse*") became the emblem of a security force erupting with such "flagrant delight (*jouissance*) [...] in the carnage."[48] The CUTV anchor was pummelled to the ground and the cameraman was batoned live on camera. Another man had a close brush with death after a plastic bullet lacerated his liver on the night of May 18. But the gravity of one man's wounds were barely a footnote to the struggle at this point. One girl's letter to a friend evoked the reigning brutality.

> It's true that I have one (two, I don't really know) ribs broken. It's also true that it wasn't pretty. Thrown against the wall, window broken, the frame coming up to my ribs, and with the cop not pulling his punches, well, crunch.[...] Even though I was injured, the adrenaline still numbed the pain, and what I had seemed like scratches compared to others: lacerated faces, certainly other ribs fractured, respiratory distresses, bruised and swollen thighs and abdomens[...]. The boy next to me in the van was practically having convulsions, certainly a cranial trauma, his face bloodied, hyperventilating, and the cops were still having fun ridiculing him, telling him to stop his joking. Really, for weeks now, unspeakable violence.[49]

In the one week after Bill 78 was passed, the unprecedented wave of mass arrests totalled over a thousand people in Montréal and Québec City alone, with police kettling 518 protesters on May 23 despite providing no warning or ability to flee.[50] Stunned by the government's historic affront to "freedom of expression, association and peaceful protest," the judicial community now mobilized like never before. Departing from the Palais de Justice on May 28 clad in the official robes of their profession, hundreds of lawyers and notaries marched downtown in a silent procession that aimed a deafening message of condemnation at Charest's Law.[51] Indeed, having attained a new summit, the state's campaign of violence and intimidation, camouflaged by government deflections against students throughout the spring, was no longer possible to deny. Yet the repression didn't stop with the brutality, the arrests or the draconian conditions for release imposed by the courts. The conditions of detention were horrendous as well. People were kept handcuffed in buses for as long as seven hours without being informed of their charges, were

Lawyers march silently through Montréal on May 28, 2012, to protest Bill 78.

prevented from calling friends and relatives, and deprived of basic necessities such as access to water, medication or bathrooms.[52] Nothing out of the ordinary in the new normal of 2012, however; Montrealers had only discovered that spring what many Canadians, including Quebecers, already had in Toronto during the G20 Summit in 2010, where over 1,200 people were arrested in two days, shattering all Canadian records.[53]

As exhibited with escalating intensity throughout the spring, the spvm had definitively taken on "the traits of a paramilitary militia, making its law and order reign without worrying about the slightest accountability toward the population it is meant 'to serve and to protect.'"[54] Many Montrealers would be forgiven for thinking they were hallucinating before the dystopic scenes that had engulfed their streets. Our festive city, its traditions steeped in pacifism, had become a battleground and our elected government, the oppressor. Many protesters would suffer symptoms of post-traumatic stress disorder in the months that followed.[55] But in the heat of rebellion, the people of Québec would not be cowed.

Montréal no longer slept, and neither would the exhausted police be left a minute's rest. From the break of dawn, one protest followed the next at an "infernal" rhythm — one at noon, one in the afternoon and all just rehearsals for the evening's battalions.[56] Night after night, tens of thousands of demonstrators flooded the streets, defying and evading the security forces as they dispersed into various demos and converged anew in repetition, marauding endlessly through the city streets until the hours preceding dawn. The CUTV stream never went silent anymore, as on Twitter, the hashtags #GGI and #manifencours had become two of the most widely used in the world. Records of police brutality raced through the cybersphere, as citizens, tracking the crowds' processions online, arrived in steady streams to reinforce the embattled marchers.[57] The raucous crowds wound their way at times all the way to Charest's home in its rich Westmount enclave, where they massed outside to launch their joyous defiance against his windows: to the tune of a schoolyard taunt (*na-na, na-na-na*), in unison, "We're more than fifty, we're more than fifty..." The new chant would become a part of the folklore of the Printemps érable. But none could capture the surging elation of a mass rebellion quite like another one, forever signed with a *carré rouge*: "*La loi spéciale, on s'en câlisse, la loi spéciale...*" In the proud profanity of the Québécois street, the people answered Charest and the police that faced them: "We don't give a fuck" about your special law. The Collectif de débrayage, which named its essay for the profane chant that embodied the movement's (and this generation's) anti-authoritarian ethos, writes that "Responding *'On s'en câlisse'* to the special law transforms into bravado what was meant as the most terrifying moment of power: the state of exception when it mobilizes its omnipotence."[58] But the Québécois, *ils s'en câlissent*. Temporary as it may have been, the people, *le peuple*, had asserted their supremacy over the law that the power wielded to oppress them. As with the injunctions, so with *loi 78*: "You may well vote a law, we are still here," they declared.[59] And Québec belongs to us.

#22mai: Arrest us all, if you can

The government had moved to assert its authority, and in response, the people had rendered its largest city ungovernable — its authority, a fantasy. All across society, people were mobilizing, as civil disobedience campaigns proliferated under various forms. Citizens overwhelmed the SPVM's phone lines with phony requests for protest approvals, outlining to the police their plans for a picnic in the park or a birthday party with more than fifty invitees. Global hacktivists Anonymous published the email addresses of SPVM officers. Public figures and celebrities lined up to condemn the historic affront against civil liberties, and the social media sphere was overloaded with an endless train of citizen outbursts that increasingly drowned the mainstream media into irrelevance.

Meanwhile, the CLASSE had broken their silence after they convoked a press conference on May 21 to lay out their response to Bill 78. The congress, declared the spokespersons, had voted to declare the emperor naked: The students would disobey. The CLASSE announced they were launching a website to invite all Quebecers to express their defiance, where thousands uploaded photos of themselves above a sign that held their name, along with a simple message: "I disobey." "Arrest us all if you can" read the site's header, "for your law provides even for the crime of opinion."[60] It was a symbolic act steeped in the traditions of civil disobedience: The strike would refuse to acknowledge the government, just as the government had refused to acknowledge the strike.[61] But more than contenting themselves with symbols alone, the gauntlet thrown down by the CLASSE had paved the way for a collective tsunami the likes of which the country had never seen.

The next day was May 22, the date of the third national march and the hundredth day since the strike had begun. Dared by the unprecedented government crackdown that lingered over the heads of protesters, the students were more determined than ever to issue Charest his final rebuke, one to match brinkmanship with brinkmanship and launch a deafening riposte fit for the historic moment. The protest call was to mark "100 days of striking, 100 days of contempt, 100 days of resistance," and the crowds did not disappoint. When the day arrived, upwards of 250,000 marchers flooded the streets for a third time running, giving renewed form to an epic revolt that showed no signs of abating. In a daring swipe at the emergency law, the CLASSE contingent led the crowds as they diverged from the route submitted to police by the establishment student federations, who joined the union leaderships in trying to contain the marchers on the authorized path.[62] To no avail. Whether most knew it or not at the time, the May 22 marchers had thus been cast in the largest act of civil disobedience in the country's history, and the police could do nothing but stand idly by as the human tide swept past.[63]

#casseroles: After the winter, society stirs

The jubilation that followed from the victory of the street over the state was short lived, and it wasn't long before the raw dynamics of power had reestablished themselves in the streets of Montréal. The very night of the May 22 march, the SPVM savagely charged the night demonstration as if only to reassert their lost command, sparking a riot that ended in 113 arrests.[64] The day had been a joyous if brief respite from the violence that pursued its frenetic race to the brink, each day bringing with it the irrepressible fear of a first casualty. Yet concurrently, in the background at first, a profound mutation of the movement had set root that seemed to flow from the street's latent desire to pull back from the edge, to avert the worst, and yet at the same time *ne pas lâcher* — to not back down. But where do we go from here?

The answer was whispered online on the evening of May 17, as Bill 78 was sparking fiery debate in the Assemblée nationale and online. Infuriated by the unprecedented drift to authoritarianism he saw unfolding, François-Olivier Chené, a CEGEP professor of political science, launched a call over Facebook and Twitter for a new form of protest unknown to Québec. Inspired by the *cacerolazos* that emerged under Pinochet's dictatorship in Chile, Chené summoned Quebecers out onto their balconies, urging them to get out their pots and pans and "bang them with all the rage" that the *loi spéciale* inspired in them. "I threw the bottle into the sea," Chené later told *Le Devoir*, "without knowing whether anyone would take up the call."[65] But that, it seemed, was all it took. Immediately, the #casseroles hashtag he launched snowballed out across social media, going viral.

In the days that followed, every night at eight o'clock, people began emerging onto the balconies that line Montréal's streets, their kitchenware held at the ready. They were heard first in Villeray, the Plateau Mont-Royal, Rosemont, and soon Hochelaga-Maisonneuve, Saint-Henri, Mile-End, Parc-Extension — the neighbourhoods of the city were springing to life with the sounds of rebellion, as there, surrounded by neighbours on all sides and the security of their homes, their indignation rang out in a collective cacophony that resounded throughout the nights.[66] The contagion swept through the city, and by May 20 the *casseroles* descended from their balconies to begin marching illegally through their neighbourhoods, in improvised processions that grew in size as residents came down from their homes, pots and utensils in hand, to melt into the parades.[67] The public spaces of the city — street corners, church lawns and squares across each and every borough — were animated as never before. With no routes or organizers to speak of, the multitudes of marches merged when they met, forming ever larger contingents of tens of thousands as they wound their way endlessly through the streets.[68] "*On s'en câlisse ... clac clac, clac clac clac ... la loi spéciale ... clac clac, clac clac clac.*" Before long, it seemed no block was silent, no street deserted by the chorus of the people's percussion, as in some neighbourhoods, the church bells in the "city of a thousand bell towers" tolled at eight o'clock to salute the non-violent resistance.[69]

The sleepy suburbs ringing Montréal — Longueuil, Saint-Basil-Le-Grand, Saint-Eustache, La Prairie — joined in next, as the tidal wave rippled out across the far reaches of the province: Sherbrooke, Trois-Rivières, Gatineau, Granby,

The CLASSE *holds a press conference on May 21, 2012, to announce that they will defy Bill 78.*

Québec City, Saguenay, Saint-Jérome, and on it went. Where the population had been bitterly divided over the students' protests, suddenly, citizens of all ages and backgrounds were coming together to defend the people's democratic rights, as the protests spread to at least fifty-five municipalities all across Québec.[70] In Montréal, rare was the neighbour who didn't smile at the sight of pots and spoons hanging from restless hands or of the giddy energy in the eyes of the passersby that carried them. As the *casseroles* unfurled across Québec to purge society's sense of collective disempowerment, an infectious and jubilant catharsis aired that once unleashed, proved impossible to contain. Neither Montréal nor Canada had ever seen a mass rebellion like this — an eruption so popular, so spontaneous, so purely and utterly *spectacular*. Bolstered by the wind of revolt at its back, the movement dared to start believing in its power to topple the government. And proud Montréal, forever irreverent, became an icon of "insubmission" that inspired the collective imagination with "the image of what an entire city in resistance could be like."[71] The affective force of those nightly happenings moved more than a few who'd grown cynical over the years. For while Canada slept, stuck in the mud of its Thatcherite atomization, Québec, all of a sudden, had sprung to life.

The *casseroles* movement transformed the mobilization by broadening the accessibility and appeal of revolt. In promising a festive ambiance free of police repression, the movement was able to reach into villages and communities, across age and social stratums — "neighbours and people from local businesses, families with small children, elderly and retired people, working adults" — that until then had remained relatively untouched by the unrest.[72] It allowed the rebellion to reach into people's homes and communities where they were and to roll them out the welcome mat lined with assurances of safety and solidarity. And when that happened, it changed everything. Charest had misjudged, quite monumentally it seemed, the depth and breadth of Quebecers' opposition to his rule, and in trying to suppress a revolt, he had sparked its widest and most determined expansion. Yet in an irony of history, Charest can perhaps find succour in his contributions to the student spring, for in an age of debilitating cynicism and political disaffection, he had unwittingly achieved the unimaginable: the repoliticization of the masses. One citizen's letter to *Le Devoir* attempted to capture the essence of the transformation.

> A fresh breeze is blowing through the streets of Montréal: Neighbours *see each other.*[...]Encounters, discussions and evening gatherings now arise casually among neighbours on the porches and balconies of Montréal. The neighbourhood will be less and less foreign. Now that is a true political victory!
>
> We must repeat this pleasant percussion [*tapage sympathique*], eventually through other forms, until the whole territory is occupied by neighbours who acknowledge each other, who speak to each other, who see each other through the chance encounters of their days and get to

know each other over the years. That is how we inhabit a space; *that is how we become citizens.*

My heart is bursting with joy.[73]

Or take this one perhaps, from the anonymous administrator of the citizen website Translating the Printemps érable, created out of frustration with the English-language media's ferociously biased reporting of the student spring. The letter was addressed "to mainstream media":

> I have lived in my neighbourhood for five years now, and this is the most I have ever felt a part of the community; the lasting impact that these protests will have on how people relate to each other in the city is deep and incredible. [...] I come home from these protests euphoric. The first night I returned, I sat down on my couch and I burst into tears, as the act of resisting, loudly, with my neighbours, so joyfully, had released so much tension that I had been carrying around with me, fearing our government, fearing arrest, fearing for the future. I felt lighter.[...]
>
> This is what Quebec looks like right now. Every night is tear gas and riot cops, but it is also joy, laughter, kindness, togetherness and beautiful music. Our hearts are bursting. We are so proud of each other; of the spirit of Quebec and its people; of our ability to resist, and our ability to collaborate.
>
> Why aren't you writing about this? Does joy not sell as well as violence? Does collaboration not sell as well as confrontation? You can have your cynicism; our revolution is sincere.[74]

In a profoundly charged and consequential sense, the *casseroles* movement had marked the consummation of the Québécois spring, and the blossoming of the communalist currents that lay embedded within its roots. Beyond the fight over tuition, beyond the confrontation between a government and the youth, the Printemps érable had become nothing less than the invitation to a deep-seated process of rebirth: a re-learning of community, a re-learning of popular sovereignty — indeed, a re-learning, in the most fundamental sense, of what politics *means* and can be made to mean again. In the wake of the *casseroles*, citizens began organizing in their communities to form neighbourhood assemblies they dubbed the Assemblées populaires autonomes de quartier (APAQ), in a direct echo of the horizontal and participative assemblies born of the Indignados and Occupy movements and of the 2001 Argentine crisis before them. In boroughs across Montréal, small flyers appeared summoning neighbours to an "egalitarian, non-racist and non-sexist" public forum to decide on the community's response to the political and police repression.[75] The assemblies, which spread outside Montréal to Laval, Longueuil, Saint-Jérome and Trois-Rivières, ultimately failed to attract significant numbers, and most faded away after the 2012 election, although some do remain active in the boroughs of Villeray, Rosemont-Petite-Patrie and Hochelaga-Maisonneuve.[76] Yet their first appearance in the Québec landscape itself spoke to the democratic effervescence born of the *casseroles*, and to the thirst at the roots of society that was all too briefly assuaged in those early days of summer. Faced with the aging heirs of the Thatcherite revolution who had radically reimagined human collectivities as mere agglomerations of individuals "empty of all sociality,"[77] masses of Quebecers stood up, at last ready to respond: There *is* such thing as society, and it is awake.

"Montréal, rebel city":
The Printemps érable becomes a global sensation

The crackdown sounded by Bill 78, and the *casseroles* movement that rose up to meet it, hadn't only transformed the struggle at home. In the wake of the spectacular wave of civil disobedience that washed over the province, the rousing tale of the populist revolt shot onto television screens and the front pages of publications around the world. The story of the Printemps érable had gone global, aided in no small part by the cultural ambassadors of Québec's rising generation who popularized the cause overseas. Québec's cinematic *wunderkind* Xavier Dolan and his full cast of *Laurence Anyways* graced the red carpet at Cannes with the red square pinned prominently to their clothes. Arcade Fire caused a stir when they sported the emblem in a performance on Saturday Night Live. Across social media, word was spreading of Québec's peaceful resistance, as for a rare time the international media turned their eyes to the small nation of Québec.

In France, where the student strike had frequently graced the front pages, pop culture magazine *Les Inrocks* launched a special edition devoted to the "Printemps érable: the coolest revolt." (Where we learn, for example, that GND apparently wears the same sunglasses as Canadian actor Ryan Gosling in *Drive*.) And in the *Courrier International* — owned by prestigious daily *Le Monde,* which devoted a full dossier on its website to the student crisis — a front-page feature appeared with a photo of a fiery young *carré rouge* marching in the *maNUfestation*, the sides of her head shaved as only square patches of red tape covered her breasts. "How the '*printemps érable*' woke up Québec," announced the teaser, above the bold headline: "Montréal: rebel city." From the United States, Australia and Indonesia to China, Russia, the Middle East and countries across Europe, dozens of publications across the world were watching as Québec's student crisis-turned-democratic uprising pursued its dramatic course. And the *carrés rouges* only had Charest to thank for their sudden celebrity.[78]

In the wake of Charest's *loi spéciale*, the peaceful resistance of this people of eight million had suddenly become an international *cause célèbre*. In the week after Bill 78 was passed, Chilean academics and student leaders, who had been protesting for free university education since 2011 in an eerie precursor to the movement of the *carrés rouges*, penned a rousing letter of solidarity under the header "¡*Todos somos quebecenses!*" ("We are all Quebecers!") Excitedly posted online and diffused on Twitter by Occupy Wall Street, the open letter linked together both people's fights against austerity and the commercialization of public education, and declared: "The struggle of students, academics and workers in Québéc is also our struggle."[79]

The sounds of solidarity soon resounded too with the clings and clangs of *casseroles* protests that emerged in countries around the world. As early as May 21, dozens of demonstrators gathered outside the Québec government's offices in New York City to protest against Bill 78, and for the first time since the student strike began, a whisper of protest briefly filtered out beyond Québec's borders to the Canadian provinces.[80] On May 30, "Casseroles Night in Canada," launched on Facebook by Montréal activist and journalist Ethan Cox, saw citizens bang pots and pans in cities across the country, drawing two thousand marchers in Toronto in their bid to channel the communitarian currents of the *casseroles* and echo the Québec students' struggle against austerity.[81] That same week, images swam through social media depicting cooking utensils and pots and pans held up in protest against the iconic backdrops of the world's great cities — 150 demonstrated outside Canada House in London's Trafalgar Square, a few hundred more in front of the Eiffel Tower and some more for a second time in New York, this time in Times Square.[82] On June 14, no fewer than seventy cities around the world joined the wave for an international day of action, as small *casseroles* protests rippled out across all continents, from Montevideo to Zagreb to Honolulu, to launch a powerful condemnation of the Québec government's descent into authoritarianism.[83] The most globally networked generation to ever exist had summoned its friends overseas, and they answered with a force to match the crash of the world catapulting into the social media age. The symbolism of the solidarity blowing in from abroad arrived as a gust of warm wind at the movement's back. And it arrived as well as a potent signal of the new interplay between distant events that is already redefining the world: On August 4, after the Chilean government banned protests on Santiago's main avenue, the *cacerolazos,* fallen silent for thirty years, rang out anew in the neighbourhoods of the capital.[84]

Formula One versus the people: The high costs of a commercial state

With the knife of Bill 78 held to the student movement's throat, the government opened a final round of negotiations on May 28. Four days later, education minister Michelle Courchesne unilaterally broke off the talks (or was perhaps ordered to) and accused the students — who were interested in pursuing the discussions, which they viewed as constructive — of intransigence.[85] Charest had appeared at the negotiating table only once, on May 29, sitting down with the students for the first time since the start of the strike in February. He was present for just over thirty minutes, and simply pronounced the gap between the two sides too great to be overcome. Of this anyway he was perhaps correct: The government's final offer proposed to reduce the tuition increase in the first year to $100 — to be offset through equivalent reductions in tax credits — while the full increase for the six subsequent years would be entirely maintained, for a total increase of $1,624: one dollar less than the exact sum of the five-year hike as initially announced.[86]

The unconvincing show of Charest's last best effort set the stage for the final wave of repression, with the security state hiting its apogee as the Canadian Grand Prix arrived in town in early June. The heavily subsidized Canadian Formula One event — whose global boss, billionaire Bernie Ecclestone, is currently on trial and facing ten years in prison for bribing a jailed banker, says Ecclestone, to buy his silence over his tax affairs[87] — enjoys the steel-plated backing of the establishment, who vaunt its supposed economic spinoffs. It is also, however, a regular magnet for environmentalist, feminist and left-wing protesters who object to its brazenly anachronistic fetishization of car culture, shameless objectification of women (with its scantily clad playmates) and destructive materialism (just for starters).

After breaking off the final round of negotiations, Minister Courchesne accused Gabriel Nadeau-Dubois of threatening to disrupt the event, after he reportedly told her "With this offer [from the government], we'll organize your Grand Prix for you."[88] The hysteria from the political and media establishment was immediate and preceded even the student leader's forthcoming clarifications: that the CLASSE aimed to take advantage of the opportunity to raise awareness of the struggle among tourists, but not to prevent its happening.[89] Even the presidents of the FEUQ and FECQ, who frequently part ways with the CLASSE on tactics, were bewildered by the government's overreaction: "From what I know," said Martine Desjardins, "the CLASSE simply has the intention to inform people, to go distribute red squares and raise awareness about the issues."[90] A simple call to the student associations would have allowed them to offer reassurance, added Desjardins. Yet given the virulence of the government's indignation, Quebecers would have been forgiven for thinking the CLASSE had threatened to set off a bomb.

It may be that the government was genuinely terrified at the thought of so lucrative an event being compromised; or it may be that Charest smelled another tactical opportunity to tar the CLASSE as violent, and pounced, with the media and economic establishments only too eager to board the bandwagon. Either way, the F1 immediately announced it was "preventatively" cancelling the Grand Prix Open House out of concerns for the safety of attendants, thereby dutifully validating and amplifying the government attack line. With the supposed threats of the CLASSE inflated enough to serve as effective cover, the police then leapt into a state of paranoid delirium to defend the perceived commercial interests at risk. A call was sent out for protesters to swarm and jam the metro line leading to Parc Jean-Drapeau, which is situated on Île Sainte-Hélène. The SPVM reacted by stationing three officers in each metro car and launching an unprecedented campaign of blanket political profiling. Illegal searches and seizures targeted anyone sporting the red square or "any youth not fitting the aesthetic canon of the F1 fan."[91] One art student carrying red paint in his bag was thus deemed suspect and expelled from the metro; one person carrying juggling balls too, in a city that's a global hub for circus arts; and without a trace of irony, one woman was detained for reading *1984* on the metro.[92]

Rampant cases of "preventative arrests" aimed at those matching the police's stereotypes inflamed social media and drew pointed interventions by legal experts who decried the unqualified illegality of such tactics.[93] There exists no concept of preventative arrests under Canadian law, even if that hasn't stopped Canadian police from increasingly cracking down on protests by invoking Article 31 of the Criminal Code, which was designed to combat proven or imminent violations of the peace. The courts have been called on to pronounce on this trend in at least three cases (all since the 1980s), with the most notable and recent delivered in 2011 by an Ontario provincial court judge in response to their widespread use during the G20 Summit in Toronto.[94] In all cases, the courts ruled that Article 31's invocation was invalid and abusive without a specifically identifiable, imminent and substantial threat. In the G20 case, the judge's scathing indictment of the "adrenalized" police force left no room for doubt, condemning the aggressive tactics as amounting to the "criminalization of dissent."[95] The troubling conclusion is that those deciding the priorities of the SPVM would seem too preoccupied with expanding their arsenal against their own citizens to bother teaching the law to those we empower to enforce it.

The SPVM erected an open-air triage and detention facility near the Biosphère outside the Parc Jean-Drapeau metro station, which it used to process and hold dozens of innocent youth who arrived on the island that also plays host to a plethora of recreational facilities. Accounts surfaced of people who were held for up to three or four hours without access to water or toilets, their hands cuffed or tie-wrapped, before being released without charges at the Angrignon metro terminal located at the opposite end of town.[96] Yet embarrassingly for the SPVM, two such "*carrés rouges,*" who were instantly swarmed by sixteen police officers and detained upon exiting the metro, were no ordinary backers of the movement, if indeed they were at all. They would later discover, in fact, that they were undercover journalists for *Le Devoir.*[97] The next morning, the newspaper's front page screamed "*Carrés rouges,* your documents!" above an explosive report that tore to shreds the SPVM's claims to be basing its interventions solely on suspicious comportment.[98] The image traced by the journalists was of a bellicose and vigilante police force that was devoted to protecting the Grand Prix from all signs of dissent, and that dripped with explicit contempt for students, as well as for legal and constitutional guarantees.

> The journalists cooperate, but return a question for each one posed [by police]. Why search us? "Because you're adorning revolutionary insignia," answers an officer, "and because I've had it with people like you." He's

wearing a gauze on his forearm, which seems to protect an injury. But isn't this profiling? "We're doing exactly that, criminal profiling," responds the same officer. Is Parc Jean-Drapeau no longer a public place? "Today, it's a private place open to the public," adds another, removing from our bags a mango, a dance season program, notebooks, pens. Nothing illegal, nothing that hints at any criminal intentions. Why can't we be here? "The organizers don't want you here." So today, the SPVM responds to the needs and desires of Grand Prix organizers? "Exactly," says officer 5323, proudly repeating it a second time after we ask again. At the request of the journalists, the two main officers provide their badge numbers, insisting that we write them down. "Take them, your notes, for the ethics complaints board and all that. You can call my boss, Mister [Commander Alain] Simoneau, he'll be happy to hear you say I'm doing a good job."[99]

The journalists were held at the outdoor detention facility for questioning and accused by the police, without any explanations, of holding "criminal intentions." It was only after providing their identification — and thus being revealed as journalists — that Catherine Lalonde and Raphaël Dallaire Ferland were released without charge but expelled from the island, in the company of a photographer they'd encountered whose photos were deleted by police without his consent.[100] At least forty-three people were "preventatively" arrested that day.[101]

At the second event site downtown, Charest's beloved Grand Prix couldn't escape the unrest that was smouldering in the streets. Society encroached from all sides. Summoned by the lately emboldened Convergence des luttes anticapitalistes (CLAC), masses of angry protesters, enraged by the indecency of the excess being flaunted in the midst of Liberal austerity, descended on the event as never before. The party strip became a battleground, as the security apparatus was mobilized to protect Crescent Street's consumerist bubble and prevent tourists from having to encounter a whiff of the crisis into which they'd breezily plunged. At a busy downtown intersection, peaceful protesters trying to enter the barricaded street were ferociously repelled by lines of armed riot police, liberally pepper-sprayed, beaten with batons and dragged across the pavement, in full view of bar patrons who looked on from the overflowing *terrasses*.[102] Police launched targeted arrests of people guilty of no more than wearing black or of sporting communist insignia, which in the eyes of police commander Alain Simoneau constituted a "clear" source of danger.[103] Some protesters had managed to infiltrate the site and were sharply expelled after erupting inside with chants of "*Travaille, consomme pis ferme ta gueule!*" ("Work, consume and shut your mouth!")[104] Yet mostly, the decibel-rattling dance music insulated the tourists' sunny afternoons from the raging crisis around them, as faintly in the distance, the seething popular anger struggled to pierce through the sonic fog: "1-2-3-4, this is fucking class war! 5-6-7-8, overthrow this fascist state!"[105] The partiers, protected by the state, were free to spend to their heart's content, unperturbed and in perfect calm, as a part of Québec's embattled democracy was writhing in pain a few metres away.

Government rhetoric persisted in its well-rehearsed hysteria through the summer, as the eerily robotic coherence of ministers' statements seemed to confirm suspicions of a meticulously choreographed Liberal strategy. The government script had scarcely changed since the start, though minister of culture Christine St-Pierre slipped into an apparent excess of zeal when she claimed the red square worn by a respected writer simply symbolized "violence and intimidation." The farcical attack, however, had grown increasingly strained with time. By then, it was being worn by an important cross-section of Québécois society that included Opposition leader Pauline Marois, artists, professors, progressives and parents of all backgrounds, and some of Québec's most lauded celebrities in high-profile international appearances. Her smear proved especially incendiary because of its context: It was uttered in response to author Fred Pellerin temporarily refusing his appointment as Knight of the Ordre national du Québec, explaining that such honours seemed inappropriate to him in the midst of a social crisis. St-Pierre's reaction sparked outrage in the cultural community, and 2,600 artists signed an open letter demanding an immediate apology. It came late, but did eventually arrive.[106]

Thirty-five days to fix the world

St-Pierre's comments were not only ill-advised, but equally ill-timed. In the greater scheme, the movement was pursuing its mutation away from street confrontations with police and toward the *casseroles'* family-friendly *tapage*. Such was the scenario leading into the vacation months, as the marches dwindled in size leading into an August electoral campaign. On August 1, however, the same day as Charest had convoked the election, one final show of strength and defiance was launched by the street across the premier's bow. That day also fell on the one hundredth day since the start of the nightly marches. After weeks of relative calm and shrinking nightly crowds, one last hurrah drew thousands into the streets, as *casseroles* marches departed from their neighbourhoods to converge downtown in "a long and joyous procession," to chants of "*Les élections, on s'en câlisse!*"[107] Invoking the "silent majority," Charest called the election for September 4 to settle the crisis once and for all, and framed the issue facing voters thus: "In Québec, is it the street that governs? [...] Or will it be employment, the economy and democracy?"[108]

The FEUQ and FECQ promised to meet him on his path, and Léo Bureau-Blouin, replaced at the head of the FECQ by Éliane Laberge in June, declared his candidacy for Pauline Marois's Parti Québécois.[109] The federations embarked on a provincial tour to prevent the re-election of the Liberals, while the CLASSE launched its own to promote its newly released manifesto, *Nous sommes avenir*. And as for Gabriel Nadeau-Dubois: He bowed out of the spotlight on August 9 after issuing his resignation, delivered in the form of an eloquently unmistakable "*à la prochaine*" that was published in *Le Devoir*. With the precise mordancy that has become his trait, GND's moving appeal reverberated with a generation's dream of a democratic future and landed as a gauntlet thrown down at the feet of the governing élites.

> The solidarities sewn across clouds of gas will not soon be undone. The outstretched hands will not release. And we will march again, for years if we must and well beyond this strike, so that one day the people of Québec may take back the reins of this country from the hands of money and the profiteers.[110]

The saga of the Printemps érable needed an election to resolve the immediate question of the tuition increase, and certainly, to restore the social peace. But the forces and ambitions that grew to full form during the student spring will not turn back and retreat into obscurity. One chapter closes only to prepare the way for the next. For there can be little doubt that Nadeau-Dubois speaks for countless others when he evokes the readiness of the youth to pursue the long march, and who feel, quite as he does, that *le combat est à venir* — the struggle has just begun.

PART THREE

TOMORROW RISES

WAR ON A GENERATION
A Legacy of Debt

Mom, I'm asking you to ask yourself, to ask everyone, in Québec City,
on the television, Dad, my little brother. Ask them. Ask them to ask
themselves again. I am not in the madness of my youth. I am among
a people in crisis. And so are all of you. Ask yourselves this. Don't
become indifferent. This is war.[1]
> — Noémie Brassard, "*À ma mère*" (my translation)

The scale of the youth anger that erupted in 2012 shocked many across Québec and
Canada. And to many who understood its origins the least, the instinctual response
was often ridicule, when not derision. To those who converted incredulity into
curiosity, however, the very strength and suddenness of the revolt were the sure
signs of deeper acrimonies that lay simmering for years and that surged to the fore
precisely because the political establishment had long refused them recognition.
It's not hard to see why: In their day, the greying members of Québec's political
classes enjoyed generous social protections, cheap public services and a promising
economic and (comparatively speaking) ecological future. Yet in the eyes of many
of Québec's students, these élites were now pulling the rug out from under the
feet of the following generation. Whether the subject was public education, social
services, the climate crisis or our natural resources, the mobilizing sentiment was
thus one and the same: a seething and even existential fear that by the time youth
grew to assume positions of power, there would simply be little left to inherit, or
to save. And the more the older generations backed the Liberals' push to privatize
the education system, the more the students' sense of being ignored and exploited
hardened into resolve, as they arose to go toe to toe against an aging establishment
that was mobilized completely in the defence of its own interests.

This potent undercurrent of the student unrest surfaced in the earliest
weeks of the strike. It appeared in the opinion pages of newspapers and online,
and in informational material produced by some of the movement's core backers, like the progressive think-tank, the Institut de recherche et d'informations
socio-économique (IRIS). Although it was not explicitly featured in the public
arguments of the student leaders during the strike, to many this undercurrent of
intergenerational resentment served as the moral substructure of the mobilization

and as an affirmation of the innate justice of their cause. The Trudeau Foundation's Pierre-Gerlier Forest recalls a seminal moment in the spring after the rejection by students of the May entente, when the issue, once the elephant in the room, came sauntering out into the glare of the spotlights.

> A new ideological dimension of the movement was revealed. This time, the issue was intergenerational equity — the notion that the benefits of the welfare state are skewed towards the baby boom generation, while their children are left with massive public debt and very few advantages. How could people who paid next to nothing to get a university degree now complain shamelessly about youth being expected to pay its "fair share"?[2]

Given the much-parroted governmental insistence on the students' "fair share," the only surprise was perhaps that it took this long for the issue to take its rightful place at the centre of the debate. Québec's students, after all, were far from the first to raise the alarm over a generationally uneven balance of debts and benefits in the Western world. As far back as 1984, sociologist and demographer Samuel H. Preston warned of a sharp turn in the United States toward a spending bias that favoured the growing cohort of the elderly at the expense of children.[3] Since then, much has been written about the financial strain affecting Western democracies, as fertility rates have plummeted while the elderly live longer without retiring later.[4] With the electoral weight of the older generations inflated as a result, the distribution of public resources in democracies has skewed to favour the old over the young and contributed to making age an increasingly dramatic political divide.[5]

None of this, however, means that intergenerational conflict is inevitable in the context of the West's aging populations.[6] It is perfectly avoidable, in fact, in the presence of political will. Such was what sociologist Fred C. Pampel concluded in 1994 when he extended Preston's investigation to a comparative study across countries. Pampel found that generational inequities in spending were strongest in countries without strong leftist parties (who tend to place a higher value on solidarity, presumably) and where a lack of official age-based representative organizations (age-based corporatism) meant that age groups were being excluded from the political structures.[7] In other words, the emergence and gravity of the generational divide depends directly on policy choices and political regimes. This was confirmed again in a study of eight democracies performed by sociologist Clara Sabbagh and political economist Pieter Vanhuysse between 1996 and 1998, which found marked perceptions of injustice by university students when it came to the sharing of wealth across generations. Tellingly, the authors found these sentiments to be less pronounced in the more expansive welfare states of continental Europe, while they were at their most acute in the Anglo-Saxon market-based systems where neoliberalism has found its most fertile soil: Canada, the United States and the United Kingdom.[8] Fifteen years later, the culmination of such mounting resentments blew out into the open during the Québec student revolt. Pierre-Luc

Brisson, a young *carré rouge* and author of *Après le printemps,* articulates the shared sentiment well.

> Numerous are the youth whom we ask to pay today to get an education, they who tomorrow will have to bear the weight of the aging population. [...] Right or wrong, we have the impression that the Baby Boom generation is making off with their golden parachutes (*se sauve avec l'assiette au beurre*), while the youth, who do not have the advantage of numbers, will have to struggle for numerous years before ever hoping to benefit from a minute fraction of the social benefits their elders once granted themselves.[9]

Clearly, issues of intergenerational justice were far from an ivory tower sideshow during the student spring. They were central. From the fall of 2011, IRIS launched conference tours across Québec to publicize their research that showed striking imbalances between students' conditions today and at the time of their parents. Their research also sought to highlight viable policy alternatives, which served to expose the ideological roots of the hike.[10] IRIS's campaign provided heavy artillery to the CLASSE, who frequently invoked their studies in class visits and distributed their pamphlets to students. The think-tank even produced a series of YouTube videos entitled "The myths around tuition," which garnered a total of 220,000 views online by the winter of 2012.[11] History, in short, was a powerful presence at the centre of the students' arsenal.

Drinking up and poisoning the well

The reports authored by IRIS painted a stark portrait: Québec's students in 2012 had to work an average of 67 percent more to pay for their studies than the group that attended universities in the 1970s, who had basked in the benefits of frozen tuition levels and the full slate of the Quiet Revolution's efforts at democratizing education.[12] Indeed, by the government's own ready admission, the hikes would have brought inflation-adjusted tuition levels *back* to 1968 — prior, that is, to the first student strike that year, which brought fuller implementation of the Parent Commission's transformative reforms.[13] And naturally, as tuition levels have risen, so too has the proportion of students who work part-time in order to pay for their studies. In 1970, only one in five Québec students worked during the school year; by 2012, four fifths of the student body worked sixteen hours a week or more, in addition to full-time summer employment.[14]

Such is the face of the advancing cultural revolution of the capitalist class, whereby life has value only when it is economically productive, to *them* — and even those who submit are incapable of stemming their rising indebtedness. Average student debt in Québec rose to $16,202 by 2009 for the final year of undergraduate studies, and the FEUQ estimates that 65 percent of students finish their undergraduate degrees with $15,000 of debt.[15] Adjusted for inflation, these numbers represent multiples greater than what any Québec cohort since the 1970s has had to contend with.[16] Indeed, with the current provincial system that makes it impossible for students to keep the grants and loans portions of their aid separate, the process is virtually designed to guarantee that students graduate with debt the second they accept help.[17] Yet far from inciting concern among the establishment, the powerful interests behind the scenes are surely satisfied with the trend: Interest fees on student loans in Québec are funnelled directly into the pockets of the largest banks, in contrast even to the federal system, which was modified in 2001 to correct for this perversion.[18] Since 1989, $1.5 billion of public funds has been transferred by the Québec government to the banks to cover the interest fees of students while they are still engaged in their studies, and $30 million is paid to them annually by students who have graduated. The bank lobbies thus have a direct interest in the indebtedness of Québec's students — as well, it would appear, as in the Liberal Party's success. Under Charest, the banks boasted impressive victories, notably gaining the abolition of the capital tax in 2007 that had been in place since 1947, a gift worth nearly a billion dollars annually, which, if allotted appropriately, could have funded the entire cost of free university education for every Quebecer.[19]

To justify this increase in youth indebtedness, the Liberal government, characteristically unconcerned with all but financial measures of success, made the claim that the investment in an undergraduate diploma provides a net return of $600,000 more in earnings over the span of an average lifetime.[20] Yet even if we were to debate in the Liberals' language of dollars and cents, one of the many evident problems with this argument, based on figures from 2006, is that it's impossible to predict future earnings based on yesterday's economy. This is particularly true in the present context of wider educational attainment, which is rapidly decreasing the value of a degree precisely as tuition fees continue to rise.[21] Today's alumni are in fact far from compensated for their inflated debt loads with salaries to match their greater qualifications. The 2006 Canadian census instead found that graduate-age Canadians (twenty-five to twenty-nine) were earning thousands less in 2005 constant dollars than those who entered the post-university job market in 1980, with young men's earnings falling from an average of $43,767 in 1980 to $37,680 in 2005, and that of women falling by $709 despite their rapidly rising educational attainment over the same period.[22]

It's been said many times, and will be said again: This may well be the first generation to be left a lower standard of living than their parents enjoyed before them. These figures, taken together, hint at exactly that and speak to a very real deterioration in students' quality of life in recent decades: to a student population that is paying more for their studies, working longer hours to pay for it, incurring more debt and once graduated, is earning less for it — but also, to a student body whose academic performance and mental and emotional health are threatened by increasing levels of stress. It is of little surprise that a study by Statistics Canada in 2008 found that full-time students who work twenty hours a week or more exhibit greater stress levels and higher levels of absenteeism, see their academic performance suffer, and are ultimately placed at greater risk of dropping out.[23] It may be naïve not to think that for the Liberals, this collateral is but a small price to pay to force more students onto the job market — and all while amassing the debt that conspires to mould them into submissive workers for many years to come.

Shackled to the treadmill: The tyranny of debt

Indeed, this is another way that raising tuition levels serves to further the market society's most totalitarian ambitions: by narrowing students' freedoms to pursue their own paths. We can see it just beneath the surface of the Liberals' "earnings premium" argument, which dabbles in averages and thereby downplays the socially significant question of *which* disciplines purchase greater salaries and which do not. A study by CIBC World Markets in 2013 found that graduates of fine and applied arts programs actually made an average of 12 percent *less* than those with only a high school diploma between 2001 and 2011.[24] According to the CIBC, just under half of all Canadian students choose what they call "underperforming" disciplines in the arts and humanities, where the added financial value of a diploma is marginal at best. These students, say the report's authors, "*aren't* getting a relative edge in terms of income prospects,"[25] and yet tuition fees for all disciplines have continued to soar, with Canada's currently standing at twice the average of the advanced industrial countries of the OECD.[26] (Québec's, after cancelling the tuition increase, now hover around the OECD average). Students within the arts and humanities — disciplines that encourage a broadening of one's social perspectives and that do more to favour independent critical thought — are being squeezed, as those who reject the market's signals to pursue their passions are punished with a much longer and more arduous path to financial emancipation. Indeed, it's of no small import that the students who stayed on strike the longest during the spring of 2012 came from the fields of the humanities and fine arts.[27]

Built in to the debt system, therefore, is a more subtle and more sinister mechanism of social engineering at work, and one that so completely encapsulates the coldly monetarist mindset of the neoliberal establishment. To graduates beginning their working lives submerged under terrifyingly unfamiliar mountains of debt, the years immediately following graduation may be the decisive phase that defines their life's trajectory. The psychological and financial stresses that bear on them as they embark on their professional development can therefore only act as pressures that conspire to funnel students down financially rewarding paths — or if the system is running at optimal efficiency, to dissuade them from ever pursuing their desires in the first place. Yet in the pathologically blinkered eyes of the current market, socially, culturally and environmentally constructive ends are most frequently assigned little value, while their destructive opposites are. Those saddled with debt are often in too vulnerable a position to risk the necessary time and effort to discover their true calling. They are quickly pushed to choose money over more fulfilling or high-minded explorations, but at high personal and collective cost indeed. For with the edges of these graduates' individualities blunted to fit neatly into ready-made economic slots, the singular inspirations and energies of too many are withdrawn from the pool of resources channelled toward collective goods — as triumphant capitalism marches onward, its boots on the necks of the youth's struggles for self-actualization.

This insidious impact of the debt system is far from accidental to present structures erected on its pillars. "The student indebtedness that was the economic origin of the crisis," says the Collectif de débrayage, "can only be understood as the obligation to adopt a conduct of guilt, the obligation to *work* to repay one's debt."[28] Indebted students begin their working lives as vassals, bonded to their creditors and forced to check their humanity at the entrance to the capitalist work mill in order to buy back their freedom. Yet the impacts of the debt system's innate tyranny may even outlive repayment, as explained best by cultural theorist and critic Noam Chomsky.

> Students who acquire large debts putting themselves through school are unlikely to think about changing society. When you trap people in a system of debt, they can't afford the time to think. Tuition fee increases are a disciplinary technique, and by the time students graduate, they are not only loaded with debt, but have also internalized the disciplinarian culture. This makes them efficient components of the consumer economy.[29]

In fewer words, a system built on debt is an effective means of enforcing the status quo. "Government by debt is a mode of production of docile workers"[30] says the Collectif de débrayage, and indeed such is the very genius of the system's built-in resilience. Those occupied with the business of getting by are deprived the luxury of pursuing socially or culturally constructive paths, as our current market, geared only toward consumption, attaches little to no value to such endeavours. They are left little time to engage in the unproductive economic crimes of artistic creation or experimentation, to pursue their own independent projects, research or critical thinking, or — dare we defend such unmitigated hedonism — to live healthy and well-rounded lives. To the paternalist élites who demanded yet more enslavement of their youth through debt, the students found courage in their numbers to finally offer up the heartfelt riposte: We are not spokes in the wheels of your destructive economy, and we will no longer apologize for wanting more from life than this.

The unpayable debt:
A gift of environmental devastation

During the Printemps érable, Quebecers were treated to the explosive impacts of these generational inequities on social harmony. Yet most remarkable of all, perhaps, was that the youth's pervasive sense of being victims to a historic injustice did *not* stop at the edge of their present and future economic precarity. Early on, the upper layer of the student revolt was peeled back to expose a seething vein of environmental discontent below. To all those willing to see, this generation had delivered the clearest sign yet of its truly global and forward-looking perspectives, and shown that the materialism often ascribed to them by others was ultimately skin-deep.

Prominent Québec author, documentary filmmaker and environmental activist Richard Desjardins was struck by the phenomenon, as he recounted in an op-ed published in *Le Monde*: "It's remarkable," he wrote, "that the student protests pertain also to the management of our natural resources. Banners and placards attest to the fact. And when on April 22, Earth Day, the two themes met, 300,000 people descended into the streets of Montréal."[31] The figure, approximate as it may be, merits repeated emphasis: nearly a third of a million people in the streets, in a city whose greater metropolitan region counts just under four million souls and in a province counting just over twice that number.[32] Never had either a Canadian Earth Day protest or the city of Montréal seen protests on such a scale. Never, for that matter, had Canada at all.

The convergence of the two issues was neither spontaneous nor accidental, but both natural and in a crucial sense, deeply inevitable. As we'll recall from the very first class-by-class visits by the CLASSE, Charest's environmental policies were placed front and centre in the association's arguments demonstrating the government's guiding values and priorities. In a speech delivered to the conference *Indignez-vous* organized by the Council of Canadians at the height of the conflict, Gabriel Nadeau-Dubois incisively invoked the broader picture when he attacked what he deemed an ideologically cohesive governing class. His words echoed the portraits of hijacked democracy painted by the likes of Alain Badiou, Erik Swyngedouw, Colin Crouch and Stéphane Hessel — and much like them, Nadeau-Dubois didn't pull his punches.

> The people who want to raise tuition levels, [...] the people who decided to impose a health surtax, the people who put in place the Plan Nord, [...] the people who are trying to prevent Couche-Tard [cornerstore] workers from unionizing, all of these people are the same. They are the same people, with the same interests, the same groups, the same political parties, the same economic institutes. These people, they are one single élite, a gluttonous élite, a vulgar élite, a corrupt élite, an élite that sees education as but an investment in human capital, that sees a tree as but a sheet of paper and that sees a child as but a future employee.[33]

For GND and the untold thousands he spoke for, the élites' agenda does not just offend our values or interests. It offends our humanity. To the CLASSE as much as their public face, the underlying clash was clear: between humanism and the cold exploitation of humans by an economy controlled by the rich; between cooperation toward a collective cause and a self-defeating and destructive competition between companies and consumers. With its eyes focused beyond the horizon, the CLASSE feared that a defeat in the fight against tuition increases would open the door to a wider commodification of the public good, from hospitals, to electricity production, to our natural resources.

> A handful of people, accountable to no one, is in the process of ravaging these spaces in total impunity, from the Plan Nord to shale gas. For these people whose vision is confined to the next quarter, nature has no value but that which is measured in economic returns [...] so myopic are they to the beauty of the common good.[34]

The environment had been paramount to the Indignados' struggle against corrupt and greedy élites in Spain, and in Québec, the issue found equal resonance among a youth whose concerns increasingly span oceans and borders and reach beyond issues of material wealth.[35] For the student marchers as much as for the influential figures and organizations that rallied to their struggle, the environmental and social impacts of the Liberals' agenda led back to one single diagnosis — and to one single establishment. We saw it in the open letter from two hundred public figures that invoked the government's Plan Nord to attack "the environmental degradation engendered by an anachronistic development model."[36] We saw it in Philippe Ducros's rousing letter "We are immense," in which he evoked the "victims of climate upheaval tied to our energy bulimia."[37] And we saw it as well in Guy Rocher's letter, when the co-author of the Parent Report asked how the government could shower such largesse on the multinationals exploiting our natural resources, while simultaneously refusing it to our own youth — a juxtaposition decried as well, and with particular venom, by Richard Desjardins in the pages of Le Monde.[38] All of these high-profile interventions served to greatly shape the public debate during the student spring. And all echoed the CLASSE's critique of an economic model that is saddling this and future generations with an impossible ecological debt that surpasses only the social and financial ones now hanging heavily around our necks.

The explosion of the environment as a central issue to the student struggle came as little surprise to Jean-Marc Léger, the president of the largest Canadian-owned polling firm, which bears his name. For Léger, it was clear that the "generation gap in Québec" was a "key factor behind" the Printemps érable. "The youth focused their anger on tuition fees, but behind that, their anger is much broader," he warned. "In my view, this movement has only just begun."[39] Léger's eyes are wide open. The students' challenge went far beyond the issue of tuition fees, and even beyond the Plan Nord, to take direct aim at the underlying dogma for

Gabriel Nadeau-Dubois speaks to a family-friendly demonstrations called by the CLASSE *on March 18, 2012.*

which both are poster children. And indeed, the source of the students' rage is not difficult to grasp. In 2011, the International Energy Agency warned that the current trajectory of the world's governments would sabotage any hopes of limiting the average rise in the Earth's temperature to supposedly manageable levels pegged by the scientific community at two degrees Celsius. The agency says that we are instead heading toward a calamitous global increase of six degrees or more by the end of the century.[40]

Decades of reports came before and more will continue to pour in, each delivered in ever shriller tones that draw an inglorious portrait of a species and its beloved "law of the house." Naomi Klein evokes the big picture with eloquence.

> Our economic system and our planetary system are now at war. Or, more accurately, our economy is at war with many forms of life on earth, including human life. What the climate needs to avoid collapse is a contraction in humanity's use of resources; what our economic model demands to avoid collapse is unfettered expansion. Only one of these sets of rules can be changed, and it's not the laws of nature.[41]

From Klein and Chomsky to former NASA scientist James Hansen and former Norwegian prime minister Gro Harlem Brundtland, who chaired the U.N. commission that coined the term "sustainable development" in the 1980s, the volume has now reached pitched levels. All agree: Global warming may lead to the end of human civilization, and in the not-too-distant future.[42] The World Bank has warned that a four degree rise in temperatures by century's end — a conservative estimate — will produce "extreme heat waves, declining global food stocks, loss of ecosystems and biodiversity and life-threatening sea level rise."[43] Sea levels may rise by one to two metres by 2100, leaving many island nations under water and major cities in great jeopardy, including New York, London, Hong Kong, Shanghai, Los Angeles, Miami, Mumbai, Vancouver and countless more.[44] There is a grave existential threat that looms over the future of our generation. Yet when these young women and men raise their heads toward the leaders entrusted with their protection, we see a political establishment that doesn't inhabit the same world. We see, instead, a unanimous community of scientists whose hands have been clutching and holding the alarm lever down for decades — and in the foreground, our elected representatives with their fingers pressed to mute. This disconnect, so often emitting airs of the surreal, can only be viewed as the inescapable backdrop to the youth-driven revolts that have swept the world to challenge the market doctrinaires. For after all, it is this new generation, and not the governing one, that will have to confront the impacts of a rapidly warming planet and yet daily perceives a governing élite displaying a callous nonchalance toward the future we will inherit. Our generation cannot help but harbour the hardening sentiment of being exploited by an élite that reaped the benefits of cheap tuition, a generous social safety net and more promising employment prospects in their day — and whose future was not then marred by an impending ecological catastrophe whose dangers have long ceased to be qualified by doubt. For the youth of Québec, as of the world, rarely, if ever, can a political issue be as personal or as visceral as this. "Behind that, their anger is much broader," warned Léger. So went his next ominous words: "You will see."[45]

II

NEW DEMOCRACY RISING
The World of the Network Generation

We will not bend beneath their blows,
we know that a pen is heavier than a stone,
that a fist is worth less than a head
and know to respond to those who sow the wind
that we are the storm.

The storm of a youth that thirsts for spring,
and that is but assuming the weighty responsibility
incumbent to our age;
that of remaking the world, in our image.[1]

— Sébastien Moses, *"De ventôse à germinal"* (my translation)

In 2012, the entrenched powers of neoliberal capitalism met Québec's student revolt — a simple student strike in any other time — with an unprecedented wall of autocracy and sparked its mutation into a collective awakening that rocked the foundations of the political establishment. Indeed, the virulence with which the élites sought to crush the youth's rise reverberated through a generation as the mark of our leaders' essential authoritarianism and laid bare the cancerous anachronisms against which the *carrés rouges* sought to define their democratic ambitions. Try as the establishment may to force this genie back into the bottle, only unexamined complacency allows us to file away the movement's legacy in the past or to turn away from the signs that point our way to a changing future. For if the spring of 2012 taught us one thing, it is that slowly but unstoppably, a new world is rising up from society's soil and stubbornly pushing its way through the widening cracks of the establishment's rotting foundations.

This was Québec's first mass movement of the twenty-first century, with its form holding up a map of the democratic culture of the generation that launched it. From the charged monikers "Printemps érable" and the lesser used "Printemps québécois," to the spectacular eruptions of red throughout the province, the #GGI's infinite array of creative and symbolic protests, the nightly #manifencours and of course, the #casseroles, most of the student movement's defining innovations and acts originated not from the top, but rather organically, from below and online:

from networked individuals, collectives and local associations. They are the ones who propelled the movement's mushrooming ever outwards and who cast its language, its iconography and ultimately, its dreams. The architecture of its expansion mirrored the decentralized "networked brains" that animated the Indignados and Occupy Wall Street. And in its triumph, the CLASSE/ASSÉ, their cultural and ideological cousin, had proven its prescience, and its pertinence.[2]

These social media-era movements are fast discrediting the twentieth-century presumption that hierarchical authority structures are a requisite for effective collective action and in doing so, may be laying the seeds of a new democratic future. For Catalan sociologist Manuel Castells, who has devoted twenty years to exploring the rise of the "network society," the reasons are evident.[3] Everything that networked movements lose in efficiency by relinquishing top-down control, he says, they more than make up for in the added energies of the grassroots, who are re-engaged, motivated and mobilized into action. It all boils down to trust. Hierarchical and delegative structures keep information and decisional authority out of the hands of the "unqualified masses," which breeds suspicion, weakens their ability to make a difference and ultimately repels their engagement. Yet open and horizontal networks replace that relationship of mistrust and exploitation with transparency, cooperation and solidarity, and thereby "undermine the need for formal leadership."[4] In short, the rise of networks, facilitated and accelerated by the social media revolution, is changing everything.

On s'en câlisse:
The democracy generation and the decline of deference

The Printemps érable was the site of an intractable and even inevitable clash that exposed a fundamental cognitive dissonance at the root of the generational divide. Beyond the diffficulty of reconciling each side's views of society, the very possibility of a dialogue was consistently undermined by their opposing languages of democracy and authority that proved essentially incompatible. We were speaking in different tongues.

Democracy, for the Liberals and their supporters, was to be expressed at the ballot box, and while people had a right to express opposition in the interval through protest, that right, their actions and arguments suggested, should be circumscribed by the need to avoid disturbing the normalcy of economic life.[5] In an article entitled "Clash of the centuries," the Trudeau Foundation's Pierre-Gerlier Forest remarked that the "tightly controlled declarations, carefully crafted press releases and formal press conferences" of the government bespoke an "obsession with titles and status" that was "typical of twentieth-century governments."[6] And indeed, Charest's belief in the absolute authority of his office seemed beyond any shred of mitigation: not by the absence of a mandate, for unlike Bourassa in 1989, the tuition increase was *not* in the party's last electoral platform; nor even, it seemed, by the lack of a democratic majority, with his party securing just under 25 percent support from eligible voters (42 percent of votes cast) in the election held four years prior — more than his PQ opposition, that is, but a far cry from a majority.

In such an idea of democracy that places order and authority above the popular will, education minister and deputy premier Line Beauchamp could feel justified in asserting, as she did during the crisis, that "the people's elected representatives are never wrong" and that "the most important thing is to respect them."[7] Engaging with and involving the one social group impacted the most by her decision was not the priority; neither was safeguarding the long-term and broad-based common good, as decided through open and collaborative deliberation. For Beauchamp, the *most* important thing was to "respect" — that is, obey — the will of the representatives, in place only because a plurality (usually a minority) of voters in their ridings made a mark by their name some years ago. In such a context, Beauchamp's comments, which sanctify the rules of the game at the expense of their spirit and fundamental end, are hard to reconcile with even the most anemic conception of the democratic ideal. But they did at least reveal an essential underlying truth: that for Beauchamp, Charest and others of their school, the supreme values of order and authority are simply so deeply rooted, culturally, as to have become ends in their own right.

The government's insistence on deference became the source of ridicule for students and members of the press, who joined Martine Desjardins in chastising Beauchamp for frequently behaving like a school headmistress.[8] Indeed the Liberals' near-caricatural channelling of the father-knows-best defence could not have been more maladroit in the circumstances, nor better calculated to reaffirm the students in their cause. For within the student movement, the rejection of hierarchical authority models was surging, as growing numbers of the rising generation turned to embrace the deeper democracy of a new age. Membership crises hit both establishment student federations during the strike, as the CLASSE, grown from 40,000 to 105,000 members to land close on the heels of the FEUQ, was propelled into the pilot's seat of the mobilization.[9] By May 28, a third of the FECQ's member associations had launched consultations on disaffiliation, representing what its most vocal critics deemed "the greatest disaffiliation consultation wave in such a short period of time in the entire history of the federation."[10] In a virulently styled open letter entitled "A corrupted federation" (*"Une fédération gangrenée"*), thirty former student association executives lambasted the organization for "a profound lack of transparency, a severe undervaluing of democracy and a flagrant lack of respect for the decisions adopted democratically by the congress or by member associations."[11] Most especially, FECQ president Léo Bureau-Blouin stood accused of refusing to endorse the abolition of tuition fees during the strike despite a clear mandate from the assemblies to do so.[12]

While numerous FECQ affiliates were voting to leave the federation, a growing chorus of critics within the FEUQ was voicing an identical vein of discontent.[13] In tendering his resignation as a member of the national executive in April 2013,

Thomas Briand-Gionest decried a severe lack of transparency and accountability and cited a controlling and top-down approach by the offices of the president and vice-president — and specifically, by Martine Desjardins. "Over the course of recent years," he wrote, "the member associations have too often been brushed aside in the decisional processes and in the diffusion of information."[14] Briand-Gionest was not alone in his views. In October 2013, Desjardin's successor as president of the FEUQ, Antoine Genest-Grégoire, resigned his post after a third association voted to disaffiliate, cutting its membership down by fourteen thousand students since before the 2012 strike. Most ironic, perhaps, was that the FEUQ's national executive, much like their counterparts at the FECQ, refused to acknowledge the results of the democratic exercises.[15] Yet accepted or not, the FECQ and FEUQ were bleeding members as a direct result of an internal crisis of representation that directly echoed the CLASSE's wider democratic critique.[16] By contrast, the provisional Coalition large de l'ASSÉ was disbanded after the strike to return to its core existence as the ASSÉ. But it now counted thirty thousand new members who had permanently joined, which means there are another thirty thousand who, whether unaffiliated anew or remaining with one of the old federations, will carry with them new expectations gained from their momentary immersion in the CLASSE's practices of direct democracy. The democratic pressures will only continue to build.

A new era, a new world:
The birth and rise of the network society

The culture of youth is changing, everywhere pulled along by the same currents of the global pond. Every day, we dive into it online. Importantly, Castells links the "culture of autonomy" shared by Twitter and the Internet back to the seeds sown by the New Left movements of the 1970s, whose libertarian and participative democratic cultures laid the grounds for the creation of the Internet on American campuses.[17] The Internet was never ideologically innocent, as those who today fight to undermine Net neutrality know well: Embedded within its architecture is a radical democratic culture that threatens the world's traditional hierarchies of power. In the decades that followed its creation, the budding network society then took root with escalating intensity, reaching a tipping point in the twenty-first century as online practices and conceptions fell in line with the Internet's essential character. It was around this time that individual modes of online interaction (like email), which simply transferred old modes wholly intact over to the new medium, made way for new "autonomous forms of social networks controlled and guided by their users."[18] The Internet had come of age, and with it a "new social morphology" that has been gradually seeping through the sands of society to change our mental maps of human interaction and organization.[19]

A glimpse at the contrasting experiences of generations is therefore incredibly revealing. While their parents were born at the slow-burning dawn of the network transformation, Québec's youth are of a generation that has grown up immersed in its most potent expressions yet. Our link to the political world, and thus our political education and socialization, is also primarily through the Internet.[20] The cumulative difference with our parents is fundamental: While the mass media sources that prior generations depended on for their political information (television, radio, print) were "predominantly linear," in political scientist Henry Milner's phrase, we in the Internet generation are accustomed to selecting and sorting our own information, to ordering it and to creating it. The impact on political culture has been nothing short of revolutionary. "Power" in this world, says Milner, "shifts from institutions to networks and from bordered territories to cyberspace, transcending geographical and hierarchical restrictions. Linearity is a thing of the past."[21] The paradigm shift has borne real implications for the way youth conceptualize democracy and authority. This fact was on sharp display during the student conflict, as Québec's students, says Milner, gave voice to something that is "implicit in social media politics": namely, "the rejection of representative democracy."[22]

This is no case of technological determinism, but the recent and exponential acceleration of a long and steady social mutation. Madeleine Gauthier is a sociologist at the Centre Urbanisation Culture Société of the Institut national de la recherche scientifique (INRS) who has specialized in youth issues for over thirty years. Gauthier aptly remarks that our generation has been raised since childhood to speak equal to equal with adults, rather than to defer to their authority for its own sake. "For them," she says, "authority comes more from competence and trust than from hierarchy. My professor colleagues will tell you, once you take the time to discuss with them and arrive at an agreement, they can become extraordinary collaborators."[23] In such a world, the very meaning of authority begins to change from a unidirectional relationship to a reciprocal one: Like puzzle pieces lying flat on a table, they aim to slot together to achieve a shared vision. The only superiority granted is confined to each person's acknowledged areas of expertise.

Gauthier's comments confirm a larger social trend that has unfolded in parallel — and is intimately linked — to the network transformation. Examined most famously by Canadian political scientist Neil Nevitt in 1996 and again in 2011, this shift has seen values of deference declining across society, propelled largely by more egalitarian and anti-authoritarian parental practices.[24] A recent Australian case study that examined self-perceived parenting styles of 550 parents echoes Nevitt's seminal work, The Decline of Deference, and found a pronounced "socio-cultural shift from conformist, authoritarian parenting, to more [...] democratic approaches."[25] In short, more than ever before, Western youth today expect a conversation rather than a decree.[26] In such light, our appropriation of the Internet as our primary medium seems perfectly natural and both confirms and fuels the wider cultural shift toward values of horizontalism and networked autonomy.

Prominent Canadian progressive Judy Rebick early noted the phenomenon too when she founded the alternative media website Rabble in 2001. From the beginning, she recounts, the majority of the site's visitors entered through the discussion board known as Babble. Yet Babble was not always a part of the project, as Rebick herself admits to not initially grasping its appeal. "Young people we consulted across the country told us 'if it's not interactive, we're not interested,'" she recalls. "But the basic desire of young people to listen to others like themselves before forming their opinions rather than to experts, politicians or columnists told me something new was happening with this younger generation — something profoundly democratic."[27] A study by Pew Research corroborates her experience. According to an American study performed in 2007, 80 percent of so-called "Net Geners" under the age of twenty-eight visit blogs regularly, while 40 percent of American teens and young adults operate their own. In 2007 alone, 64 percent of this generation in the U.S. said they engaged in some form of content creation online, though this number may be far higher today, as this already marked a jump of 10 percent over the previous year.[28]

The return of society: The bottom-up communitarianism of the twenty-first century

The interactive, horizontal and decentralized world of the network generation is the image of a new social vision whose values were everywhere in the air through the six months of the student crisis. Critics on the right often painted the student movement with the laughably anachronistic brush of Marxism and its variants — intellectually lazy referents that only answered their preexisting need to swiftly dismiss and suppress all criticisms of holy capitalism. Yet the communitarianism channelled by the *carrés rouges* was born not of nostalgia. On the contrary: Solidarity, that ideal traditionally carried by the left, and personal liberty, that ideal traditionally carried by the right, are melding into a contemporary paradigm that's now finding its voice within the forums of the social media generation.

This new communitarianism shares the right's disdain for bureaucracies and top-down modes of control, replacing them with the diffuse autonomy of networks where citizens, no longer bound by physical space or political borders, seek out the online hands to hold as they pool talents and energies toward a collective cause. Society is indeed undergoing a profound metamorphosis, and "The Internet," writes the Collectif de débrayage, "is the order of the anthropological mutation."[29] This is the global communitarian resurgence to which we bear witness, forced by the winter that our anti-biological, anti-social and anti-environmental economic model has bestowed to a generation suffocating in its grip. In this rapidly decaying landscape, the incapacity of arbitrary and élite-governed nation-states to address the dire crises threatening our future is daily laying bare the catastrophic failures of our power structures — and spurring grassroots and globalized movements that seek to reclaim control over our collective destiny.

In these societies grown increasingly atomized and anonymized under the cultural, economic and social systems of the capitalist class, online networks are arising to rescue the faded ideal of a common good based on timeless human and social needs. Castells has written that "the legacy of networked social movements will have been to raise the possibility of *re-learning* how to live together."[30] In the wake of the *casseroles* movement, his words ring out with an eerie prescience and hint that the sources of this metamorphosis may run even deeper. Paolo Gerbaudo, author of *Tweets and the Streets*, has similarly remarked that "In front of a crisis of public space, social media have become *emotional* conduits for reconstructing a sense of togetherness among a spatially dispersed constituency, so as to facilitate its physical coming together."[31] And British author George Monbiot has poignantly dubbed the post-Thatcher ("there is no such thing as society") era, unprecedented in our species' history, as "The Age of Loneliness."[32] So I believe what they are all saying is this: We are thirsty. And that this emotional need may well be the voices of instinct and evolution speaking to us. For where we evolved within extended families, tribes, villages and later neighbourhoods, we have become individual consumers and taxpayers dependent only upon the market and competing amongst ourselves to maximize our personal gains. Where once public spaces were inherently social and political, those that remain too often serve as supporting infrastructure for the marketized city-space, rest stops along the way from commercial hub A to B, when not transformed wholesale into commercial malls themselves. Chased from its physical realm, the human community has sought shelter in the safe spaces found online — just long enough, that is, for the collective to reconstitute itself and to organize to take back its physical domain. But before any of this can begin to happen, we must first re-learn all that we've forgotten.

This is where we can begin if we aim to grasp the overwhelming dominance of the pro-*carrés rouges* within Québec's youth population and the intense social polarization that forced us into a bitter face-off with our elders. In the symmetrical markers of the strike's peak at 304,242 students on March 22 and the similar number that (despite not all being on strike anymore) voted to reject the entente in May, we hear a consistent and resounding majority of Québec's roughly 423,000 post-secondary students who swam ardently against the tide of the prevailing commercialist culture.[33] All public opinion polling performed during the strike showed that the resonance of the students' discourse and goals extended to the wider youth population as well. In separate polls conducted by Léger Marketing, CROP and Forum Research all between February and May 2012, youth aged eighteen to twenty-four (and with slightly lesser margins, eighteen to thirty-four) consistently backed the *carrés rouges* by margins that fluctuated between 58–74 percent, while those aged fifty-five and older opposed it by equally strong margins.[34] These polls, moreover, likely understate the dominance of the anti-hike side among youth, for they included only those aged eighteen or over and thus omitted much of the CEGEP population, which played an absolutely central and frontline role in the mobilization.

Place Jacques-Cartier in Vieux-Montréal appears deserted after the national march held on March 22, 2012.

Critics of the students often answered that opposition to the tuition increase signified nothing more than the selfish collective's "we won't pay." Yet by every string of available evidence, this knee-jerk and defensive attack must reflect the individualist values and worldviews of its sources more than its targets. *Le combat est avenir*, youth retorted. And for that future, a massive number of Québec's students were ready to, and nearly did, sacrifice an entire semester — and for university students, an average of over $1,100 in tuition fees — so that later generations of students might benefit from an accessible and humanist public education.[35] They were ready to, and often did, sacrifice hundreds and even thousands of dollars in fines for defying police repression, as well as their future opportunities in exposing themselves to the threat of criminal accusations.[36] And they were ready to, as too many did, sacrifice their "mental and physical health in investing body and soul in practices of insubmission"[37] and in going toe to toe, almost always unarmed, against the cold and faceless machine of state brutality. If the obvious question that imposes itself next is "why?", the answer can only come in the form of another question: If not the very ones who stand to inherit the destruction, then who will speak up on behalf of the future?

Already in October of 2010 — before both the student revolt and the consciousness-changing moment of Occupy Wall Street — an online Léger Marketing survey of 3,060 Quebecers provided strong hints of a backlash brewing among youth. Among those aged eighteen to twenty-four, 43 percent sought a Québec further to the left, "more communitarian and with greater solidarity," as well as with fewer divisions between social classes. Another 41 percent sought a Québec with a certain balance between state intervention and private enterprise, yet they envisaged that endpoint as "more social-democratic" than the status quo. Loud and clear, this rising generation is saying that the pendulum has swung too far away from collective stewardship and that the unprecedented capture of wealth and power by the rich must be reversed: On the opposite end of the spectrum, a paltry 8 percent argued for less regulation and a larger space for private enterprise, while only 9 percent of this anti-authoritarian youth favoured a stronger emphasis on law and order.[38]

There is nothing in these results to surprise, and other polls have also shown strong youth support for new leftist parties like Québec Solidaire, which is itself a child of the twenty-first century alter-globalization movement, with its focuses on communitarianism and direct democracy aligned closely with the ASSÉ's.[39] Indeed, if the mobilization lasted for as long as it did, it was precisely because Québec's students possessed a sense of history and knew what they were fighting for. We saw the youth's struggles reverberate in the cogent arguments of the student leaders who never shied from a reasoned riposte to the basest attacks; it was read in the opinion pages, blogs and social media sphere where the *carrés rouges* often distinguished themselves in deploying substance against slander; and it was seen in the hand-drawn slogans held high in the streets, which spoke in favour of a world in which we might find a safe future. This was a movement with both heart and intellectual heft, and its fateful eruption from within the youth population ought not to inspire defensive retrenchment from our elders. If anything, in fact, it ought to inspire hope, along with an earnest introspection — and an offer of aid. For within the very fabric of the Printemps érable lived a renewed faith in the promise of a fuller democracy, in the urgency of a collective dream and in the necessity, but more, the *possibility*, of reknitting society's torn and lonesome threads for a more human age.

For our generation, it's clear that the world the neoliberals built holds little hope. Yet faced with an establishment that's closed to our ideals and a demographic reality that drowns us out, those who will most fully bear the brunt of today's actions are left with little to do but band together and take to the streets. Our critics often fumed at the inconveniences caused; one hand-drawn placard launched our frustrated retort: "Sorry to disturb you, we're just trying to change the world."[40] Indeed, if Québec had never before known a protest movement of this magnitude, it may well be that the stakes had never seemed so high. Beneath the surface of the students' daily disturbances lay a *cri du coeur*, an impassioned plea from those who will soon assume historic burdens. While youth may not have the strength of a democratic majority, we, as the citizens of tomorrow, do have a moral right. It's time the future was lent an attentive ear.

NOUS SOMMES À VENIR
The World to Come

To find our words again. The words we've hidden behind others.
Citizens behind clients, knowledge behind merchandise, we behind
each of us. [...]
  Everywhere are walls and limits. Thinking outside the box
is arduous, but there are many among us who want the horizon.
And who still believe.[1]
                    — Catherine-Alexandre Briand, "*Ça sent la poussière*" (my
                                                        translation)

Jean Charest's political demise was wrongfully predicted on too many occasions
to count, yet every time he re-emerged in full control over his adversaries. Faced
with an army of young amateurs in 2012, he mobilized the full slate of the state's
coercive powers to crush the most imposing reservoir of resistance standing in
his way — and lost. On September 4, 2012, the Liberal government was defeated,
and Charest resigned as party leader following his ouster from his electoral riding
in Sherbrooke, which he had represented for fourteen years. Parti Québécois
leader Pauline Marois assumed office as Québec's first woman premier after her
party won by a hair's breadth, garnering just under a third of the popular vote. By
ministerial decree, Marois immediately cancelled the tuition increase, abrogated
Law 12 (formerly Bill 78) and convened a summit on post-secondary education to
address the issues raised during the student spring. The new government launched
a commission of inquiry to examine the actions of all players during the Printemps
érable, which released its thorough 450-page report in May 2014 that contained
twenty-eight recommendations, twenty-one of which targeted police abuses. The
Printemps érable had come to an end, if not a definitive one.
  When placed against the backdrop of its contemporaries across Europe and
North America, Québec's *carrés rouges* may thus boast immediate political victories of
uncommon proportions, and nor were these the only ones: The once-mighty CREPUQ,
which had represented university administrations since 1963 and become an ardent
champion of privatization policies, narrowly averted dissolution after all but one of
its members threatened to quit owing to disputes over tuition fees and the organization's role. The pull of the students' arguments on the debate within the academic

community had driven a wedge into the heart of the former monolith. It emerged from its crisis in January 2014 as the new Bureau de coopération interuniversitaire, with its mandate limited to cooperation between administrations and provision of common services. From now on, each administration will speak for itself in the public domain, and its role as a lobby group, neoliberal or otherwise, is over.[2]

These victories belong to the youth of Québec and to the emergent culture of democratic organizing and decision-making proper to the network generation of the new century. After years of weakness and retreat in the face of the neoliberal juggernaut, the Printemps érable announced the resurgence of Québec's student movement as a central political actor and of its capacity, unparalleled anywhere on the continent, to be the social motor that once helped build modern Québec. It is through the institutional strength, resources and organizational reach of Québec's student associations that they were able to educate, engage and mobilize a generation into mounting a historic offensive against élite power; and it is through their proud heritage and cultural recognition that the space and weight of their voice in the public debate was assured.

If our generation in Québec is to win its fight to restore democratic control over our common resources and reverse the establishment's tide of commercialization, it will be through the outlet of the student associations — and particularly, at this point in time, the ASSÉ. It was on the inestimably important foundations built by the Québec youth of yesteryear that they, their modern heir, sparked a mass awakening that made Montréal a battleground in the defining fight of our times. Built with the bricks and mortar of the student movement and the designs of this century's centreless networks, the students erected a structure able to withstand a torpedo aimed by a premier directly at its foundations, stare down the militarized brigades of capitalist power and rally the people to their side to topple an autocrat. In 2012 the student movement recovered both its voice and its muscle, and must not now turn back.

The tenacious edifice of the One Percent

Much changed on the ground in those days of spring, but the lasting and concrete victories of the student movement pale in comparison. When placed in historical perspective, the limits of the students' triumphs in fact speak to the tenacity of an establishment and the resilience of the neoliberal élite's insidious and omnipresent structures of hegemony. In such a context, the days after the election of the PQ couldn't help but arrive as a rude awakening to the betrayed revolutionaries of the Printemps érable.

The Marois government, whose string of reversals and betrayals were of an uncommon effrontery for a government so new, excelled largely at punctuating the definitive rupture of the youth with the political establishment. The decisive actions announced in the aftermath of the election proved but a fleeting mirage. While Law 12 was abrogated, the government took no issue with its municipal equivalents in Montréal and Québec City. They remain in place and are selectively enforced by police, whose growing powers of discretion serve as a channel for their mounting prejudices against activists and youth.[3] The *Sommet sur l'enseignement supérieur,* criticized by the student federations, boycotted by the ASSÉ and protested by ten thousand students who agreed with the ASSÉ's labelling of it as a charade,[4] served largely to legitimate the PQ's decision to index tuition fees to inflation. And on a dizzying panoply of campaign promises that aired long stifled hopes for a pushback against the neoliberal advance — from raising taxes on corporations and the rich, to increasing royalties on mining companies, to imposing a complete moratorium on shale gas exploration — the PQ caved in and reversed course almost instantly in the face of opposition from the Liberals and CAQ and high-powered lobbying efforts by industry and moneyed interests.[5]

The PQ had set out more to save the status quo than challenge it, and in the immediate term seems to have achieved a resounding success. The deception confirmed the predictions of the CLASSE, for whom — contrary to the presidents of the FEUQ and FECQ, who were both defeated as PQ candidates in 2014 — Marois was but the second face of the same corrupted coin they had railed against; a short-term necessity, but never the answer to their aspirations. Sadly, events since have proven them all too correct. After a turbulent eighteen months in office defined by rightward policy reversals and an electoralist embrace of ethnic nationalism, the PQ was dealt an even more catastrophic rebuke than the Liberals. The party plummeted to 25 percent to hit its lowest level of support since its first election in 1970, and Pauline Marois, like Charest before her, was ousted from the legislature she sat in for nearly three decades. Riding a virulent backlash against fears of a third referendum on independence and the PQ's anachronistic identity politics, the Liberals, now under the leadership of Charest's one-time health minister Philippe Couillard, returned to power with a majority government. As of writing, the Liberals have sworn off raising tuition levels further (for now), but have otherwise relaunched their austerity drive with a renewed audacity. Popular opposition is steadily mounting. On October 31, 2014, thousands marched through Montréal and over eighty thousand students went on strike to protest austerity, joined by the Coalition Main Rouge, which regroups over one hundred civil society organizations (including the ASSÉ and labour unions).[6] The flyers that appeared in the streets in the days before announced that "Austerity will not cut our revolt" and directed citizens to a new website: printemps2015.org. The next chapter is pending.

A power struggle on the horizon?

The electoral jousts between the two heads of the neoliberal Cerberus may serve their purpose of occasionally renewing the façade of legitimacy in the eyes of the public at large. Yet for the youth to whom this charade of representative alternation means little, the discontent will not be assuaged. Few if any among the protesters likely expected structures of power so tenacious to crumble so readily. Indeed having grown up knowing nothing but the market society of the neoliberals, the *carrés rouges* could not have been so naïve. Yet the incapacity of so historic a mobilization to spur larger reflections must nonetheless sound an alarm on the degree to which our élites have cemented their control — and more portentously, the extent to which the older electorates who support their parties, the Liberals and Parti Québécois, are turning a deaf ear to the straining voices of the rising youth.

The truly historic nature of the 2012 revolt can inspire little doubt. Former Québec premier and longtime Lévesque minister Jacques Parizeau was among the many high-powered commentators who lined up, even before the crisis had ended, to vaunt the strike as a pivotal moment marking Québec's social and intellectual revival.[7] For this elder statesman and stalwart of the Quiet Revolution, the Printemps érable announced nothing less than the "extraordinary awakening of a generation," conjuring his fondest memories of that seminal phase that helped build modern Québec. "The Quiet Revolution, whose achievements we constantly laud, it [was] a youth revolution," reminds Parizeau, now eighty-four. "The atmosphere at that time was irresistible," to the point that Premier Daniel Johnson, Senior, of Duplessis's conservative Union Nationale, was "swept up in the movement." Parizeau turned his eyes to the masses overflowing in the streets, as his excitement could barely be contained. "And now," he told *Le Devoir*, "it feels like that."[8]

Parizeau's parallel may well be apt. Yet to hear esteemed members of Québec's greying political alumni attest to the fact serves only to call attention to the screeching asymmetry in the outcomes of each movement. This must resound as a clarion call to all Quebecers who hold social and intergenerational harmony at heart. For if the students of Québec were forced to such extremes in 2012 only to cancel a tuition increase, it is partly that youth today have neither the strength of numbers nor social or political clout they once had[9] — and l argely that the contemporary élites' power is more deeply entrenched, more virulently defended and more widely supported, tacitly and actively, by the aging electorate.

Yet if the Printemps érable signalled anything at all, it was that we, the agents of renewal who wait ever more impatiently to take our destinies into our own hands, will not be bullied or bowed, and not even by the most overwhelming odds. The next chapter can only be decided by how far the ruling class is ready to go to stave off the challenge from their eventual successors and how long the older generations will continue to back the agendas that directly imperil the youth's future — and to refuse the outstretched hands of a generation that would like too much to count our parents and grandparents among our friends and allies. It was this very real prospect of a war between generations, consistently suggested by his company's polling results, that pushed Jean-Marc Léger to issue an uncommon plea in *Le Devoir*.

> The Baby Boom generation that has controlled Québec since the 1960s continues to impose its vision. They don't accept the emergence of another group that doesn't think the same way as they do. [...] The youth are waking up, do not crush them. It is they, tomorrow, who will be the

premiers of Québec, the doctors, the lawyers.[...] It is they who will govern society.[...] We must allow the other generation to take power.[10]

This generation — that "doesn't think the same way" — came into its own in the spring of 2012, and we will not soon return to our tutelage. "We see them everywhere deciding to occupy public space, meaning there where we can't not see them and can't not hear them," observes Madeleine Gauthier.[11] She is right to trace that arc. For even if the immediate causes of the student strike were deeply domestic, ultimately, nothing truly is anymore — not for us. The horizontal networking that is emerging as our generation's hallmark was the same force that propelled the movements of the Arab Spring across the Middle East, the Indignados across Europe and the Occupiers across the world. And closer to home, Québec's *casseroles* had barely fallen silent when the indigenous youth of Canada rose up in December of 2012 to defend their resources from corporate exploitation. With a renewed force and confidence bestowed by the tools and aspirations of a new age, the country's First Nations stood up to refuse widening assaults on their treaty rights and announced that this land's first inhabitants would be #IdleNoMore. The movement has since spread to indigenous communities across the United States, where native peoples are fighting on the front lines against corporate aggressions.

This twenty-first-century democratic resurgence fuelled the Chilean student revolts from 2011 to 2013 and helped return Socialist president Michelle Bachelet to power in 2014, backed by student leader Camila Vallejo, on an emboldened agenda of implementing free education and reducing the country's stark inequalities.[12] It sparked Mexico's #YoSoy132 youth rebellion in 2012 against the political influence of the country's media oligopoly and against an illegitimate president elevated to office with their support despite flagrant violations of electoral law. It gave birth to the Turkish insurrection of the summer of 2013 against the emboldened autocracy of the Islamist capitalists in power,[13] and the Brazilian protests that erupted in parallel against the largesse showered on FIFA's international sports event at the expense of the people's welfare. All were forged in the contemporary underground of social media and bathed in the grassroots, communitarian and participatory culture of its currents. All, despite differing contexts and levels of gravity, marked the mass awakening of societies arising to challenge the class-based agendas of their élites and to fight back against the deployment of state autocracy and violence in the service of their élites' narrow interests.

From the online underground to the street and beyond: A generation rises

"Regardless how the current conflict ends," predicted history professors Piroska Nagy and Martin Peticlerc at the height of the conflict, "the student strike carries [...] the seeds of a radical project engendering the democratic transformation of Québécois society."[14] Yet seeds so transformative are not sown overnight. In the old forums and media of the establishment generation, business as usual continues its onward stroll, wistfully oblivious to the ground that's shifted beneath its feet. But in the online underground of the Internet generation, new synergies are being woven every day, sprouting up from the fertile soil laid during the student spring.

Ricochet, launched in the fall of 2014, is just one outpost of this landscape being slowly recarved. An independent, not-for-profit, bilingual and crowdfunded media "born of the Maple Spring of 2012,"[15] the web-based outlet's imposing roster of talent includes Gabriel Nadeau-Dubois, Anne Lagacé Dowson (formerly of the CBC), former Rabble editor Derrick O'Keefe, Anarchopanda's real-life alias Julien Villeneuve (a CEGEP professor) and the co-founder of Idle No More Québec, Melissa Mollen Dupuis. Already, the organization has attracted the high-profile support of Naomi Klein and hosted the Montréal launch of her latest book, *This Changes Everything: Capitalism vs. the Climate*, where Nadeau-Dubois gave the introduction. Ricochet is the face of a new Québec rising, uniting anglophones and francophones from across Canada behind a project to "reinvent independent media"[16] and provide a new counterweight to the corporate press. The Printemps érable offered a potent demonstration of how the mainstream media is being drowned out by the expanding array of online alternatives to become but one voice in the global chorus. In a context where each generation relies increasingly on different modes of media for their information and arguments, the emergence of projects like Ricochet will only widen the chasm between the youth and our elders and heighten the tensions opposing our aspirations.

This youth, in the words of the Collectif de débrayage, "conceives of itself in all confidence as the true carrier of the contemporary, destined in time to sweep away the old world of discipline and authority."[17] The 2012 mobilization was a major step along this path, which we can start to grasp only once we reflect on the depth and breadth of the experiences it produced. Gabriel Nadeau-Dubois suggests a good place to start when he writes that the "strike was one of the largest projects of civic education that Québec has ever known. For one year, in hundreds of assemblies, tens of thousands of people debated the future of an institution and its place in society."[18] He is likely not exaggerating the impacts when he argues that through force of debating in the assemblies, students internalized the culture and mores of horizontal deliberation. Indeed, the participative conception of democracy it nurtured will only harden youth's rejection of top-down impositions.

Beyond the students who packed the assemblies, there will likely be transformative impacts on the broader youth population as well. Numerous studies in Europe and North America have suggested that people who engage in protest activities become more politicized, in which case the student spring may have become the entry point into politics for tens of thousands of youth who descended into the streets for the first time.[19] There, they learned new tactics that laid the grounds for a twenty-first-century protest culture that will continue to adapt and evolve with the conflicts to come. From the usual imperative of staying united, social media bestowed the masses with a collective intelligence that enabled multiple dispersions and regroupings to evade the police; from the imperative of planned routes and organization, it lent the possibility of spontaneous and spatially diffused marches that outwitted and overwhelmed the police's old modes of command and control. For nearly six months, tens or even hundreds of thousands of young Quebecers — a significant proportion in a nation of eight million — were trained in the democratic modes of a new age and crossed the Rubicon that once divided deference from resistance. And whether it was in the 2.0 tactics of mobilization and outreach, the diverse, decentralized and often creative forms of public protest, the constant and often caustic interactions on social media — or crucially, the first encounters on the receiving end of state brutality — the pedagogic imprint left behind will take years to be fully measured.

These innovations have laid the map of a new world now emerging and exposed the unshakeable tenacity of a youth with little left to lose. The resistance of the establishment may only forestall, but not prevent, this long and necessary march toward a changing of the guard. Yet should the élites opt again for oppression and confrontation over conciliation, they will find on their paths a generation ready to rise again. For indeed if the 2012 mobilization was the "victory of a generation armed with a complete mastery of contemporary communications tools,"[20] the next can only showcase one grown wiser, harder and more politically astute from its battles in the trenches of the student spring. "It's said that generations are formed when they are twenty years old," reflected Nadeau-Dubois one year on from the strike. "The largest social movement in Québec's history has marked us and has instilled an entire generation with a way of viewing politics that will be determinant for the rest of their lives."[21]

What will remain of the Printemps érable? Likely a great deal indeed. More, perhaps, with each day that passes where the élites persist in their discredited march to the tune of their insular interests and ideals. More with each destructive action they take that imperils the common resources and ecosystems on which the greying future will depend. And more, without any shadow of a doubt, with each young *carré rouge* that steps forth from the shadows to assume their full place in society and demand a just tomorrow for them and their children to be. Ignore it as the élites may, history has taken a step forward. Failing to acknowledge the rising tide will carry a cost that will grow steeper with each new day of denial. For trapped within its echo chamber, a political establishment long since fissured from the people seems incapable of keeping its ear to the streets and its finger on the popular pulse — or its eyes on the *casseroles* hanging restlessly in the cupboards.

NOTES

Introduction

1 According to the Gini index of income inequality, Québec is a notably more equal society than Canada, while both are significantly more equal than the United States. See Conference Board of Canada, "Income Inequality," at <conferenceboard.ca/hcp/details/society/income-inequality.aspx>; and Lamoureux and Bourque 2010: 4.

2 A Forum Research poll of 1,589 Quebecers conducted by random automated phone calls on February 23, 2012, found opposition to the tuition increase at 66 percent within the 18–34 age demographic, while the 55+ group supported it by 57 percent. The wide-ranging poll, with a margin of error estimated at +/- 2.5 percent, 19 times out of 20, may be found on the FECQ's page on Scribd: <scribd.com/doc/82987495/Quebec-Issues-Poll-Forum-Research>. A CROP poll of 1,000 web respondents conducted March 15–19 found the 18–34 group opposing the tuition hike by a margin of 60 percent, with 55+ respondents supporting it by a margin of 61 percent. The non-probabilistic poll has no margin of error; the complete poll and methodology may be viewed at <ledevoir.com/documents/pdf/sondageFECQ.pdf>. Those findings are corroborated by three Léger polls with smaller sample sizes, between 400–613 web respondents conducted on March 22, March 29 and May 11. These found opposition to the tuition hike among the younger 18–24 cohort at 74 percent, 58 percent and 69 percent respectively, with support from those aged 55 and older at 74 percent, 62 percent and 66 percent. The fluctuation is likely attributable in large part to larger margins of error, at +/- 4 percent (March 22) and 4.9 percent (March 29 and May 11), 19 times out of 20. All three are available on Léger's website, in order: <legermarketing.com/admin/upload/publi_pdf/Sondage_express_Journal_de_Montreal_Greve_etudiante_22_mars_2012.pdf>; <legermarketing.com/admin/upload/publi_pdf/Sondage_express_Journal_de_Montreal_Greve_etudiante_29_mars_2012.pdf>; <legermarketing.com/admin/upload/publi_pdf/Sondage_JDM_Greve_etudiante_11_mai_2012.pdf>. For a full discussion, see Chapter 11.

3 Throughout this book, the terms ASSÉ and CLASSE will often appear to be interchangeable, but this is inaccurate. The ASSÉ is the permanent core around which the provisional Coalition large de l'ASSÉ was formed in December 2011, to be disbanded in November of 2012 after the strike had ended. The term CLASSE is therefore used only to refer to the organization during this time frame. Otherwise, the ASSÉ is used.

Chapter 1

1 Rocher 2004: 7.
2 Lacoursière 2007: 17.
3 Dickinson and Young 2008: 369.
4 Ibid.: 337–38.
5 Ibid.: 329; Pigeon n.d.b.
6 Dickinson and Young 2008: 326.
7 Roberts 1963: 3–5.

NOTES

8   Dickinson and Young 2008: 331; Roberts 1963: 3–5.

9   Pigeon n.d.b; Dickinson and Young 2008: 303, 345, 353.

10   Ayotte-Thompson and Freeman 2012: 4; see also Pigeon n.d.a.

11   CBC online n.d.

12   Guay n.d.a.

13   Dickinson and Young 2008: 351–52.

14   Ibid.: 345, 349, 351.

15   Pigeon n.d.a; Paquet 2011: 51–52.

16   *Commission royale d'enquête sur l'enseignement dans la province du Québec* (Parent Report), vol. 5, paragraph 600 (my translation).

17   Parent Report, vol. 5, paragraphs 611–21.

18   Parent Report, vol. 5, paragraph 590 (my translation).

19   Bélanger 1984: 5, 7. For a brief discussion, see Marsan 2005: 49–52.

20   Bélanger 1984: 5, 7–8.

21   Marsan 2005: 61–62.

22   Bélanger 1984: 8; Lacoursière 2007: 18; ASSÉ 2005: 5; Marsan 2005: 52.

23   Lacoursière 2007: 18; Marsan 2005: 50–52; Bélanger 1984: 8.

24   Bélanger 1984: 9, 14, 24–25, 28–29; Lacoursière 2007: 19; Marsan 2005: 51–52.

25   See Lacoursière 2007: 19; Ayotte-Thompson and Freeman 2012: 4.

26   Doray and Pelletier 1999: 39.

27   Lacoursière 2007: 19–20; ASSÉ 2005: 5; Renaud 1996: 19; Bélanger 1984: 6–7, 27; Ayotte-Thompson and Freeman 2012: 4.

28   Lacoursière 2007: 20; Renaud 1996: 22; Marsan 2005: 52. For more on the strike, see Bélanger 1984: 39–43.

29   Bélanger 1984: 6, 17.

30   See the United Nations Office of the High Commissioner for Human Rights 1976.

31   Renaud 1996: 29.

32   Bélanger 1984: 14, 47–49; Lacoursière 2007: 20; Marsan 2005: 52–56; Renaud 1996: 46–47.

33   Bélanger 1984: 180–81.

34   Lacoursière 2007: 69; Bélanger 1984: 196.

35   Ayotte-Thompson and Freeman 2012: 4; Lacoursière 2007: 20; ASSÉ 2005: 5. For a fuller chronology and discussion, see also Renaud 1996: 23–36; and Bélanger 1984: 54–55, 69–75, 79, 91, 104, 116.

36   Lacoursière 2007: 20–22; Renaud 1996: 20; Bélanger 1984: 42, 135.

37   Lacoursière 2007: 69. For (much) more on the ANE(E)Q, see Bélanger 1984: 80–196.

38   Bélanger 1984: 93–101, 191.

39   Lacoursière 2007: 23; ASSÉ 2005: 6.

40   Lacoursière 2007: 25.

41   Ibid. 33–34 (my translation).

42   For more on the divergences that led to the proliferation of associations, see Lacoursière 2007: 23–24 and Bélanger 1984: 162–63, 188–93.

43   Lacoursière 2007: 25; Bélanger 1984: 171.

44   Bélanger 1984: 193–95.

45   For a fuller discussion, see Lacoursière 2007: 25; ASSÉ 2005: 7.

46   Lacoursière 2007: 27.

47   Ibid.: 62–63.

48   Ibid.: 60–63; see also St-Pierre and Ethier 2013: 92–94.

49   St-Pierre and Ethier 2013: 93–94.

50   Lacoursière 2007: 35–36, 43, 45; ASSÉ 2005: 7–8; Renaud 1996: 37–40.

51   Lacoursière 2007: 35–36, 43, 45; Renaud 1996: 39.

52   Lacoursière 2007: 37; Renaud 1996: 39.

53   Lacoursière 2007: 46; Renaud 1996: 40–41.

54   Renaud 1996: 41.

55   Lacoursière 2007: 84; ASSÉ 2005: 11.

56   Lacoursière 2007: 46–48, 82–90; ASSÉ 2005: 11–13.

57   Lacoursière 2007: 112. See also ASSÉ 2005: 11–16; Renaud 1996: 42–45.

58   Lacoursière 2007: 69–73; Renaud 1996: 47.

59   Renaud 1996: 36–37; Marsan 2005: 46.

60   For a fuller discussion of the new approach, see Lacoursière 2007: 148–56; Renaud 1996: 36–37; Marsan 2005: 64.

61   Lacoursière 2007: 148–56.

62   Lacoursière 2007: 72. See FEUQ, "Structure" at <feuq.qc.ca/a-propos/structure/> and FECQ, "Structure" at <fecq.org/structure>.

63   Lacoursière 2007: 148.

64   Ibid.: 87, 91, 96; Renaud 1996: 45.

65   Lacoursière 2007: 96, 100.

66   Ibid.: 135.

67   Ibid.: 103. Renaud (1996: 45) thus labels the federations "the student right."

68   Lacoursière 2007: 117–20; Renaud 1996: 45. For more on the MDE, see Le Mouvement pour le droit à l'éducation (MDE) 2005: 81–101.

69   For more on the creation of the ASSÉ and its alter-globalization mobilizations, see Moysan-Lapointe 2003: 102–107.

70   St-Pierre and Ethier 2013: 78–79. For an indepth account of the ASSÉ's origins, see Moysan-Lapointe 2003: 102–107; Lacoursière 2007: 167–69. For an indepth account of the rise of horizontalism and network structures of organization as originated within the alter-globalization movement, see Juris 2008.

71   Lacoursière 2007: 163. For complete statutes and regulations, see ASSÉ 2013: 8–9.

72   The ASSÉ's website makes explicit reference to the French students' *Charte de Grenoble* and its foundational ideal of the student as a young intellectual worker. See <asse-solidarite.qc.ca/asse/principes/>.

73   Frappier, Poulin and Rioux 2012: 61. For a discussion of the banks' role in the Québec loans and grants system, see Pineault 2006: 31 and Ancelovici and Dupuis-Déri 2014: 13–14.

74   Côté 2006: 23; Lapan 2006: 18. For a fuller chronology of events, see Chiasson-Lebel 2006: 72–80.

75   Chiasson-Lebel 2006: 75.

76   Lacoursière 2007: 171–72; Frappier, Poulin and Rioux 2012: 62.

77   Lacoursière 2007: 168.

78   Ibid.: 168–72; Lafrance 2006: 38. For more on the divergence of tactics, see Chiasson-Lebel 2006: 74–79.

79   Lacoursière 2007: 170. For more on the ASSÉ's demands and tactics, see Frappier, Poulin and Rioux 2012: 63; Lapan 2006: 15–17, 19; Boustany, García and Picard 2006: 42–43; Coutu and Dion 2006: esp. 48–49; Chiasson-Lebel 2006: 72, 75–78.

80 Lapan 2006: 17.

81 Lacoursière 2007: 170–71; Lapan 2006: 16–17.

82 Lemay and Laperrière 2012: 428.

83 Frappier, Poulin and Rioux 2012: 64–65.

84 Chiasson-Lebel 2006: 74-5; Lacoursière 2007: 171. See also Boustany, García and Picard 2006: 42.

85 Radio-Canada 2005. See also Frappier, Poulin and Rioux 2012: 65–66; Lacoursière 2007: 172.

86 Chiasson-Lebel 2006: 78–79; Lacoursière 2007: 172; Frappier, Poulin and Rioux 2012: 65.

87 Chiasson-Lebel 2006: 79; Frappier, Poulin and Rioux 2012: 66.

88 See Côté 2006 for a discussion of the strike's failure; for recriminations against the FEUQ see Coutu and Dion 2006: 52–53.

89 Lacoursière 2007: 173.

90 Ibid.: 174.

91 Barrette 2012: 63.

Chapter 2

1 Lavarenne 2013: 32 (my translation).

2 Martin and Tremblay-Pépin 2011: 8.

3 Doray and Pelletier 1999: 55.

4 Ratel 2006: 90. See also Doray and Pelletier 1999: 55–63.

5 La Presse canadienne 2012b. For the previous portfolios, see Radio-Canada 2011c.

6 Gingras, Godin and Trépanier 1999: 85–86.

7 Martin and Ouellet 2011: 104–105; see also Gingras, Godin and Trépanier 1999: 70, 82, 86, 90–91; Doray and Pelletier 1999: 55–56.

8 Doray and Pelletier 1999: 56, 62; Boisvert 1997: 55–58; see also Ratel 2006: 86.

9 Martin and Ouellet 2011: 28; Ministère de l'éducation, du loisir et du sport (MELS) 2011: 11.

10 Martin and Tremblay-Pépin 2011: 5.

11 Martin and Ouellet 2011: 106–107.

12 Massumi 2012. See also Martin and Ouellet 2011: 104, 109. For a wider discussion on the integration from the 1980s onward between research and educational policies and economic objectives, see Doray and Pelletier 1999: 55–56. See also Gingras, Godin and Trépanier 1999: 70, 82, 86, 90–91.

13 Boisvert 2013; Seymour et al. 2012.

14 Boisvert 2013.

15 Hémond, Maltais and Umbriaco 2010: 5.

16 Ibid.: 5–6.

17 The Îlot Voyageur project engaged by UQÀM is the most well-known of these misman-agement debacles. Four professors at Université de Montréal condemned the "useless" satellite campuses and real estate misadventures of Québec's universities in an op-ed piece published in Le Devoir. See Seymour et al. 2012; see also Boisvert 2013.

18 Hémond, Maltais and Umbriaco 2010: 4, 6, 12.

19 The starving of education that has resulted from these transformations led 2,400 academics to sign an open letter in support of the CLASSE's campaign during the 2012

strike; see Guilmain, Le Saux and Thellen 2012. See Chapter 6 for a fuller discussion of the Professeurs contre la hausse.

20 Martin and Ouellet 2011: 28. For more on the increase in bureaucratic costs associated with managing research funds and the rerouting of funds away from pedagogic activities, see Martin and Ouellet 2011: 98, 106–107. See also Boisvert 1997: 1–3, 48–49.

21 Boisvert 1997: 90.

22 For a thorough discussion and explanation of the "*réseau universitaire fantôme*," see Boisvert 1997: 29–40.

23 Boisvert 1997: 16, 35.

24 MELS 2011: 4.

25 Ibid.: 3.

26 Martin and Ouellet 2011: 31–32. The authors are citing 2008–09 figures from the Québec government; see Ministère de l'éducation, du loisir et du sport (MELS) and Ministère de l'enseignement supérieur, de la recherche, de la science et de la technologie (MESRST) 2013: 40; MELS 2011: 11.

27 Fédération des associations étudiantes universitaires québécoises en éducation permanente (FAEUQEP) 2013: 6; see also Ouimet 2012.

28 Bergeron 2012a.

29 For a wider discussion on the misfunding of universities, see Boisvert 1997: 63.

30 Boisvert 1997: 1–3.

31 Martin and Ouellet 2011: 29 and Martin and Tremblay-Pépin 2011: 9.

32 Giroux 2006: 185 (my translation).

33 Boisvert 1997: 49.

34 Cited in Posca 2013 (my translation).

35 Posca 2013.

36 Boisvert 1997: 49 (my translation).

37 Ibid.

38 Martin and Tremblay-Pépin 2011: 9. This figure presumably includes her total base salary and only part of her additional benefits, as outlined in note 50.

39 A 2012 report by the FEUQ listed the salaries and additional benefits of eighteen university presidents in Québec as of August 2010. McGill University's Heather Munroe-Blum sat atop the pinnacle with $358,173 in salary plus $360,045 in additional "benefits," while the Université de Montréal's Luc Vinet followed close behind with $339,031 (and $24,327 in benefits). See Fédération étudiante universitaire du Québec (FEUQ) 2012: 3–4. Radio-Canada engaged in the same investigation and found similar numbers; see Radio-Canada 2012i and CBC News online 2010; see also CBC News online 2012 and Serebrin 2011.

40 Radio-Canada found that Concordia University's budget for salaries exploded by 180 percent in this period, but the administration explained that it was due to a modification in their manner of calculating the figure. See Radio-Canada 2012i.

41 Posca 2013.

42 Lacoursière 2007: 91; Vierstraete 2007: 40.

43 See Doray 2012.

44 Vierstraete 2007: 40.

45 MELS and MESRST 2013: 44.

46 Martin and Pépin-Tremblay 2011: 3.

47   Cited in Dufour 2012.
48   Martin and Tremblay-Pépin 2011: 16.
49   Dufour 2012.
50   Gervais 2014.
51   Finances Québec 2011: 39–49.
52   Martin and Tremblay-Pépin 2011: 11–14; Doray 2012. In 2009, average debt in Québec for students enrolled in their final year of an undergraduate degree (and who took out loans) was $16,600 compared to a Canadian average of $29,327, with the discrepancy attributable to much higher tuition levels in the rest of the country. In tune with the sharp climb in Québec after 1989, Statistics Canada's data shows that the province posted the second highest increase in the country for student debt levels between 1986 and 1995. Note that all figures have been adjusted by the author to represent 2014 constant dollars. See Council of Ministers of Education, Canada (CMEC) 2000: chapter 3.5, section F.
53   Martin and Tremblay-Pépin 2011: 11–14.
54   Cited in Nadeau-Dubois 2013a: 91 (my translation).
55   Cited in Nadeau-Dubois 2013a: 180–81. The excerpt from Charest's autobiography is cited in Robitaille 2012a; Beauchamp is cited in TVA Nouvelles 2012.
56   It is Nadeau-Dubois (2013a: 180) who uses the term "rhetorical invention" (my translation).
57   The French term "judiciarisation" has no direct equivalent in English, so I have simply anglicized the original word. It refers to the process whereby the courts are tasked with intervening in a conflict that could have been resolved via other (in this case political) means.
58   Massumi 2012. See also Martin and Ouellet 2011: 23.
59   Massumi 2012; Assemblée nationale du Québec 2012: 6.
60   Julien 2012: 153 (my translation).
61   Ibid.
62   See Martin and Ouellet 2011: 73.
63   This passage is related in Nadeau-Dubois 2013a: 89. Original source: Derrida 2011: 11 (my translation, emphasis added).
64   This passage is also related in Nadeau-Dubois 2013a: 90. Original source: Woodsworth 2009.
65   Related in Nadeau-Dubois 2013a: 91. Also available in Gervais 2011. My translation.
66   Nadeau-Dubois 2013a: 91.
67   Cited in Klein 2014: 60.
68   While less clear than the CLASSE/ASSÉ's full-throated defence of humanist ideals, the FEUQ does officially espouse a "humanist education as a societal choice," as described in the FEUQ's mission statement published on their website (see <feuq.qc.ca/a-propos/>). The quote on the educational model comes from Julien 2012: 153 (my translation).
69   For a more expansive discussion of this transformation in the state's conception of education, see Hurteau, Hébert and Fortier 2010: 27; Massumi 2012; Martin and Pépin-Tremblay 2011; Lamoureux 2012; and Lamarre 2012.

Chapter 3

1   Hessel 2010: 14 (my translation).
2   Downey 2007: 108.
3   Swyngedouw 2011: 371.
4   Crouch 2004: 4.
5   Deriving from tsarist Russian, Merriam-Webster defines a "Potemkin village" as an "impressive façade or show designed to hide an undesirable fact or condition."
6   Badiou and Finkielkraut 2010: 35 (my translation).
7   Badiou 2012: esp. 15–17.
8   Swyngedouw 2011: 371.
9   Ibid.
10 Žižek 2002: 303.
11 For more on the impact of neoliberal reforms on our democracies, see Purcell 2008 and Giroux 2004.
12 *The Economist* 2012.
13 Ibid.; Popiden 2012.
14 Popiden 2012.
15 Stepanova 2011: 1.
16 Ibid.; *The Economist* 2012.
17 Huang 2011; Stepanova 2011: 2.
18 Stepanova 2011: 1–2.
19 Ibid.; Shapiro 2009; Huang 2011.
20 Levinson and Coker 2011.
21 Huang 2011.
22 Sadiki 2012.
23 Hessel 2010: 9 (my translation).
24 Ibid.: 10–11.
25 Hessel 2011: 16.
26 Hessel 2010: 12 (my translation).
27 *Le Monde* 2013.
28 Kotz 2009: 305–308; Crotty 2009: 563–65.
29 Marques 2011.
30 Ibid.
31 See Silva 2011: 58–61.
32 Oikonomakis and Roos 2013: 8.
33 See Silva 2011: 60–61.
34 For more on the Indignados, see Castells 2012: 110–55 and Gerbaudo 2012: 76–101.
35 Silva 2011: 61. See also Castells 2012: 110–55 and Gerbaudo 2012: 76–101.
36 Carrión 2011: 32.
37 Cala 2011; Robinson 2011: 8.
38 Robinson 2011: 8.
39 Silva 2011: 62.
40 Baiocchi and Ganuza 2012: 43.
41 Silva 2011: 61; Robinson 2011: 8; Carrión 2011: 30; Cala 2011: 3.
42 Baiocchi and Ganuza 2012: 42.
43 For more on the Indignados, see Castells 2012: 110–55 and Gerbaudo 2012: 76–101.

44 Pechtelidis 2011: 449.
45 Ibid.: 459.
46 Ibid.: 461.
47 Ibid.: 452.
48 Silva 2011: 63.
49 Vradis and Dalakoglou 2011: 336.
50 Silva 2011: 63; Gourgouris 2011.
51 Douzinas 2011.
52 Gourgouris 2011.
53 Douzinas 2011.
54 Gourguris (2011) relates the Greek protesters' demand for "immediate democracy" — deliberately articulated to retain a double meaning of both "democracy now" and of a democracy that is direct and without mediation.
55 Schwartz 2011.
56 Eifling 2011.
57 Roy 2011.
58 Schwartz 2011.
59 Kroll 2011.
60 See Takethesquare.net, specifically <howtocamp.takethesquare.net/2012/03/06/how-to-cook-a-non-violent-revolution-v2-0/>.
61 Hardt and Negri 2011.
62 DiMaggio and Street 2011: 11.
63 Ibid.
64 Tormey 2012: 134.
65 For more on Occupy Wall Street's discourse and development, see Castells 2012: 156–217; Gerbaudo 2012: 102–33.
66 Oikonomakis and Roos 2013: 1.
67 Hurteau, Hébert and Fortier 2010: 37; Martin and Tremblay-Pépin 2011: 17.
68 Schepper and Handal 2012: 1.
69 Finances Québec 2011: 23.
70 Martin and Pépin-Trembay 2011: 17.
71 The Argentine revolt that erupted in 2001 in response to the collapse of the banking sector in the Latin American nation was another crucial precursor to ows and the Indignados. The protest cries of the Argentine street at the time, captured in the mantra "*Que no quede ni uno solo!* ("Not one should remain!") in retrospect rang as a prescient warning to governments the world over who might surrender their country — and with it, their democratic legitimacy — to the power of global financial and corporate élites. See Sitrin 2011: 9.
72 Coalition large de l'Association pour une solidarité syndicale (CLASSE) 2012 (my translation).
73 Ibid.

Chapter 4

1 Tillard and Miville-Allard 2013: 9 (my translation).
2 Charest 2002.
3 Pineault 2012: 37.

4 Ibid.

5 For a discussion of Québec's neo-corporatist model, see Pineault 2012: 36–37.

6 For a discussion of the neoliberal model of state-society relations that Charest imported, see Dufour 2012a: 11–12.

7 Pineault 2012: 39.

8 Dufour 2012a: 12.

9 Montpetit 2006: 137.

10 Dufour 2012a: 12.

11 Bélanger 1984: 193–95.

12 See ibid.

13 See Julien 2012: 156 (my translation); see also Forest 2013: 47.

14 Chouinard 2004; Radio-Canada 2004.

15 Chouinard 2004.

16 Ibid.; Lessard 2012a.

17 Guay n.d.b.

18 Ibid.

19 Centre de documentation sur l'éducation des adultes et la condition féminine (CDEACF) 2007; LCN 2007; Dutrisac 2007.

20 In 2003, a series of anti-union legislation was pushed through the Assemblée nationale this way, launching large-scale mobilizations; see Frappier, Poulin and Rioux 2012: 59. In 2004, an emergency law was passed imposing a collective agreement on public sector workers with average 1.2 percent annual raises (far below inflation) (Frappier, Poulin and Rioux 2012: 61).

21 Pineault. 2012: 38.

22 St-Pierre and Ethier 2013: 23.

23 This comes from the 2008 Montmarquette Report. See Montmarquette, Facal and Lachapelle 2008: XVI–II, 8, 14–15. The full report and a condensed version are both available in English at <groupes.finances.gouv.qc.ca/GTTSP/index_en.asp>. See also Dutrisac 2008.

24 Montmarquette, Facal and Lachapelle 2008: XV.

25 See Comité consultatif sur l'économie et les finances publiques 2009.

26 Montmarquette, Facal and Lachapelle 2008: XVI.

27 Ibid.: XV–XVI.

28 Canada Revenue Agency n.d.; Revenu Québec n.d. For international corporate tax rate comparisons, see KPMG n.d.

29 Hurteau, Hébert and Fortier 2010: 37. See Brown and Mintz 2012: esp. 26–28 and Fortier 2013.

30 Richer 2012.

31 Hurteau, Hébert and Fortier 2010: 36.

32 La Presse canadienne 2010b.

33 Castonguay 2011.

34 Frappier, Poulin and Rioux 2012: 38.

35 See table in Hurteau, Hébert and Fortier 2010: 36. For more on the trend away from progressive taxation and the rise in income inequalities, see Fortier and Tremblay-Pépin 2013: esp. 7–9.

36 Couturier and Schepper 2010: 6, 29. See also Fortier and Tremblay-Pépin 2013: esp. 6–9.

38 Pineault 2012: 30.
39 For an indepth analysis of the plan, see Schepper and Handal 2012.
40 Gouvernement du Québec 2011; Desjardins 2012. See also Shields 2013.
41 Vérificateur général du Québec 2009: ch. 2, p. 3.
42 Dutrisac 2010a.
43 Dutrisac 2009.
44 Robitaille 2010a; Robillard 2010b; Robillard 2010a. See also Marrissal 2010.
45 Dutrisac 2011; Descôteaux 2011.
46 Larocque and Robillard 2010; La Presse canadienne 2010a.
47 Robitaille 2010a.
48 Dutrisac 2010b.
49 Myles and Bourgault-Côté 2013.
50 Robitaille 2010b; Boisvert 2010; Kathleen Lévesque 2012.
51 Chouinard 2010.
52 Radio-Canada 2011f.
53 Radio-Canada 2012b.
54 Duchesneau 2011: section 2.1 (my translation). See also Larouche and de Pierrebourg 2011.
55 Duchesneau 2011: section 7 (my translation).
56 Ibid.: section 12.2 (my translation).
57 Ibid.: sections 6, 10.1, 10.4, 11.2, 12.1, F (my translation). See also Noël 2011.
58 Larouche and de Pierrebourg 2011; Radio-Canada 2011b.
59 Noël 2011.
60 Duchesneau 2011: section 12.1.
61 Larouche and de Pierrebourg 2011 (my translation).
62 Duchesneau 2011: section 12.1.
63 Lessard 2013.
64 Duchesneau 2011: section 9.2.
65 See Duchesneau 2011: sections 5.3, 6 and 9.2.
66 Duchesneau 2011: section 12.1 (my translation).
67 de Grandpré 2013.
68 La Presse canadienne 2011b; Radio-Canada 2011a.

Chapter 5

1   Moses 2013: 175 (my translation).
2   Pineault 2012: 39.
3   St-Pierre and Ethier 2013: 23.
4   Ibid. (my translation).
5   Ibid.: 23–24.
6   Pineault 2012: 38.
7   St-Pierre and Ethier 2013: 23–24.
8   Ibid.: 56–57.
9   Lemay and Laperrière 2012: 428.
10 While 63,000-strong, TaCEQ, born in 2009, is not considered a truly national student association as its members are limited to Laval, Sherbrooke and McGill universities.

This fact, in addition to its limited nature as a discussion group and facilitator rather than a robust association (e.g., members pay no fees), explains the lack of attention brought to this organization in accounts of the student spring. The TaCEQ also represented a minute proportion of student strikers in the spring of 2012, estimated at 6 percent. See M. Robert 2012: 31.

11   Gervais 2010.

12   St-Pierre and Ethier 2013: 56.

13   Barrette 2012: 65.

14   Dufour 2012a: 19–21.

15   Ibid.: 23.

16   Cited in Lefebvre 2013.

17   For an explanation of the diversity (and escalation) of tactics model, see St-Pierre and Ethier 2013: 47–57.

18   St-Pierre and Ethier 2013: 58–59; M. Robert 2012: 31.

19   See Radio-Canada 2012g and La Presse canadienne 2012g; see also St-Pierre and Ethier 2013: 58–61.

20   St-Pierre and Ethier (2013: 59) claim the FEUQ upheld the entente while the FECQ did not, since it repeatedly criticized actions of CLASSE affiliates and offered to sit down with the government without them present. This view is corroborated by Frappier, Poulin and Rioux (2012: 85, 101–102), who explicitly credit Desjardins and Nadeau-Dubois with maintaining student unity.

21   Barrette 2012: 65.

22   Lemay and Laperrière 2012: 428; St-Pierre and Ethier 2013: 28.

23   La Presse canadienne 2011a.

24   Barrette 2012: 65 (my translation).

25   St-Pierre and Ethier 2013: 24–25.

26   Frappier, Poulin and Rioux 2012: 22–23.

27   St-Pierre and Ethier 2013: 26–27.

28   Ibid.: 28.

29   Ibid.

30   Frappier, Poulin and Rioux 2012: 96; St-Pierre and Ethier 2013: 92.

31   Nadeau-Dubois 2013a: 109–18.

32   St-Pierre and Ethier 2013: 25, 98–103.

33   Ibid.

34   St-Pierre and Ethier 2013: 123.

35   Martin and Tremblay-Pépin 2011: 17; Couturier, Hurteau and Pépin-Tremblay 2010: 2, 8–9, 12.

36   St-Pierre and Ethier 2013: 134. For more on corruption under Charest, see Chapter 4.

37   Radio-Canada 2011e; FECQ 2012.

38   Radio-Canada 2011e.

39   Gervais 2012e; Sanschagrin and Gagnon 2014: 290; Collectif de débrayage 2013: 54. For more on the PQ's turn toward austerity at the expense of its social-democratic traditions and base, see Bernier 2005: 146–47, 152.

40   Fédération étudiante universitaire du Québec (FEUQ) 2011.

41   See Desjardins 2013: 108–15.

42   St-Pierre and Ethier 2013: 103–105.

43 Ibid.: 47–48.

44 Ibid.: 135. The two student federations have official policies in favour of Québec independence dating back to the 1995 referendum yet refrained from evoking the issue during the 2012 crisis.

45 St-Pierre and Ethier 2013: 47–57.

46 Ibid.: 63–65.

47 Ibid.: 57–58.

48 Ibid.: 61–62.

49 Ibid.: 92, 114.

50 Nadeau-Dubois 2013a: 36.

51 St-Pierre and Ethier 2013: 30.

52 Ibid.: 114–15.

53 M. Robert 2012: 31.

54 Ibid.

55 Nadeau-Dubois confirms the lesson learned in an interview with France's *Paris Match*; see Dancoing 2012.

56 St-Pierre and Ethier 2013: 139. For a discussion of the symbol, see Gaudreau 2012; Blanchard 2014. For the FECQ leadership, the red square apparently signified the urgency of the situation and the need to halt the increase (i.e., evoking the red of a stop sign); see FECQ, "*Pourquoi le carré rouge?*" at <fecq.org/Pourquoi-le-carre-rouge>. The FEUQ's Martine Desjardins preferred the denotation of indebtedness, as cited in Agence QMI and TVA Nouvelles 2012.

57 St-Pierre and Ethier 2013: 152.

58 Ibid.: 149–52.

59 Ibid.: 151, 161–62, 171.

60 Ibid.: 171–72.

61 Ibid.: 156–59.

62 There exist many meanings to the term "*maNUfestations.*" See St-Pierre and Ethier 2013: 162–63 and Poulin 2012. *MaNUfestation* is a play on words that modifies the French word for demonstration by replacing the "ni" in "*manifestation*" with a "*nu*" for "nude."

63 St-Pierre and Ethier 2013: 162–63. See also *Urbania*'s special summer 2012 edition, *Rouge*, produced in collaboration with the École de la montagne rouge and the National Film Board, available for free at <urbania.ca/magazines/3182/greve>. An interactive online companion art piece was also created at <rouge.onf.ca>.

64 St-Pierre and Ethier 2013: 186–87. For a thorough discussion of the rise of networks, see Chapter 11.

65 St-Pierre and Ethier 2013: 185, 189.

66 Ibid.: 186–89.

67 Ibid.: 197.

68 Ibid.: 189.

69 This will be discussed at length in Chapter 7.

70 St-Pierre and Ethier 2013: 186, 188, 192–95.

71 Cited in Downey 2007: 121; see also Van Alstyne and Brynjolfsson 2005: 851–68.

72 St-Pierre and Ethier 2013: 189–90. For more on the online dominance of the CLASSE and its allies, see Chapter 6. Largely free of political and corporate control (despite thus far, ownership), it is the resulting autonomy of Internet (and especially social media)

spaces that is identified by Manuel Castells as key to incubating the networked social movements of recent years (see Castells 2012: 221–24).

Chapter 6

1   Briand 2013: 19 (my translation).
2   These are all taken from columns published in the *Journal de Montréal* and *Journal de Québec*, both owned by Québécor. Joseph Facal was the one who inferred a similarity between the CLASSE, Pyongyang and Havana. See Nadeau-Dubois 2013a: 134, 137.
3   Tremblay-Pépin 2013b.
4   Tremblay-Pépin 2013a.
5   A study by Influence Communication in December 2012 found that Québec's media space is dominated overwhelmingly by those on the right of the political spectrum. See Nadeau-Dubois 2013a: 142–44.
6   Some of the most excessive attacks on students from the corporate media are related in Nadeau-Dubois 2013a: 129–44.
7   La Presse canadienne 2012i.
8   Bonenfant, Glinoer and Lapointe 2013: 156–57, 184, 202. For a discussion of the union leaderships' positioning (and hence, motives) during the student crisis, see "*Les syndicats ont-ils manqué le Printemps québécois?*" in Bonenfant, Glinoer and Lapointe 2013: 156–57.
9   Guilmain, Le Saux and Thellen 2012 (my translation).
10   Bonenfant, Glinoer and Lapointe 2013: 39.
11   The text, originally published in *Le Devoir*, is reproduced in its entirety in Bonenfant, Glinoer and Lapointe 2013: 39–41. For more on the discourse and development of the Indignados movement, see Castells 2012: 110–55; Gerbaudo 2012: 76–101; Silva 2011: 58–65; Baiocchi and Ganuza 2012: 42–45; and Carrión 2011: 30–32. For more on Occupy Wall Street, see Castells 2012: 156–217; Gerbaudo 2012: 102–33; and Hardt and Negri 2011.
12   Guilmain, Le Saux and Thellen 2012.
13   Ibid.
14   Ibid.
15   Gervais 2012h.
16   See Parents contre la hausse, <parentscontrelahausse.org> (my translation).
17   Ibid. (my translation).
18   Ibid. (my translation; emphasis mine).
19   Bonenfant, Glinoer and Lapointe 2013: 59; Bélair-Cirino 2012c.
20   Bonenfant, Glinoer and Lapointe 2013: 200.
21   See Gervais 2012d (my translation).
22   The comment was made during the press conference announcing the letter. See Ève Lévesque 2012 (my translation).
23   Collective of authors 2012 (my translation).
24   Ibid.
25   Ibid.
26   See Bonenfant, Glinoer and Lapointe 2013: 76–79.
27   Morin 2012.
28   Bonenfant, Glinoer and Lapointe 2013: 152.

29 Ibid.: 223.
30 Gervais 2012f (my translation).
31 Leroux, Nadeau and Rocher 2012; Rocher and Perrier 2012; Gervais 2012f.
32 Ducros 2012 (my translation).
33 Pineault 2012: 45.
34 St-Pierre and Ethier 2013: 189–90.
35 There is scant research on Twitter users in the peer-reviewed literature, but private sector data analysis enterprises have been more active in pursuing such research, such as the study cited above performed by Beevolve, a company specializing in social media monitoring.
36 A June 2009 study performed by Sysomos, a company specializing in social media monitoring for businesses, found a similar pattern among Twitter users, with 65 percent of all self-disclosed Twitter users being under the age of twenty-five; see Cheng, Evans and Singh 2012. A May 2012 report by Pew Research found that 31 percent of Internet users aged 18–24 used Twitter, and that 20 percent use it on a "typical day." Those aged 25–44 used it half as much, with use between 16–17 percent and "typical day" usage between 9–11 percent. Twitter use continues to drop off as age rises, with the 45–64 group at 9 percent usage (4 percent on a "typical day") and 65 and above users at 4 percent ("typical day" usage 1 percent) (Smith and Brenner 2012).
37 See Bonenfant, Glinoer and Lapointe 2013: 69–70.
38 Ibid.: 144. See also Barrette 2012: 109.
39 See Le Devoir 2012a (my translation).
40 Note that an unknown but likely significant volume of tweets would not show up in his analysis if marked with no hashtag (often the case in user-to-user exchanges) or with rarely used ones. See Le Devoir 2012a.
41 To view the graphs and learn more about his methodology, see Beauschene 2012a and 2012c; see also Le Devoir 2012a.
42 Le Devoir 2012a.
43 See Beauschene 2012b. A histogram in the graph also illustrates the volume of tweets plotted chronologically against key events of the spring, revealing a steady trend of intensification as the crisis wore on. The daily peak of 11,733 tweets was attained on May 18 following passage of Bill 78 (discussed in Chapter 9).
44 St-Pierre and Ethier 2013: 187.
45 Bonenfant, Glinoer and Lapointe 2013: 94.

Chapter 7

1 Faubert 2013: 84 (my translation).
2 To view a selection of the École's work, see the special summer 2012 edition of *Urbania* called *Rouge*, produced in collaboration with the École de la montagne rouge and the National Film Board; available online at <urbania.ca/magazines/3182/greve>. See also Doyon 2012; Petrowski 2012b. Some more instances of their work are reproduced in Petrowski 2012a.
3 Montréal has been North America's only UNESCO-designated City of Design since 2006 (part of the Creative Cities Network), with the municipal government managing its own Bureau de Design. See <mtlunescodesign.com/en/about>.
4 Olivier and Lamoureux 2014: 209–10. See Bonenfant, Glinoer and Lapointe 2013: 14–17.

5   For the Jon Lajoie song, see St-Pierre and Ethier 2013: 62. For more on "Speak Red," see Bonenfant, Glinoer and Lapointe 2013: 38 and for the "*Lipdub rouge*," 164.

6   To view this meme, see Bonenfant, Glinoer and Lapointe 2013: 61. Another featured the same photo of Beauchamp, with the caption: "Refuses to sit at the same table with the CLASSE. Eats her breakfast with the mafia"; see St-Pierre and Ethier 2013: 202 (my translation).

7   Anarchopanda's real-life alias is Julien Villeneuve, a philosophy professor at Collège de Maisonneuve and self-described "anarcho-pacifist" who supports free university education. See Guerchani 2012.

8   Olivier and Lamoureux 2014: 245–49.

9   See Bonenfant, Glinoer and Lapointe 2013: 14, 18–19, 22–23, 24–26, 30–31, 33, 64.

10   See Bonenfant, Glinoer and Lapointe 2013: 54–55 and Olivier and Lamoureux 2014: 224.

11   Simard 2012.

12   Collectif de débrayage 2013: 64.

13   Ménard, Grenier and Carbonneau 2014: 123.

14   Ibid.

15   See Collectif de débrayage 2013: 67–68; Ménard, Grenier and Carbonneau 2014: 123.

16   Bonenfant, Glinoer and Lapointe 2013: 30. See also Teisceira-Lessard 2012c.

17   Bonenfant, Glinoer and Lapointe 2013: 30; see also Teisceira-Lessard 2012c; Gervais 2012i.

18   The CLASSE privileges assembly votes over referenda because of the deliberative component, which they consider central to the democratic process, but each local association has the autonomy to decide on their own mechanisms for consultation. See St-Pierre and Ethier 2013: 77–78.

19   Bonenfant, Glinoer and Lapointe 2013: 20.

20   Ibid.: 20, 33, 40, 60–61, 124, 127. On May 14, riot police deployed pepper spray at Collège Édouard-Montpetit, and a student at Collège Rosemont suffered a concussion after being struck by a baton (Bonenfant, Glinoer and Lapointe 2013: 212).

21   See Ménard, Grenier and Carbonneau 2014: 123.

22   Collectif de débrayage 2013: 72.

23   Nadeau-Dubois 2013a: 175–76.

24   Collectif de débrayage 2013: 72–73.

25   Nadeau-Dubois 2013a: 45.

26   All strike results come from Nadeau-Dubois 2013a: 57.

27   Nadeau-Dubois 2013a: 45; Ménard, Grenier and Carbonneau 2014: 36.

28   Dufour 2012a: 6; Nadeau-Dubois 2013a: 46.

29   Young anglophones in Québec are today overwhelmingly bilingual. In 2011, Statistics Canada reported that the bilingualism of anglophone Quebecers attained a peak of over 75 percent at age fifteen, sat at 68 to 70 percent at ages twenty to twenty-five and decreased slightly to drop off significantly after age sixty-five, when it dipped below 50 percent (Lepage and Corbeil 2013).

30   Collectif de débrayage 2013: 68 (my translation).

31   Ibid.: 68–69.

32   Ibid.: 68.

33   Radio-Canada 2012l.

34 Collectif de débrayage 2013: 71; Bonenfant, Glinoer and Lapointe 2013: 20, 24–27, 40, 43, 47–51.
35 Nicoud 2012.
36 Ibid.
37 See Savard and Cyr 2014: 64–65.
38 Nicoud 2012.
39 Savard and Cyr 2014: 64–65.
40 See Savard and Cyr 2014: 64 (my translation).
41 Poirier 2012 (my translation).
42 For a brief discussion of the violence frame in the media, see Ancelovici and Dupuis-Déri 2014: 22–23.
43 See Ancelovici and Dupuis-Déri 2014: 23; Savard and Cyr 2014: 65–66.
44 See Savard and Cyr 2014: 65–66.
45 Collectif de débrayage 2013: 76–77.
46 Lemonde et al. 2013: 308.
47 Ibid.
48 McCarthy 2012; Collectif de débrayage 2013: 77–78.
49 Collectif de débrayage 2013: 77.
50 Ibid.: 78–79.
51 St-Pierre and Ethier 2013: 186.
52 Gervais 2012g.
53 Bonenfant, Glinoer and Lapointe 2013: 53; Olivier and Lamoureux 2014: 215.
54 Gervais 2012e (my translation).
55 Lagacé 2012 (my translation).
56 La Presse canadienne 2012h (my translation); Bonenfant, Glinoer and Lapointe 2013: 53.
57 La Presse canadienne 2012h.
58 Lagacé 2012 (my translation); Lemay and Laperrière 2012: 429. See also Bonenfant, Glinoer and Lapointe 2013: 60.
59 Collectif de débrayage 2013: 115 (my translation).
60 La Presse canadienne 2012h.
61 Radio-Canada 2012l.
62 Collectif de débrayage 2013: 90.
63 Ibid.: 89.
64 Ibid.
65 Lemoine and Ouardi 2010: 65 (my translation).
66 Collectif de débrayage 2013: 91; Olivier and Lamoureux 2014: 223.
67 Bonenfant, Glinoer and Lapointe 2013: 32–35, 54–57, 61.
68 Collectif de débrayage 2013: 98. See Chapter 4 for a discussion of the politicization of the appointments process by Charest.
69 Lemonde et al. 2013: 311–13; Dupuis-Déri and L'Écuyer 2013: 333.
70 Dupuis-Déri and L'Écuyer 2013: 333.
71 Lemonde et al. 2013: 311.
72 Ibid.: 325 (my translation).
73 Ibid.: 298. For more on the *Act respecting the accreditation and financing of students' association*, see Chapter 1.
74 Collectif de débrayage 2013: 98.

75 Ibid.: 94–100; Lemonde et al. 2013: 295–300.
76 Lemonde et al. 2013: 325 (my translation).
77 Ibid.: 297.
78 Nadeau-Dubois 2013a: 183–84.
79 Collectif de débrayage 2013: 96.
80 Dupuis-Déri and L'Écuyer 2013: 336.
81 Collectif de débrayage 2013: 156 (my translation). The Collectif describes the scenes in May from Rosemont and Lionel-Groulx CEGEPs.
82 Bonenfant, Glinoer and Lapointe 2013: 91; see also Chouinard and Journet 2012.
83 Bonenfant, Glinoer and Lapointe 2013: 100–101; Radio-Canada 2012k (my translation).
84 FECQ and FEUQ 2012; Radio-Canada 2012h.
85 Bonenfant, Glinoer and Lapointe 2013: 108–109; Breton 2012.
86 Radio-Canada 2012j.
87 Bonenfant, Glinoer and Lapointe 2013: 114.
88 Radio-Canada 2012g.
89 Bonenfant, Glinoer and Lapointe 2013: 132–33. For more on police repression and brutality during the student spring, see Ligue des droits et libertés et al. 2013 and Ménard, Grenier and Carbonneau 2014: esp. 198–245, 269–307, 317–38.

Chapter 8

1   Beaulieu-April 2013: 65 (my translation).
2   Collectif de débrayage 2013: 103–104.
3   Ibid.: 103.
4   Bonenfant, Glinoer and Lapointe 2013: 133.
5   See Larouche 2012; Agence QMI 2012.
6   Ménard, Grenier and Carbonneau 2014: 55.
7   Petrowski 2012b.
8   Many clips of the *Jour de la Terre* march are available on YouTube, where you can view the predominance of red squares and anti-hike slogans throughout the crowd. See also Guillemette 2012a; for photos, see Bonenfant, Glinoer and Lapointe 2013: 134–37.
9   Guillemette 2012a.
10 Bonenfant, Glinoer and Lapointe 2013: 148, 150.
11 Collectif de débrayage 2013: 117 (my translation).
12 Ibid.: 119 (my translation).
13 Ibid.
14 Nadeau-Dubois 2013a: 123 (my translation).
15 Collectif de débrayage 2013: 117.
16 Ménard, Grenier and Carbonneau 2014: 59.
17 Collectif de débrayage 2013: 119–20.
18 Bonenfant, Glinoer and Lapointe 2013: 150–51. See Radio-Canada 2012f; St-Pierre and Ethier 2013: 186.
19 Radio-Canada 2012f (my translation).
20 Allard 2012 (my translation).
21 Ibid.
22 Bonenfant, Glinoer and Lapointe 2013: 151; Radio-Canada 2012f.

23 Bonenfant, Glinoer and Lapointe 2013: 152.

24 This was the protest chant heard at the nightly marches.

25 Collectif de débrayage 2013: 128.

26 Ibid.: 129.

27 Judith Butler in a lecture delivered in Venice on September 7, 2011. A transcript has been made available care of the European Institute for Progressive Cultural Policies. See <eipcp.net/transversal/1011/butler/en>.

28 The "crisis of public space" is discussed in Gerbaudo 2012: 11, 105–106. As early as 1992, the "destruction of any truly democratic urban space" by the policies and processes of neoliberalism was decried by Davis (1992: 156), while Don Mitchell, in 1995, proclaimed the "end of public space" in the United States. See Mitchell 1995: 108; see also Brenner and Theodore 2002.

29 Bonenfant, Glinoer and Lapointe 2013: 227, 231.

30 For a full account of police abuses, see Ligue des droits et libertés et al. 2013 and Ménard, Grenier and Carbonneau 2014:esp. 198–245, 269–307, 317–38. See also Santerre and Lachapelle 2012; La Presse canadienne 2012e; Myles and Bélair-Cirino 2012.

31 Ménard, Grenier and Carbonneau 2014: 232.

32 Ibid.

33 Ménard, Grenier and Carbonneau 2014: 167–68, 232–33.

34 Lemonde et al. 2013: 308; Dupuis-Déri and L'Écuyer 2013: 329.

35 Collectif de débrayage 2013: 129.

36 Shields and Guillemette 2012.

37 Ibid.

38 Collectif de débrayage 2013: 142.

39 Ibid.: 146 (my translation).

40 Ibid.: 145–46.

41 Boivin 2012.

42 Ibid.

43 Santerre and Lachapelle 2012.

44 Ligue des droits et libertés et al. 2013: 11; Dupuis-Déri and L'Écuyer 2013: 353–54.

45 "Whose street? Our street!" is a common protest chant heard in Québec.

46 Massumi (2012) echoes the critiques of Badiou, Crouch and others pertaining to the democratic crisis engendered by neoliberalism, as discussed in Chapter 3.

47 Bonenfant, Glinoer and Lapointe 2013: 191.

48 Ibid.: 206.

49 Savard and Cyr 2014: 78.

50 See a first-hand account reproduced in Collectif de débrayage 2013: 130.

51 Savard and Cyr 2014: 78 (my translation).

52 Ibid.

53 This first-hand account is reproduced in full in Collectif de débrayage 2013: 130–34.

54 Savard and Cyr 2014: 78.

55 For a detailed account of the Victoriaville riot and the resulting injuries, see Ménard, Grenier and Carbonneau 2014: 238–45; see also Bilodeau, Duchaine and Journet 2012. The student who lost an eye authored an op-ed piece in *Le Devoir* one year later: see Valade 2013.

56 Lemonde et al. 2013: 317.

57   Ibid.: 315.
58   Collectif de débrayage 2013: 134.
59   Ibid.
60   Ibid.: 135 (my translation).
61   Ibid.
62   Ibid.: 136.
63   Bonenfant, Glinoer and Lapointe 2013: 184. For more, see Radio-Canada 2012d.
64   Radio-Canada 2012d.
65   Collectif de débrayage 2013: 135 (my translation).
66   Robitaille 2012c.
67   Collectif de débrayage 2013: 136.
68   Bonenfant, Glinoer and Lapointe 2013: 230.
69   Auger 2012.
70   Collectif de débrayage 2013: 136 (my translation).

Chapter 9

1   Andraos 2013: 63 (my translation).
2   In the estimation of Dufour and Savoie (2014: 7), the student conflict of 2012 was the worst crisis to hit Québec in sixty years.
3   Collectif de débrayage 2013: 168.
4   Dutrisac 2012c (my translation).
5   Bonenfant, Glinoer and Lapointe 2013: 234 (my translation). See Salvet 2012b.
6   Dutrisac 2012c (my translation).
7   Radio-Canada and La Presse canadienne 2012.
8   Bonenfant, Glinoer and Lapointe 2013: 216.
9   Ménard, Grenier and Carbonneau 2014: 38, 116, 365. The Ménard Report, ordered by the PQ government of Pauline Marois in 2012, concluded that the student crisis could probably have been averted had the government had recourse to mediation. See Ménard, Grenier and Carbonneau 2014: 365.
10   Radio-Canada 2012c.
11   Bonenfant, Glinoer and Lapointe 2013: 252 (my translation).
12   Collectif de débrayage 2013: 169.
13   Dufour 2012b (my translation).
14   Collectif de débrayage 2013: 164 (my translation).
15   Collective of authors 2012b (my translation). See also Nadeau 2012b.
16   Collective of authors 2012b.
17   Pineault 2012: 46.
18   Collectif de débrayage 2013: 164.
19   Ibid.
20   Ibid. (my translation).
21   Ibid.
22   Ibid. (my translation).
23   See Assemblée nationale du Québec 2012: article 11. Emphasis added.
24   Ibid.: article 16.
25   Ibid.: division V.
26   Ibid.: articles 17, 26, 30.

27   Ibid.: article 15.
28   Collectif de débrayage 2013: 169 (my translation).
29   La Presse canadienne 2012f.
30   Bonenfant, Glinoer and Lapointe 2013: 227, 231.
31   Collectif de débrayage 2013: 170 (my translation).
32   Ibid.: 169 (my translation).
33   Ibid.: 167.
34   Ibid.: 159 (my translation).
35   Ibid.: 167.
36   Ibid.
37   Dufour and Savoie 2014: 7.
38   Collectif de débrayage 2013: 170 (my translation and emphasis).
39   Bergeron 2012b (my translation).
40   Journet 2012 (my translation).
41   Bergeron 2012b (my translation).
42   Profs contre la hausse 2012.
43   Nadeau 2012; Myles and La Presse canadienne 2012; Canadian Civil Liberties
      Association 2012; Gervais 2012c; Amnesty International 2012.
44   Robitaille 2012b (my translation).
45   Nadeau-Dubois 2013a: 164 (my translation).
46   Robitaille 2012b (my translation).
47   An eye-witness account is reproduced in Collectif de débrayage 2013: 176.
48   Collectif de débrayage 2013: 178 (my translation).
49   Reproduced in Collectif de débrayage 2013: 189 (my translation).
50   Lemonde et al. 2013: 320.
51   La Presse canadienne 2012d (my translation); Lemonde et al. 2013: 323.
52   Collectif de débrayage 2013: 184; Lemonde et al. 2013: 320.
53   See Lemonde et al. 2013: 308, 317.
54   Collectif de débrayage 2013: 77 (my translation).
55   Dupuis-Déri and L'Écuyer 2013: 333.
56   Collectif de débrayage 2013: 177.
57   Ibid.: 181.
58   Ibid.: 179 (my translation).
59   Ibid.
60   Ibid.: 172 (my translation).
61   Ibid.
62   Ibid.: 209.
63   Gervais and Bélair-Cirino 2012.
64   Collectif de débrayage 2013: 210.
65   Bélair-Cirino 2012a (my translation).
66   See Drapeau-Bisson, Dupuis-Déri and Ancelovici 2014: 151; see also Hachey 2012
      and Porter, Bélair-Cirino and Guillemette 2012.
67   Collectif de débrayage 2013: 185.
68   Ibid.: 187.
69   Ibid.: 186.
70   Savard and Cyr 2014: 82.
71   Collectif de débrayage 2013: 188 (my translation).

72   Sterne 2012. See also Drapeau-Bisson, Dupuis-Déri and Ancelovici 2014: 150.

73   Lutfi 2012 (emphasis and translation mine).

74   "An Open Letter to the Mainstream Media," by the anonymous administrator of Translating the Printemps érable, May 27, 2012. Available via Occupy, along with a videoclip of the *casseroles*: <occupy.com/article/montreal-open-letter-mainstream-media>.

75   Drapeau-Bisson, Dupuis-Déri and Ancelovici 2014: 161–67.

76   Ibid.: 177–79.

77   Beauchemin, Bourque and Duchatel 1995: 31.

78   *Le Devoir* has assembled a press review of foreign coverage of the Printemps érable up to June 12, 2012. See *Le Devoir* 2012b.

79   Collective of authors 2012a. A fairly decent English translation of the text is available on the website of Occupy Wall Street: <occupywallst.org/article/todos-somos-quebequenses-we-are-all-quebecois/>.

80   Drapeau-Bisson, Dupuis-Déri and Ancelovici 2014: 161.

81   Ibid.: 160.

82   Le Huffington Post Québec 2012.

83   Drapeau-Bisson, Dupuis-Déri and Ancelovici 2014: 160–61; Mazataud 2012.

84   Collectif de débrayage 2013: 257.

85   Journet and Lessard 2012.

86   Bonenfant, Glinoer and Lapointe 2013: 255–57.

87   Reuters 2014.

88   Guillemette 2012b.

89   Ibid.

90   Ibid.

91   Collectif de débrayage 2013: 211 (my translation). Under Canadian law, police must have a warrant to engage in searches of individuals, without which they are illegal. The only exceptions are in cases of a flagrant offence, of a search carried out after a legal arrest or if the threatening object is plainly visible. See Lemonde et al. 2013: 317.

92   Lemonde et al. 2013: 315; Collectif de débrayage 2013: 211.

93   Sylvestre 2012; Robert 2012.

94   La Presse canadienne 2012c; Sylvestre 2012.

95   Lemonde et al. 2013: 315–17. See also Switzer 2011 and CBC News 2011b.

96   Lemonde et al. 2013: 314–15.

97   Lalonde and Ferland 2012 (my translation of headline).

98   Lemonde et al. 2013: 314.

99   Lalonde and Ferland 2012.

100 Ibid.

101 Lemonde et al. 2013: 43.

102 Montpetit 2012.

103 Lemonde et al. 2013: 314 (my translation).

104 Collectif de débrayage 2013: 212.

105 Montpetit 2012.

106 Nadeau 2012a (my translation). For the reaction, see Dutrisac 2012a.

107 Loosely translated: "We don't give a fuck about the elections!" See Collectif de débrayage 2013: 229.

108 Radio-Canada 2012a (my translation).

109 Teisceira-Lessard 2012a; Lessard 2012b.
110 Nadeau-Dubois 2012 (my translation).

Chapter 10

1 Brassard 2013: 189 (my translation).
2 Forest 2013: 50.
3 Preston 1984: 435–57.
4 Tepe and Vanhuysse 2008: esp 1–2; Myles and Pierson 2001: 305–33; Busemeyer, Goerres and Weschle 2009: 195–212; International Monetary Fund (IMF) 2004; Organization for Economic Co-operation and Development (OECD) 1996; World Bank 1994.
5 Sabbagh and Vanhuysse 2006: 639; Tepe and Vanhuysse 2008: 2; Busemeyer, Goerres and Weschle 2009.
6 Esping-Andersen and Sarasa 2002: 5–21; Pampel 1994: 153–95; Tepe and Vanhuysse 2008.
7 Esping-Andersen and Sarasa 2002; Pampel 1994; Tepe and Vanhuysse 2008.
8 See Sabbagh and Vanhuysse 2006: esp. 658. Pampel's 1994 results are very similar, finding age inequality in spending.
9 Brisson 2012: 34 (my translation).
10 St-Pierre and Ethier 2013: 131.
11 St-Pierre and Ethier 2013: 97–99, 131 (my translation).
12 Martin and Tremblay-Pépin of IRIS analyzed historic data from the province's Commission des normes du travail and the Ministère de l'éducation and compared the number of full-time (40-hour) weeks paid at minimum wage required to pay for education. Their calculations show a 1978 student working four weeks — the base year was chosen to reflect the achievements of the Quiet Revolution — while a student in 2012 has to work 67 percent more, or 6.7 weeks. See Martin and Tremblay-Pépin 2011: 13.
13 Finances Québec 2011: 21; see also Radio-Canada 2011d.
14 Fédération étudiante universitaire du Québec (FEUQ) 2011: 3.
15 Martin and Tremblay-Pépin 2011: 11; Blanchet 2012.
16 This compares to a Canadian average of $29,327, with the discrepancy attributable to much higher tuition levels in the rest of the country. With the 1986 Canadian average of $10,016, we may therefore presume, in spite of lack of equivalent historical data, that Québec's at the time was far lower owing to the tuition freeze and that the rise in debt in Québec has been similarly drastic in keeping with the sharp climb after 1989. Statistics Canada's data corroborates this hypothesis, with Québec posting the second highest increase in student debt levels for the period between 1986 and 1995. Note that all figures have been adjusted by the author to represent 2014 constant dollars. See Martin and Tremblay-Pépin 2011: 11 and Council of Ministers of Education, Canada (CMEC) 2000: chapter 3.5, section F.
17 Collectif de débrayage 2013: 58.
18 Pineault 2006: 31.
19 Martin and Tremblay-Pépin 2011: 17; Radio-Canada 2012e.
20 Julien 2012: 153; Finances Québec 2011: 26.
21 Strapagiel 2013.

22 Statistics Canada 2008: 19; for a summary, see McFeat 2008.
23 See Martin and Ouellet 2011: 88–89.
24 Strapagiel 2013.
25 Cited in Strapagiel 2013, emphasis added.
26 Strapagiel 2013.
27 Dufour 2012a: 6.
28 Collectif de débrayage 2013: 125 (my translation).
29 Cited in Hartlep and Eckrich 2013: 82.
30 Collectif de débrayage 2013: 125 (my translation).
31 Desjardins 2012.
32 The 2011 census established the population of Montréal's metropolitan census area, which extends deep into the north, south and west shores off Montréal island, at 3,824,221 inhabitants; see Statistics Canada 2011.
33 Gabriel Nadeau-Dubois, in a speech given to the conference *Indignez-vous* presented by the Council of Canadians at Montréal's Monument-National on April 7, 2012. For an excerpt, see *La Presse* 2012 (my translation).
34 CLASSE 2012 (my translation). Also available in English at <stopthehike.ca/manifesto/>.
35 See Castells 2012: 123.
36 Collective of authors 2012c (my translation).
37 Ducros 2012.
38 Gervais 2012f; Desjardins 2012.
39 Peritz 2012; Jean-Marc Léger cited in Bélair-Cirino 2012b.
40 CBC News online 2011a. For the 2013 report showing that nothing has remotely improved, see International Energy Agency (IEA) 2013.
41 See Klein 2014: 21.
42 See Klein 2014: 22; Chomsky 2014.
43 World Bank 2012.
44 Klein 2014: 18.
45 Jean-Marc Léger cited in Bélair-Cirino 2012b (my translation).

Chapter II

1 Moses 2013: 175 (my translation).
2 Klaudia Alvárez (2011), the communications coordinator for Democracia Real Ya, described the movement as a "*cerebro en red*" (networked brain) defined by "*inteligencias conectadas*" (connected intelligences). For an indepth analysis of both 15-M and OWS and their decentralized, networked forms, see Castells 2012: 110–217; for a slightly more nuanced take, which stresses the de facto (but not formal) leadership role of organizers, see Gerbaudo 2012: 76–133.
3 See Castells 1996, 2000, 2001, 2004, 2009 and 2012; for a full list of Castell's works and lectures, see <manuelcastells.info/en/CastellsMCV_eng.pdf>.
4 Castells 2012: 225.
5 Forest 2013: 47.
6 Ibid.: 47–48.
7 Cited in Julien 2012: 156.
8 Martine Desjardins used this expression on April 24; see Radio-Canada 2012f. *La*

NOTES

Presse editorialist Nathalie Petrowski echoed the criticism on April 30; see Petrowski 2012c.

9   Leydet 2012; Duchaine 2012.

10 Collective of authors 2012 (my translation); see also Teisceira-Lessard 2012b.

11 Collective of authors 2012 (my translation).

12 Ibid.

13 Boulianne 2013.

14 Gervais 2013b (my translation).

15 Different media reports offer competing calculations, but all agree on the associations that voted to leave. The 14,000 figure comes from *Le Soleil*. See Thériault 2013; Lamontagne 2013; Boulianne 2013. For the FEUQ's refusal to acknowledge the results of the disaffiliation votes, see Fédération étudiante de l'Université de Sherbrooke (FEUS) 2014. For the FECQ's refusal to acknowledge the results, see Gervais 2012b.

16 See Gervais 2012b and 2012a.

17 Castells 2012: 230–31; Castells 2009: 116–36; Gerbaudo 2012: 22. See also Castells 2001 and Markoff 2006.

18 Castells 2012: 231.

19 Castells 1996: 469. For another thorough account of the network society's many manifestations, see Barney 2004: esp. 25–33, 176–81.

20 Milner 2013: 32.

21 Ibid.

22 Ibid.: 31.

23 Cited in Desrosiers 2012b (my translation).

24 See Nevitt 2011: 6–7, 9–11. For a more indepth (but less current) analysis, see Nevitt 1996.

25 Campbell and Gilmore 2007.

26 Nevitt 2011: 9.

27 Rebick 2013: 43.

28 Lenhart et al. 2007: 45.

29 Collectif de débrayage 2013: 269 (my translation).

30 Castells 2012: 246.

31 Gerbaudo 2012: 159 (emphasis added).

32 Monbiot 2014.

33 300,000 students rejected the preliminary entente arrived at between the government and student representatives in May. See Auger 2012.

34 A Forum Research poll of 1,589 Quebecers conducted by random automated phone calls on February 23, 2012, found opposition to the tuition increase at 66 percent within the 18–34 age demographic, while the 55+ group supported it by 57 percent. The wide-ranging poll, with a margin of error estimated at +/-2.5 percent, 19 times out of 20, may be found on the FECQ's page on Scribd: <scribd.com/doc/82987495/Quebec-Issues-Poll-Forum-Research>. A CROP poll of 1,000 web respondents conducted March 15–19 found the 18–34 group opposing the tuition hike by a margin of 60 percent, with 55+ respondents supporting it by a margin of 61 percent; the non-probabilistic poll has no margin of error. The complete poll and methodology may be viewed at <ledevoir.com/documents/pdf/sondageFECQ.pdf>. Those findings are corroborated by three Léger polls with smaller sample sizes of between 400–613 web respondents, conducted on March 22, March 29 and May 11. These found opposition

to the tuition hike among the younger 18–24 cohort at 74 percent, 58 percent and 69 percent respectively, with support from those aged 55 and older at 74 percent, 62 percent and 66 percent. The fluctuation is likely attributable in large part to larger margins of error, at +/- 4 percent (March 22) and 4.9 percent (March 29 and May 11), 19 times out of 20. All three are available on Léger's website, in order: <legermarketing. com/admin/upload/publi_pdf/Sondage_express_Journal_de_Montreal_Greve_ etudiante_22_mars_2012.pdf>; <legermarketing.com/admin/upload/publi_pdf/ Sondage_express_Journal_de_Montreal_Greve_etudiante_29_mars_2012.pdf>; <legermarketing.com/admin/upload/publi_pdf/Sondage_JDM_Greve_etudi-ante_11_mai_2012.pdf>.

35   Collectif de débrayage 2013: 126–27 (my translation).

36   Ibid.

37   Ibid.

38   The poll contained a margin of error estimated at +/- 1.77 percent, 19 times out of 20. For more details on methodology and the results, see Léger Marketing 2010: 58.

39   Support from those aged 18–24 for leftist party Québec Solidaire (QS) was at 22 percent in June 2014 according to one poll of 500 youth performed by CROP, compared to 8 percent received by the party in the April 2014 election. The true mark of leftist support among youth is difficult to ascertain, however, owing to QS's sovereignist stance and the lack of a leftist federalist alternative in the province; 69 percent in the same poll said they would vote "No" in a referendum on Québec independence. See Gagnon 2014. Support of those aged 18–24 for QS was at 18 percent in another poll by Léger in March 2014. See Bourgoin 2014.

40   Olivier and Lamoureux 2014: 209 (my translation).

Conclusion

1   Briand 2013: 19 (my translation).

2   Conférence des recteurs et des principaux des universités du Québec (CREPUQ) 2013; Bureau de coopération interuniversitaire (BCI) 2014. See also Mathieu 2013, Chouinard 2013 and Gervais 2013a.

3   In August 2014, public sector union members angry about pension reforms — which affected police, among other municipal employees — lit a bonfire in the streets in front of city hall and ransacked the council chambers. The SPVM officers on duty stood by and did nothing as their colleagues engaged in acts far more serious than those that invited violent repression during the student spring of 2012. See Normandin 2014; Bruemmer and Laframboise 2014. In April 2013, SPVM police chief Marc Parent said he would not enforce Bylaw P6 in the case of a hockey victory by the Canadiens, which are frequently met with rowdy (and at times destructive) marches through the streets of Montréal. "We know very well that at that moment, we're not there to demand an itinerary from anyone. It's not organized, it's spontaneous, and we know that very well," said Parent. See Radio-Canada 2013a (my translation). Montréal will devote at least $110,000 to defend its Bylaw P6 against a constitutional challenge, despite having dropped charges against at least 650 individuals for lack of evidence. See Champagne 2014.

4   Dutrisac 2013b; Radio-Canada 2013b; Zabihiyan 2013.

5   La Presse canadienne 2012j; La Presse canadienne 2012a; Parti Québécois 2012;

NOTES

Sioui and Bergeron 2012; Salvet 2012a; Chouinard 2013; La Presse canadienne 2014; Journet 2013; Dutrisac 2013a; Nadeau and Shields 2013; Shields 2013. The PQ's reversal on shale gas attracted the ire of Gabriel Nadeau-Dubois, who penned a virulent critique in Le Huffington Post Québec in which he called on the PQ to "enter the twenty-first century" (Nadeau-Dubois 2013b; my translation).

6   See Bédard-Wien 2014.

7   For discussions (in French) of the "awakening" of the spring, see (former Lévesque minister, Lise) Payette 2012; Ducros 2012; Dutrisac 2012b; Ricard 2012.

8   Dutrisac 2012b (my translation).

9   Sanschagrin and Gagnon 2014: 284.

10   Jean-Marc Léger quoted in Bélair-Cirino 2012b (my translation).

11   Madeleine Gauthier cited in Desrosiers 2012a (my translation).

12   See Long 2014. See also BBC News online 2013.

13   In Turkey, a violent crackdown on protests over a development project on downtown Istanbul's Taksim square — Prime Minister Recep Tayyip Erdoğan wanted to build an Ottoman-inspired shopping mall over the adjacent Gezi Park — sparked its mushrooming out into an unprecedented democratic contestation that saw hundreds of thousands challenge the government's authoritarianism. See Associated Press 2013; for more on the context and events since, see Letsch 2014.

14   Cited in Ancelovici and Dupuis-Déri 2014: 356 (my translation).

15   This was taken from the pre-launch website of Ricochet and has since been removed. Find out more at <ricochetmedia.ca/en>.

16   See Ricochet Media at <ricochetmedia.ca/en>.

17   Collectif de débrayage 2013: 269 (my translation).

18   Nadeau-Dubois 2013a: 55–56.

19   Dufour 2012a: 29.

20   Collectif de débrayage 2013: 269.

21   Gabriel Nadeau-Dubois cited in Gervais 2013c (my translation).

REFERENCES

Agence QMI. 2012. "Charest jette de l'huile sur le feu puis nuance ses propos." April 20. At <fr.canoe. ca/infos/quebeccanada/politiqueprovinciale/archives/2012/04/20120420-143438. html>.

Agence QMI and TVA Nouvelles. 2012. "Lutte contre la hausse des frais de scolarité — Mobilisations estivales et carré rouge." June 10. At <tvanouvelles.ca/lcn/infos/national/ archives/2012/06/20120610-124518.html>.

Allard, Marc. 2012. "Line Beauchamp 'jette de l'huile sur le feu,' réagit la CLASSE." Le Soleil, April 25.

Alvárez, Klaudia. 2011. Nosotros los indignados: Las voces comprometidas del #15-M. Barcelona: Destino.

Amnesty International. 2012. "Quebec Law Breaches Canada's International Human Rights Obligations." Press release, May 25. At <amnesty.org/en/news/quebec-law-breaches-canada-s-international-human-rights-obligations-2012-05-26>.

Ancelovici, Marcos, and Francis Dupuis-Déri. 2014. "Retour sur le 'printemps érable'." In Marcos Ancelovici and Francis Dupuis-Déri (eds.), Un Printemps rouge et noir. Montréal: Écosociété.

Andraos, Maryse. 2013. "À bas les masques, Big Brother." In Fermaille (ed.), Fermaille: Anthologie. Montréal: Moult Éditions.

ASSÉ (Association pour une solidarité syndicale étudiante). 2013. Statuts et règlements de l'Association pour une solidarité syndicale étudiante. Montréal: ASSÉ.

____. 2005. "Chronologie approximative du mouvement étudiant québécois." In ASSÉ (ed.), Recueil de textes sur l'histoire du mouvement étudiant. Montréal: ASSÉ.

Assemblée nationale du Québec. 2012. Bill 78. An Act to Enable Students to Receive Instruction from the Postsecondary Institutions They Attend. May 18. At <publicationsduquebec.gouv. qc.ca/dynamicSearch/telecharge.php?type=5&file=2012C12A.PDF>.

Associated Press. 2013. "Recep Tayyip Erdoğan Dismisses Turkey Protesters as Vandals." Guardian, June 9.

Auger, Samuel. 2012. "Mobilisation étudiante: Le rejet massif de l'entente confirmé." Le Soleil, May 12.

Ayotte-Thompson, Megan, and Leah Freeman. 2012. "Accessibility and Privatization: The Quebec Student Movement." Social Policy, Fall.

Badiou, Alain. 2012. Circonstances, 7. Sarkozy: Pire que prévu/Les autres: Prévoir le pire. Paris, Lignes.

Badiou, Alain, and Alain Finkielkraut. 2010. L'Explication: Conversation avec Aude Lancelin. Paris: Lignes.

Baiocchi, Gianpaolo, and Ernesto Ganuza. 2012. "No Parties, No Banners: The Spanish Experiment with Direct Democracy." Boston Review 37, 1 (Jan/Feb).

Barney, Darin. 2004. The Network Society. London: Polity.

Barrette, Yanick. 2012. Le printemps érable: Les fondements d'un changement. Montréal: self-published.

BBC News online. 2013. "Ex-president Michelle Bachelet Wins Chile Poll Run-off." December 16. At <bbc.com/news/world-latin-america-25387340>.

BCI (Bureau de coopération interuniversitaire). 2014. "La Conférence des recteurs et des princi-paux des universités du Québec (CREPUQ) devient le Bureau de coopération interuniversi-taire (BCI)." Press release, January 10. At <crepuq.qc.ca/spip.php?article1472&lang=en>.

Beauchemin, Jacques, Gilles Bourque and Jules Duchastel. 1995. "Du providentialisme au néolibéralisme: De Marsh à Axworthy. Un nouveau discours de légitimation de la régulation

REFERENCES

sociale." *Cahiers de recherche sociologique* 24. Montréal: Départment de Sociologie, UQÀM.

Beaulieu-April, Zéa. 2013. "Entre l'amorce et la suite." In Fermaille (ed.), *Fermaille: Anthologie.* Montréal: Moult Éditions.

Beauschene, Oliver H. 2012a. "Visualisation de la #GGI — Mise à jour!" *Collaborative Cybernetics,* June 28. At <olihb.com/2012/06/28/visualisation-de-la-ggi-mise-a-jour/>.

___. 2012b. "Visualisation — Structure d'influence du conflit étudiant." *Collaborative Cybernetics,* June 4. At <olihb.com/2012/06/04/visualisation-structure-dinfluence-conflit/>.

___. 2012c. "Visualisation des tweets de la grève étudiante." *Collaborative Cybernetics,* April 3. At <olihb.com/2012/04/03/visualisation-des-tweets-de-la-greve-etudiante/>.

Bédard-Wien, Jérémie. 2014. "There's Something Brewing in Québec." *Ricochet,* October 31. At <ricochet-media/en/155/theres-something-brewing-in-quebec>.

Beevolve Inc. n.d. "An Exhaustive Study of Twitter Users Across the World." At <beevolve.com/twitter-statistics/#a2>.

Bélair-Cirino, Marco. 2012a. "Grand tintamarre contre la loi 78 — Les casseroles s'en mêlent." *Le Devoir,* May 24.

___. 2012b. "Point chaud: Face-à-face des générations." *Le Devoir,* May 22.

___. 2012c. "Anciens, actuels et futurs universitaires se mobilisent — Une semaine décisive s'amorce." *Le Devoir,* March 19.

Bélanger, Pierre. 1984. *Le mouvement étudiant québécois: Son passé, ses revendications et ses luttes (1960–1983).* Montréal: ANEQ.

Bergeron, Patrice. 2012a. "Le gouvernement Charest avait une étude suggérant que les universités ne sont pas sous-financées." *Le Devoir,* November 8.

___. 2012b. "Le Québec se rapproche d'un 'État totalitaire,' disent les syndicats." *Le Soleil,* May 18.

Bernier, Luc. 2005. "Who Governs in Québec? Revolving Premiers and Reforms." In Luc Bernier, Keith Brownsey and Michael Howlett (eds.), *Executive Styles in Canada: Cabinet Structures and Leadership Practices in Canadian Government.* Toronto: University of Toronto Press.

Bilodeau, Émilie, Gabrielle Duchaine and Paul Journet. 2012. "Victoriaville: Une dizaine de blessés, une centaine d'arrestations." *La Presse,* May 4.

Blanchard, Raymond. 2014. "Le Carré rouge: Historique d'un symbole." Fédération des étudiantes et étudiants du Campus universitaire de Moncton (FÉÉCUM), April 10. At <feecum.ca/index.php/178-le-carre-rouge-historique-d-un-symbole>.

Blanchet, Jean-Nicolas. 2012. "Endettement inévitable ou train de vie excessif?" *Agence QMI* September 3. At <argent.canoe.ca/nouvelles/affaires/etudiants-endettement-inevitable-ou-train-de-vie-excessif-9032012>.

Boisvert, Gabriel. 2013. "L'éducation à l'ère du clientélisme. Mémoire en vue du Sommet sur l'enseignement supérieur." Association des étudiantes et étudiants en droit à l'Université de Montréal (AED), February.

Boisvert, Hugues. 1997. *L'université à réinventer.* St-Laurent, QC: Éditions du Renouveau Pédagogique.

Boisvert, Yves. 2010. "Une obligation de résultat." *La Presse,* February 24.

Boivin, Mathieu. 2012. "Amir Khadir arrêté à Québec." *Le Soleil,* June 5.

Bonenfant, Maude, Anthony Glinoer and Martine-Emmanuelle Lapointe. 2013. *Le printemps québécois: Une anthologie.* Montréal: Écosociété.

Boulianne, Louis-Philippe. 2013. "La FEUQ décapitée." *Impact Campus* October 8.

Bourgoin, Hugo. 2014. "Les jeunes divisés." TVA Nouvelles March 25. At <tvanouvelles.ca/lcn/infos/national/electionsquebec2014/archives/2014/03/20140325-053632.html>.

Boustany, Badih, Rodrigo García and Renaud Picard. 2006. "La CASSÉÉ: La voix radicalement humaine de la grève étudiante." In Colllectif Carré Rouge (ed.), *Carré rouge: La grève étudiante du printemps 2005.* Montréal: Self-published.

Brassard, Noémie. 2013. "À ma mère." In Fermaille (ed.), *Fermaille: Anthologie*. Montréal: Moult Éditions.

Brenner, Neil, and Nik Theodore. 2002. *Spaces of Neoliberalism: Urban Restructuring in North America and Western Europe*. Malden, MA: Blackwell.

Breton, Pascale. 2012. "Des professeurs réclament la démission de Line Beauchamp." *La Presse*, April 13.

Briand, Catherine-Alexandre. 2013. "Ça sent la poussière." In Fermaille (ed.), *Fermaille: Anthologie*. Montréal: Moult Éditions.

Brisson, Pierre-Luc. 2012. *Après le printemps*. Montréal: Poètes de Brousse.

Brown, Robert D., and Jack Mintz. 2012. "Chapter 1: The Big Picture." In Heather Kerr, Ken McKenzie and Jack Mintz (eds.), *Tax Policy in Canada*. Toronto: Canadian Tax Foundation.

Bruemmer, René, and Kalina Laframboise. 2014. "Bill 3 Protesters Storm City Hall." *The Gazette* August 19.

Busemeyer, Marius R., Achim Goerres and Simon Weschle. 2009. "Attitudes Towards Redistributive Spending in an Era of Demographic Ageing." *Journal of European Social Policy* 19, 3 (July).

Butler, Judith. 2011. "Bodies in Alliance and the Politics of the Street." *European Institute for Progressive Cultural Policies* September. At <eipcp.net/transversal/1011/butler/en>.

Cala, Andrés. 2011. "Inspired by Arab Spring, Spain's Youthful 15-M Movement Spreads in Europe." *Christian Science Monitor* May 20.

Campbell, Jennifer, and Linda Gilmore. 2007. "Intergenerational Continuities and Discontinuities in Parenting Styles." *Australian Journal of Psychology* 59, 3. Author's unabridged version at <eprints.qut.edu.au/13165/1/13165.pdf>.

Canada Revenue Agency. n.d. "Corporation Tax Rates." At <cra-arc.gc.ca/tx/bsnss/tpcs/crprtns/rts-eng.html>.

Carrión, Maria. 2011. "Spain's Young People Turn Indignant." *Progressive* August 1.

Castells, Manuel. 2012. *Networks of Outrage and Hope: Social Movements in the Internet Age*. Polity: Cambridge.

____. 2009. *Communication Power*. Oxford: Oxford University Press.

____. 2004. *The Network Society: A Cross-Cultural Perspective*. Cheltenham: Edward Elgar Publishing.

____. 2001. *The Internet Galaxy*. Oxford: Oxford University Press.

____. 2000. "Materials for an Exploratory Theory of the Network Society." *British Journal of Sociology* 51, 1.

____. 1996. *The Rise of the Network Society*. Oxford: Blackwell.

Castonguay, Alec. 2011. "79% des Québécois sont insatisfaits de Charest." *Le Devoir*, March 14.

CBC News online. 2012. "Concordia University Fined $2M for Excessive Severance Packages." March 9. At <cbc.ca/news/canada/montreal/concordia-university-fined-2m-for-excessive-severance-packages-1.1162974>.

____. 2011a. "Time for Climate Change Fix Running Out, IEA Warns." November 9. At <cbc.ca/news/business/time-for-climate-change-fix-running-out-iea-warns-1.1048216>.

____. 2011b. "Toronto G20 Policing Too Aggressive, Judge Says." August 12. At <cbc.ca/news/canada/toronto/toronto-g20-policing-too-aggressive-judge-says-1.1014295>.

____. 2010. "Concordia President Let Go Abruptly." December 23. At <cbc.ca/news/canada/montreal/concordia-president-let-go-abruptly-1.874257>.

CBC online. N.d. "The Quiet Revolution." *Canada: A People's History*. At <cbc.ca/history/EPISCONTENTSE1EP16CH1PA1LE.html>.

CCLA (Canadian Civil Liberties Association). 2012. "CCLA Denounces Drastic, Broad Infringements of Fundamental Constitutional Rights in Quebec Bill 78." Press release,

REFERENCES

May 22. At <ccla.org/2012/05/22/ccla-denounces-drastic-broad-infringements-of-fundamental-constitutional-rights-in-quebec-bill-78/>.

CDEACF (Centre de documentation sur l'éducation des adultes et la condition féminine). 2007. "*Frais de scolarité: 61% des Québécois s'opposent au dégel proposé par Jean Charest.*" March 12. At <cdeacf.ca/actualite/2007/03/12/frais-scolarite-61-quebecois-sopposent-de-gel-propose-jean>.

Champagne, Sarah R. 2014. "Règlement P-6: Nouveaux chefs d'accusation abandonnés contre 27 manifestants." *Le Devoir,* October 25.

Charest, Jean. 2002. "Priorités du Parti libéral du Québec — Des baisses d'impôt de 27% d'ici cinq ans." *Le Devoir,* September 13.

Cheng, Alex, Mark Evans and Harshdeep Singh. 2012. "Inside Twitter: An In-depth Look Inside the Twitter World." *Sysomos Inc.,* June.

Chiasson-Lebel, Thomas. 2006. "Analyser la grève étudiante du printemps 2005." In Collectif Carré Rouge (ed.), *Carré rouge: La grève étudiante du printemps 2005.* Montréal: Self-published.

Chomsky, Noam. 2014. "Are We Approaching the End of Human History?" *Moyers & Company,* September 9. At <billmoyers.com/2014/09/09/noam-chomsky-are-we-approaching-the-end-of-human-history/>.

Chouinard, Marie-Andrée. 2013. "Québec coupe en catimini dans l'aide sociale." *Le Devoir,* March 2.

Chouinard, Tommy. 2013. "La CREPUQ éclate." *La Presse,* May 1.

____. 2010. "Duchesneau à la tête d'une unité anticollusion." *La Presse,* February 23.

____. 2004. "Sondage Léger Marketing-Le Devoir-CKAC-The Globe and Mail — Les Québécois regrettent leur choix." *Le Devoir,* January 24.

Chouinard, Tommy, and Paul Journet. 2012. "Québec élargit son programme de prêts pour études secondaires." *La Presse,* April 5.

CLASSE (Coalition large de l'Association pour une solidarité syndicale étudiante). 2012. "Nous sommes avenir: Le manifeste de la CLASSE." CLASSE manifesto. July. At <bloquonslahausse. com/laclasse/manifeste/>.

CMEC (Council of Ministers of Education, Canada). 2000. *Education Indicators in Canada: Report of the Pan-Canadian Education Indicators Program 1999.* Ottawa: CMEC. At <publications. cmec.ca/stats/pceip/1999/Indicatorsite/english/pages/page18e.html>.

Collectif de débrayage. 2013. *On s'en câlisse. Histoire profane de la grève printemps 2012.* Montréal and Genève-Paris: Sabotart and Entremonde.

Collective of authors. 2012. "Une fédération gangrenée." Open letter from FECQ deserters, November. At <ledevoir.com/documents/pdf/lettre_ouverte_LMG.pdf>.

____. 2012a. "¡Todos somos quebecenses! We Are All Québécois!" Open letter from Chilean students and academics, May 29. At <occupywallst.org/article/todos-somos-quebequen-ses-we-are-all-quebecois/>.

____. 2012b. "Une loi scélérate et une infamie." May 18. At <ledevoir.com/documents/pdf/ historiens_loi.pdf>.

____. 2012c. "Nous sommes avec les étudiants. Nous sommes ensemble." *Voir,* May 1.

Comité consultatif sur l'économie et les finances publiques. 2009. *Le Québec face à ses défis.* Québec City: Gouvernement du Québec.

Commission royale d'enquête sur l'enseignement dans la province de Québec. 1966. *Rapport Parent: Rapport de la Commission royale d'enquête sur l'enseignement dans la province de Québec.* Volume 5. Québec City: Gouvernement du Québec.

Côté, Jean-Sébastien. 2006. "Orgeuil, réification et hamburger: Retour sur cette grève-échec." In Collectif Carré Rouge (ed.), *Carré rouge: La grève étudiante du printemps 2005.* Montréal:

Self-published.

Coutu, Benoît, and Richard Dion. 2006. "À la défense de la démocratie: Un monde menacé." In Collectif Carré Rouge (ed.), Carré rouge: La grève étudiante du printemps 2005. Montréal: Self-published.

Couturier, Eve-Lyne, Philippe Hurteau and Simon Pépin-Tremblay. 2010. Budget 2010: Comment financer les services publics? Montréal: l'Institut de recherche et d'informations socio-économiques (IRIS), March.

Couturier, Eve-Lyne, and Bertrand Schepper. 2010. Qui s'enrichit, qui s'appauvrit, 1976–2006. Montréal and Ottawa: IRIS and Canadian Centre for Policy Alternatives (CCPA).

CREPUQ (Conférence des recteurs et des principaux des universités du Québec). 2013. "Les chefs d'établissement universitaire adoptent une structure organisationnelle axée sur la concertation et les services communs." Press release, September 19. At <crepuq.qc.ca/ spip.php?article1466&lang=en>.

Crotty, James. 2009. "Structural Causes of the Global Fnancial Crisis: A Critical Assessment of the 'New Financial Architecture.'" Cambridge Journal of Economics 33.

Crouch, Colin. 2004. Post-Democracy. London: Polity.

Dancoing, Lucie. 2012. "Gabriel Nadeau-Dubois: 'Je ne suis pas un leader.'" Paris Match August 9.

Davis, Mike. 1992. "Fortress Los Angeles: The Militarization of Urban Space." In M. Sorkin (ed.), Variations on a Theme Park. New York: Noonday Press.

de Grandpré, Hugo. 2013. "Les québécois préoccupés par la corruption." La Presse, February 11.

Derrida, Jacques. 2001. L'université sans condition. Paris: Galilée.

Descôteaux, Bernard. 2011. "Garderies — Odeurs de scandale." Le Devoir, December 3.

Desjardins, Martine. 2013. "Des années au coeur de la tempête couge." In Marie-Ève Surprenant and Mylène Bigaouette, Les femmes changent la lutte. Montréal: Éditions du Remue-Ménage.

Desjardins, Richard. 2012. "On prend aux jeunes l'argent nécessaire à la 'conquête du Nord.'" Le Monde, July 6.

Desrosiers, Éric. 2012a. "Ras-le-bol des idées néolibérales." Le Devoir, May 26.

_____. 2012b. "Résumer le conflit à un choc des générations serait une façon commode d'en évacuer l'aspect idéologique." Le Devoir, May 24.

Le Devoir. 2012a. "Grève 2.0: Analyse des twitts de la grève étudiante." July 7.

_____. 2012b. "La crise étudiante dans l'oeil de la presse étrangère." June 12. At <ledevoir.com/ societe/education/350798/la-crise-etudiante-dans-l-oeil-de-la-presse-etrangere>.

Dickinson, John A., and Brian Young. 2008. A Short History of Québec. Montréal: McGill-Queen's University Press.

DiMaggio, Anthony, and Paul Street. 2011. "Occupy Wall Street, Mass Media and Progressive Change in the Tea Party Era." Economic & Political Weekly 46, 47 (November 19).

Doray, Pierre. 2012. "Droits de scolarité — Gels et dégels: Un bref rappel historique." Le Devoir, March 23.

Doray, Pierre, and Patrick Pelletier. 1999. "Les politiques publiques et l'université: Quelques points de repère historiques (1960–1998)." In Paul Beaulieu and Denis Bertrand (eds.), L'État québécois et les universités: Acteurs et enjeux. Sainte-Foy: Presses de l'Université du Québec.

Douzinas, Costas. 2011. "Greek Protests Show Democracy in Action." Guardian, February 7.

Downey, John. 2007. "Participation and/or Deliberation? The Internet as a Tool for Achieving Radical Democratic Aims." In Lincoln Dahlberg and Eugenia Siapera (eds.), Radical Democracy and the Internet: Interrogating Theory and Practice. New York: Palgrave Macmillan.

Doyon, Frédéric. 2012. "Design — Échos graphiques de l'École de la montagne rouge." Le Devoir, November 21.

Drapeau-Bisson, Marie-Lise, Francis Dupuis-Déri and Marcos Ancelovici. 2014. "La grève est

REFERENCES

étudiante, la lutte est populaire!" In Marcos Ancelovici and Francis Dupuis-Déri (eds.), *Un printemps rouge et noir: Regards croisés sur la grève étudiante de 2012*. Montréal: Écosociété.

Duchaine, Gabrielle. 2012. "La CLASSE a le vent dans les voiles." *La Presse*, May 5.

Duchesneau, Jacques. 2011. *Rapport de l'Unité anticorruption*. Québec City: Ministère des transports.

Ducros, Philippe. 2012. "Nous sommes immenses." *Le Devoir*, May 30.

Dufour, Pascale. 2012a. "La rue contre les urnes? Mouvement étudiant et représentation politique." Author's unabridged version of article published in *Savoir/Agir* 22 (December).

____. 2012b. "Ténacité des étudiants québécois." *Le Monde, diplomatique*, June.

Dufour, Pascale, and Louis-Philippe Savoie. 2014. "Quand les mouvements sociaux changent le politique. Le cas du mouvement étudiant de 2012 au Québec." *Canadian Journal of Political Science* 43, 3 (September). Author's version used for citations.

Dupuis-Déri, Francis, and David L'Écuyer. 2013. "Printemps de la matraque. Répression et autorépression." In Marcos Ancelovici and Francis Dupuis-Déri (eds.), *Un Printemps rouge et noir: Regards croisés sur la grève étudiante de 2012*. Montréal: Écosociété.

Dutrisac, Robert. 2013a. "Le nouveau régime de redevances minières — Québec se contente de 50 millions de plus." *Le Devoir*, May 7.

____. 2013b. "Les étudiants sont déçus, mais ne s'estiment pas grands perdants." *Le Devoir*, February 27.

____. 2012a. "Violence et carrés rouges — Les artistes indignés par la ministre St-Pierre." *Le Devoir*, June 13.

____. 2012b. "Crise étudiante — Charest exaspère Parizeau." *Le Devoir*, May 28.

____. 2012c. "Crise sociale — Charest n'admet aucun tort." *Le Devoir*, May 7.

____. 2011. "Garderies: La sélection libérale décriée." *Le Devoir*, December 1.

____. 2010a. "Nomination des juges: Charest a changé la donne." *Le Devoir*, April 15.

____. 2010b. "Financement du Parti libéral du Québec — Charest ment comme il respire, dit Bellemare." *Le Devoir*, March 24.

____. 2009. "Éthique: Charest assouplit les règles." *Le Devoir*, April 29.

____. 2008. "Pour en finir avec la 'culture de la gratuité'." *Le Devoir*, April 11.

____. 2007. "Dégel rapide des droits de scolarité." *Le Devoir*, April 24.

The Economist. 2012. "Food and the Arab Spring: Let Them Eat Baklava." March 17.

Eifling, Sam. 2011. "Adbusters' Kalle Lasn Talks about OccupyWallStreet." *The Tyee* October 7. At <thetyee.ca/News/2011/10/07/Kalle-Lasn-Occupy-Wall-Street/>.

Esping-Andersen, Gösta, and Sebastian Sarasa. 2002. "The Generational Conflict Reconsidered." *Journal of European Social Policy* 12, 1 (February).

FAEUQEP (Fédération des associations étudiantes universitaires québécoises en éducation permanente). 2013. *Le financement et la gouvernance des universités*. Brief presented for the preparatory phase of the *Sommet sur l'enseignement supérieur*. January 14.

Faubert, Amélie. 2013. "Éclaircies." In Fermaille (ed.), *Fermaille: Anthologie*. Montréal: Moult Éditions.

FECQ (Fédération étudiante collégiale du Québec). 2012. "La hausse des frais de scolarité: Une nouvelle taxe à la classe moyenne." Press release, March 21. At <newswire.ca/en/story/941527/hausse-des-frais-de-scolarite-une-nouvelle-taxe-a-la-classe-moyenne>.

FECQ (Fédération étudiante collégiale du Québec) and FEUQ (Fédération étudiante universitaire du Québec). 2012. "Grève étudiante: Le premier ministre encourage la violence, selon la FECQ et la FEUQ." Press release, April 13.

FEUQ (Fédération étudiante universitaire du Québec). 2012. "Cutting in the Fat: University Budgets." Montréal: FEUQ. April 10.

____. 2011. *Argumentaire résumé sur la hausse des frais de scolarité*. Montréal: FEUQ.

FEUS (Fédération étudiante de l'Université de Sherbrooke). 2014. "La FEUS dénonce la non-reconnaissance par la FEUQ des désaffiliations du MAGE-UQAC et de l'AGECAR." Press release, February 20. At <feus.qc.ca/la-feus-denonce-la-non-reconnaissance-par-la-feuq-des-desaffiliations-du-mage-uqac-et-de-lagecar/>.

Finances Québec. 2011. *Budget 2011–2012 — A Fair and Balanced University Funding Plan: To Give Québec the Means to Fulfil its Ambitions.* Québec City: Gouvernement du Québec.

Forest, Pierre-Gerlier. 2013. "Clash of the Centuries: What Happened When Quebec's 20th Century Government Encountered its 21st Century Social Movement." *Inroads* 32 (Winter).

Fortier, Francis. 2013. "Les taux d'impositions des entreprises au Québec." IRIS blog, April 4. At <iris-recherche.qc.ca/blogue/les-taux-dimposition-des-entreprises-au-quebec>.

Fortier, Francis, and Simon Tremblay-Pépin. 2013. *Les Québécois·es: Les plus imposé·es en Amérique du Nord?* Montréal: IRIS. February.

Frappier, André, Richard Poulin and Bernard Rioux. 2012. *Le printemps des carrés rouges: Lutte étudiante, crise sociale, loi liberticide, démocratie de la rue.* Ville Mont-Royal: M Éditeur.

Gagnon, Katia. 2014. "Les jeunes et la souveraineté: La génération 'Non.'" *La Presse,* June 2.

Gaudreau, Valérie. 2012. "Le tour du carré rouge." *Le Soleil,* March 31.

Gerbaudo, Paolo. 2012. *Tweets and the Streets: Social Media and Contemporary Activism.* London: Pluto Press.

Gervais, Lisa-Marie. 2014. "Une étude donne raison aux carrés rouges." *Le Devoir,* September 2.

____. 2013a. "L'UQ veut sauver ce qui reste de la CREPUQ." *Le Devoir,* May 29.

____. 2013b. "Grogne à la FEUQ." *Le Devoir,* April 12.

____. 2013c. "Point chaud — 'J'étais très conscient qu'on ne contrôlait rien du tout.'" *Le Devoir,* March 18.

____. 2012a. "La vague de désaffiliation à la FECQ se poursuit." *Le Devoir,* December 7.

____. 2012b. "Vague de désaffiliation à la FECQ." *Le Devoir,* November 24.

____. 2012c. "L'ONU fait la leçon à Québec sur sa loi spéciale." *Le Devoir,* May 31.

____. 2012d. "Droits de scolarité: Plus de 200 personnalités demandent un moratoire." *Le Devoir,* May 1.

____. 2012e. "Qui sont les leaders du mouvement étudiant?" *L'Actualité* April 12.

____. 2012f. "La lutte des étudiants est juste, dit Guy Rocher. L'un des penseurs du système d'éducation québécois prône l'abolition des droits de scolarité." *Le Devoir,* April 11.

____. 2012g. "200,000 fois 'Entendez-nous!'" *Le Devoir,* March 23.

____. 2012h. "Hausse des droits de scolarité — Au tour des parents de se joindre à la lutte." *Le Devoir,* March 19.

____. 2012i. "La machine étudiante s'ébranle." *Le Devoir,* February 12.

____. 2011. "Appel à l'union des milieux universitaires et d'affaires." *Le Devoir,* October 7.

____. 2010. "Universités: Rupture à Québec." *Le Devoir,* December 7.

Gervais, Lisa-Marie, and Marco Bélair-Cirino. 2012. "Loi 78: La rue choisit la désobéissance pacifique." *Le Devoir,* May 23.

Gingras, Yves, Benoît Godin and Michel Trépanier. 1999. "La place des universités dans les politiques scientifiques et technologiques canadiennes et québécoises." In Paul Beaulieu and Denis Bertrand (eds.), *L'État québécois et les universités: Acteurs et enjeux.* Sainte-Foy: Presses de l'Université du Québec.

Giroux, Aline. 2006. *Le pacte faustien de l'université.* Montréal: Liber.

Giroux, Henri A. 2004. *The Terror of Neoliberalism: Authoritarianism and the Eclipse of Democracy.* Boulder, CO: Paradigm Publishers.

Gourgouris, Stathis. 2011. "Democratic Dreams Rage in Athens." *Al Jazeera,* July 21. At <aljazeera.com/indepth/opinion/2011/07/201171985335665864.html>.

REFERENCES

Gouvernement du Québec. 2011. "304 millions de dollars de droits miniers en 2010–2011: En une seule année, le Québec récolte plus que le total des 10 années précédentes!" Press release, September 15. At <newswire.ca/en/story/841621/304-millions-de-dollars-de-droits-miniers-en-2010-2011-en-une-seule-annee-le-quebec-recolte-plus-que-le-total-des-10-annees-precedentes>.

Guay, Jean-Herman. N.d.a. "Adoption d'une mesure rendant la fréquentation scolaire obligatoire jusqu'à seize ans." *Bilan du siècle.* At <bilan.usherbrooke.ca/bilan/pages/evenements/21198.html>.

_____. n.d.b. "Élections québécoises de 2007." *Bilan du siècle.* At <bilan.usherbrooke.ca/bilan/pagesElections.jsp?annee=2007>.

Guerchani, Sarra. 2012. "Vedette des manifestations étudiantes: Qui est Anarchopanda?" *Agence QMI,* May 23. At <tvanouvelles.ca/lcn/infos/regional/montreal/archives/2012/05/20120523-051454.html>.

Guillemette, Melissa. 2012a. "Annulation de la 'journée portes ouvertes' — Le Grand Prix est-il allé trop vite?" *Le Devoir,* June 4.

_____. 2012b. "Un grand cri du peuple." *Le Devoir,* April 23.

Guilmain, Benoit, Anne-Marie Le Saux and Stéphane Thellen. 2012. "Nous sommes tous étudiants! Manifeste des Professeurs contre la hausse." *Le Devoir,* March 14.

Hachey, Isabelle. 2012. "Le mouvement des casseroles s'amplifie encore." *La Presse,* May 25.

Hardt, Michael, and Antonio Negri. 2011. "The Fight for Real Democracy at the Heart of Occupy Wall Street." *Foreign Affairs online* October 11.

Hartlep, Nicholas D., and Lucille L.T. Eckrich. 2013. "Ivory Tower Graduates in the Red: The Role of Debt in Higher Education." *Workplace: A Journal for Academic Labor* 22 (January).

Hémond, Élaine, Martin Maltais and Michel Umbriaco. 2010. *Le fonds des immobilisations des universités. Une nouvelle cohérence à trouver entre vocations, budgets et réalités. Rapport-synthèse.* Montréal: Fédération québécoise des professeures et professeurs d'université. October. At <fqppu.org/assets/files/FQPPU_Immobilisations.pdf>.

Hessel, Stéphane. 2011. "Time for Outrage." Trans. Damion Searles. *The Nation,* March 7–14.

_____. 2010. *Indignez-vous!* Montpellier: Indigène.

Huang, Carol. 2011. "Facebook and Twitter Key to Arab Spring Uprisings: Report." *The National* (United Arab Emirates) June 6.

Le Huffington Post Québec. 2012. "Mouvement étudiant: Les casseroles dans les rues de Londres." Video. May 31. At <quebec.huffingtonpost.ca/2012/05/31/grve-tudiante-casseroles-londres_n_1560102.html>.

Hurteau, Philippe, Guillaume Hébert and Francis Fortier. 2010. *La révolution tarifaire au Québec.* Montréal: Institut de recherche et d'informations socio-économiques (IRIS). October.

IEA (International Energy Agency). 2013. *Tracking Clean Energy Progress 2013: IEA Input to the Clean Energy Ministerial.* Paris: IEA Publications.

IMF (International Monetary Fund). 2004. *World Economic Outlook.* Washington DC: International Monetary Fund.

Journet, Paul. 2013. "Le PQ reprend les investissements du Plan Nord libéral." *La Presse,* May 7.

_____. 2012. "Une loi de 'mononcles impuissants' contre une génération, clament les syndicats." *La Presse,* May 18.

Journet, Paul, and Denis Lessard. 2012. "Charest et Courchesne critiquent les étudiants pour l'impasse." *La Presse,* May 31.

Julien, Frédéric. 2012. "Le printemps érable comme choc idéologique." *Culture et conflits* 87 (Autumn).

Juris, Jeffrey S. 2008. *Networking Futures: The Movements against Corporate Globalization.* Durham, NC: Duke University Press.

Klein, Naomi. 2014. *This Changes Everything: Capitalism vs. the Climate*. Toronto: Knopf Canada.

Kotz, David M. 2009. "The Financial and Economic Crisis of 2008: A Systemic Crisis of Neoliberal Capitalism." *Review of Radical Political Economics* 41, 3 (Summer).

KPMG. n.d. "Corporate Tax Rate Table." At <kpmg.com/global/en/services/tax/tax-tools-and-resources/pages/corporate-tax-rates-table.aspx>.

Kroll, Andy. 2011. "How Occupy Wall Street Really Got Started." *Mother Jones* October 17.

Lacoursière, Benoît. 2007. *Le mouvement étudiant au Québec de 1983 à 2006*. Montréal: Sabotart.

Lafrance, Xavier. 2006. "L'histoire s'écrit dans la rue." In Collectif Carré Rouge (ed.), *Carré rouge: La grève étudiante du printemps 2005*. Montréal: Self-published.

Lagacé, Patrick. 2012. "Impressionant." *La Presse*, March 23.

Lalonde, Catherine, and Raphaël Dallaire Ferland. 2012. "Carrés rouges, vos papiers!" *Le Devoir*, June 11.

Lamarre, Thomas. 2012. "Outlaw Universities." *Theory & Event* 15, 3 (online supplement). At <muse.jhu.edu/journals/theory_and_event/v015/15.3S.lamarre.html>.

Lamontagne, Nora. 2013. "Un avenir incertain pour la FEUQ." *Le Collectif* October 4.

Lamoureux, Diane. 2012. "La grève étudiante, un révélateur social." *Theory & Event* 15, 3 (online supplement). At <muse.jhu.edu/journals/theory_and_event/v015/15.3S.lamoureux.html>.

Lamoureux, Josée, and Gilles L. Bourque. 2010. "Les inégalitées au Québec: Si la tendance se maintient..." *Note d'intervention de l'Institut de recherche en économie contemporaine* (IRÉC), 10 (October).

Lapan, Julien. 2006. "Les raisons d'un mouvement: Réflexions sur les causes de la grève étudiante." In Collectif Carré Rouge (ed.), *Carré rouge: La grève étudiante du printemps 2005*. Montréal: Self-published.

Larocque, Sylvain, and Alexandre Robillard. 2010. "Charest menace de poursuivre Bellemare." *La Presse*, April 12.

Larouche, Vincent. 2012. "Fortes réactions aux blagues de Jean Charest." *La Presse*, April 20.

Larouche, Vincent, and Fabrice de Pierrebourg. 2011. "Rapport sur la collusion: 'Une ampleur insoupçonnée.'" *La Presse*, September 14.

Lavarenne, Catherine. 2013. "Giorgio." In Fermaille (ed.), *Fermaille: Anthologie*. Montréal: Moult Éditions.

LCN. 2007. "Sondage: 2 Québécois sur 3 n'approuvent pas le dégel." November 25. At <tvanouvelles.ca/infos/national/archives/2007/11/20071125-132217.html>.

Lefebvre, Sarah-Maude. 2013. "'La CLASSE s'invitait dans nos manifestations.'" *Journal de Montréal* April 7.

Léger Marketing. 2010. "Le Québec de mes rêves: Rapport d'étude Novembre 2010." *Agence QMI*, November.

Lemay, Violaine, and Marie-Neige Laperrière. 2012. "Contestation étudiante et soubresauts étatiques: Le printemps québécois sous une perspective droit et société." *Canadian Journal of Law and Society* 27, 3.

Lemoine, Stéphanie, and Samira Ouardi. 2010. *Artivisme. Art, action politique et resistance culturelle*. Paris: Alternative.

Lemonde, Lucie, Andrée Bourbeau, Véronique Fortin, Émilie Joly and Jacinthe Poisson. 2013. "La répression judiciaire et législative durant la grève." In Marcos Ancelovici and Francis Dupuis-Déri (eds.), *Un printemps rouge et noir: Regards croisés sur la grève étudiante de 2012*. Montréal: Écosociété.

Lenhart, Amanda, Mary Madde, Aaron Smith and Alexandra Macgill. 2007. "Teens and Social Media." Special report. *Pew Research Centre's Internet and American Life Project*, December 19.

REFERENCES

Lepage, Jean-François, and Jean-Pierre Corbeil. 2013. *L'évolution du bilinguisme français-anglais au Canada de 1961 à 2011*. Ottawa: Statistics Canada, Ministry of Industry. May. At <statcan. gc.ca/pub/75-006-x/2013001/article/11795-fra.htm>.

Leroux, Georges, Christian Nadeau and Guy Rocher. 2012. "L'argument de la 'juste part' des étudiants — Lettre ouverte aux professeurs d'université." *Le Devoir*, March 14.

Lessard, Denis. 2013. "PLQ: Le financement sectoriel à l'agenda de Jean Charest." *La Presse*, May 8.

____. 2012a. "Les hauts et les bas des gouvernements Charest." *La Presse*, September 8.

____. 2012b. "Léo Bureau-Blouin candidat du PQ." *La Presse*, July 24.

Letsch, Constanze. 2014. "A Year After the Protests, Gezi Park Nurtures the Seeds of a New Turkey." *Guardian*, May 29.

Lévesque, Ève. 2012. "Grève étudiante: Plusieurs personnalités en appui aux étudiants." *Agence QMI*. May 1. At <fr.canoe.ca/cgi-bin/imprimer.cgi?id=1157194>.

Lévesque, Kathleen. 2012. "Chronologie de l'Unité anticollusion du Ministère des Transports." *Le Devoir*, June 18.

Levinson, Charles, and Margaret Coker. 2011. "The Secret Rally that Sparked an Uprising." *Wall Street Journal*, February 11.

Leydet, Dominique. 2012. "Grève étudiante et démocratie: D'une crise à l'autre." *Theory & Event* 15, 3 (online supplement). At <muse.jhu.edu/journals/theory_and_event/v015/15.3S. leydet.html>.

Ligue des droits et libertés, Association des juristes progressistes and ASSÉ (Association pour une solidarité syndicale étudiante). 2013. *Répression, discrimination et grève étudiante: Analyse et témoignages*. April.

Long, Gideon. 2014. "Chile's Student Leaders Come of Age." BBC News online, March 11. At <bbc.com/news/world-latin-america-26525140>.

Lutfi, Jaber. 2012. "Lettre   Victoire collatérale." *Le Devoir*, May 23.

Markoff, John. 2006. *What the Dormouse Said: How the Sixties Counterculture Shaped the Personal Computer Industry*. New York: Penguin.

Marques, Susana Moreira. 2011. "Portugal: No Country for Young Men?" *OpenDemocracy* March 26. At <opendemocracy.net/susana-moreira-marques/portugal-no-country-for-young-men>.

Marrissal, Vincent. 2010. "Le DGE et les donateurs compulsifs." *La Presse*, March 19.

Marsan, Benoit. 2005. "Pourquoi le syndicalisme étudiant." In ASSÉ (eds.), *Recueil de textes sur l'histoire du mouvement étudiant*. Montréal: ASSÉ. (Orig. pub. 2000.)

Martin, Éric, and Maxime Ouellet. 2011. *Université Inc*. Montréal: Lux Éditeurs.

Martin, Éric, and Simon Tremblay-Pépin. 2011. *Do We Really Need to Raise Tuition? Eight Misleading Arguments for the Hikes*. Montréal: l'Institut de recherche et d'informations socio-économiques (IRIS). May.

Massumi, Brian. 2012. "Of Capitulation and Buying Out." *Theory & Event* 15, 3 (online supplement). At <muse.jhu.edu/journals/theory_and_event/v015/15.3S.massumi.html>.

Mathieu, Annie. 2013. "Université du Québec: 10 des 11 établissements menacent de quitter la CREPUQ." *Le Soleil*, April 30.

Mazataud, Valérian. 2012. "Tintamarre mondial de casseroles." *Le Devoir*, June 14.

McCarthy, Shawn. 2012. "Ottawa's New Anti-Terrorism Strategy Lists Eco-Extremists as Threats." *Globe and Mail*, February 10.

McFeat, Tom. 2008. "Income Gaps Grow, As Canada's Have-Nots Get Left Behind." CBC News online, May 1. At <cbc.ca/news/business/income-gaps-grow-as-canada-s-have-nots-get-left-behind-1.764487>.

MDE (Le mouvement pour le droit à l'éducation). 2005. "Le mouvement pour le droit à l'éducation (MDE)." In ASSÉ (eds.), *Recueil de textes sur l'histoire du mouvement étudiant*. Montréal: ASSÉ.

MELS (Ministère de l'éducation, du loisir et du sport). 2011. "L'éffort financier pour les universités en 2008–9: Comparaison entre le Québec et les autres provinces canadiennes." *Bulletin statistique de l'éducation* 40 (March). At <lapresse.ca/html/1618/Bulletin.pdf>.

MELS (Ministère de l'éducation, du loisir et du sport) and MESRST (Ministère de l'enseignement supérieur, de la recherche, de la science et de la technologie). 2013. *Indicateurs de l'Éducation — Édition 2012*. Québec City: Gouvernement du Québec.

Ménard, Serge, Bernard Grenier and Claudette Carbonneau. 2014. *Rapport de la Commission spéciale d'examen des évènements du printemps 2012*. Québec City: Gouvernement du Québec.

Milner, Henry. 2013. "Social Media Politics: Are the New Movements, from Quebec to Wall Street, Compatible with Representative Democracy?" *Inroads* 32 (Winter).

Mitchell, Don. 1995. "The End of Public Space? People's Park, Definitions of the Public, and Democracy." *Annals of the Association of American Geographers* 85, 1.

Monbiot, George. 2014. "The Age of Loneliness Is Killing Us." *Guardian*, October 14.

Le Monde. 2013. "'Indignez-vous!', mini-livre et maxi-succès." February 27.

Montmarquette, Claude, Joseph Facal and Lise Lachapelle. 2008. *The Right Fees to Live Better Together*. Report of the Task Force on Fees for Public Services. Québec City: Gouvernment du Québec.

Montpetit, Éric. 2006. "La légitimité démocratique et le projet de réingénierie du gouvernement Charest." In F. Pétry, E. Bélanger and L.M. Imbeay (eds.), *Le parti libéral: Enquête sur les réalisations du gouvernement Charest*. Lévis: Les Presses de l'Université Laval.

Montpetit, Jonathan. 2012. "The Class Struggle Comes to Crescent Street, Montreal's Notorious Party Strip." *Huffington Post Canada* June 8. At <huffingtonpost.ca/2012/06/08/the-class-struggle-comes-_n_1579953.html>.

Morin, Jacques-Yvan. 2012. "Une hausse qui freinera le développement du Québec." *Le Devoir*, March 22.

Moses, Sébastien. 2013. "De ventôse à germinal." In Fermaille (ed.), *Fermaille: Anthologie*. Montréal: Moult Éditions.

Moysan-Lapointe, Héloïse. 2005. "L'ASSÉ depuis sa création." In ASSÉ (eds.), *Recueil de textes sur l'histoire du mouvement étudiant*. Montréal: ASSÉ. (Orig. pub. 2003.)

Myles, Brian, and Marco Bélair-Cirino. 2012. "Charest approuve le travail policier." *Le Devoir*, June 12.

Myles, Brian, and Guillaume Bourgault-Côté. 2013. "Gilles Vaillancourt, gangster?" *Le Devoir*, May 10.

Myles, Brian, and La Presse, canadienne. 2012. "Projet de loi 78: Des atteintes injustifiées aux libertés fondamentales, selon le Barreau." *Le Devoir*, May 18.

Myles, John, and Paul Pierson. 2001. "The Comparative Political Economy of Pension Reform." In Paul Pierson (ed.), *The New Politics of the Welfare State*. Oxford: Oxford University Press.

Nadeau, Jean-François. 2012a. "Le carré rouge de Fred Pellerin: 'Violence et intimidation,' affirme la ministre de la Culture." *Le Devoir*, June 9.

____. 2012b. "Les historiens dénoncent la loi." *Le Devoir*, May 18.

Nadeau, Jessica. 2012. "La loi 78 porte atteinte à la Charte des droits." *Le Devoir*, July 18.

Nadeau, Jessica, and Alexandre Shields. 2013. "Le Nord pour tous: Le PQ mécontente les écologistes et les industriels." *Le Devoir*, May 8.

Nadeau-Dubois, Gabriel. 2013a. *Tenir tête*. Montréal: Lux Éditeur.

____. 2013b. "Partenaires dans la catastrophe? Le ministre Blanchet doit entrer dans le 21e siècle." *Huffington Post Québec* May 23. At <quebec.huffingtonpost.ca/gabriel-nadeaudubois/exploitation-petrole-anticosti_b_3327901.html>.

____. 2012. "Lutte étudiante — Pourquoi je démissionne." *Le Devoir*, August 9.

REFERENCES

Nevitt, Neil. 2011. "The Decline of Deference Revisited: Evidence After 25 Years." Paper presented at "Mapping and Tracking Global Value Change: A Festschrift Conference for Ronald Inglehart," University of California, Irvine, March 11.

____. 1996. *The Decline of Deference: Canadian Value Change in Cross National Perspective.* Peterborough, ON: Broadview Press.

Nicoud, Annabelle. 2012. "Chronologie des coups d'éclats étudiants." *La Presse*, May 11.

Noël, André. 2011. "Le rapport Duchesneau pour les nuls." *La Presse*, October 1.

Normandin, Pierre-André, and Marie-Michèle Sioui. 2014. "Saccage à l'hôtel de ville." *La Presse*, August 18.

OECD (Organization for Economic Co-operation and Development). 1996. *Ageing in OECD Countries: A Critical Policy Challenge.* Paris: OECD.

Oikonomakis, Leonidas, and Jérôme E. Roos. 2013. "'Que No Nos Representan': The Crisis of Representation and the Resonance of the Real Democracy Movement from the Indignados to Occupy." Paper presented at "Street Politics in an Age of Austerity: From the Indignados to Occupy," Université de Montréal, February 20–21.

Olivier, Marie-Claude G., and Ève Lamoureux. 2014. "Artistes en grève sociale illimitée." In Marcos Ancelovici and Francis Dupuis-Déri (eds.), *Un Printemps rouge et noir.* Montréal: Écosociété.

Ouimet, Michèle. 2012. "Financement des universités: Une bonne question." *La Presse*, December 13.

Pampel, Fred C. 1994. "Population Aging, Class Context, and Age Inequality in Public Spending." *American Journal of Sociology* 100, 1 (July).

Paquet, Gilles. 2011. "Révolution tranquille et gouvernance: Trois chantiers — éducation, santé et culture." In Guy Berthiaume and Claude Corbo (eds.), *La Révolution tranquille en héritage.* Montréal: Éditions du Boréal.

Parti Québécois. 2012. "Abolition de la taxe santé: Une pilule difficile à avaler." Press release, March 15. At <newswire.ca/en/story/937923/abolition-de-la-taxe-sante-une-pilule-difficile-a-avaler>.

Payette, Lise. 2012. "Les Québécois aux rayons X." *Le Devoir*, June 22.

Pechtelidis, Yannis. 2011. "December Uprising 2008: Universality and Particularity in Young People's Discourse." *Journal of Youth Studies* 14, 4 (June).

Peritz, Ingrid. 2012. "Quebec Protests Adopt a Latin Flavour." *Globe and Mail* May 25.

Petrowski, Nathalie. 2012a. "L'École de la montagne rouge, la contestation par l'image." *Courrier international* 1131 (July 5–11).

____. 2012b. "Une grève signée École de la montagne rouge." *La Presse*, May 5.

____. 2012c. "Printemps érable." *La Presse*, April 30.

Pigeon, Mathieu. n.d.a. "Education in Québec, Before and After the Parent Reform." McCord Museum. At <mccord-museum.qc.ca/scripts/explore.php?Lang=1&tableid=11&tablen ame=theme&elementid=107__true&contentlong>.

____. n.d.b. "The Quiet Revolution." McCord Museum. At <mccord-museum.qc.ca/scripts/explore.php?Lang=1&tablename=theme&tableid=11&elementid=109__ true&contentlong>.

Pineault, Éric. 2012. "Quebec's Red Spring: An Essay on Ideology and Social Conflict at the End of Neoliberalism." *Studies in Political Economy* 90 (Autumn).

____. 2006. "Libérons-nous du statut quo!" In Collectif Carré Rouge (ed.), *Carré rouge: La grève étudiante du printemps 2005.* Montréal: Self-published.

Poirier, Fannie. 2012. "Nuit du 7 mars: 'J'ai vu mon État policier.'" *Voir*, March 10.

Popiden, Sandra. 2012. "Will the Arab Spring Succeed in Bringing Bread, Freedom and Dignity?" *Bridgewater Review* 31, 2 (December).

Porter, Isabelle, Marco Bélair-Cirino and Mélissa Guillemette. 2012. "Le mouvement des casseroles se répand aux quatre coins de Montréal et du Québec." *Le Devoir*, June 29.

Posca, Julia. 2013. "La CREPUQ et le financement des universités." *Raisons sociales* (October 3). At <raisons-sociales.com/articles/la-crepuq-et-le-financement-des-universites/>.

Poulin, Alexandre. 2012. "Le manifeste de la grande maNUfestation." *Le Huffington Post Québec*, June 8. At <quebec.huffingtonpost.ca/alexandre-poulin/manifeste-grande-manufestation_b_1582508.html>.

La Presse. 2012. "Un tremplin pour une contestation radicale." April 28.

La Presse, canadienne. 2014. "Compression des dépenses at hausse des tarifs des garderies." *Le Devoir*, February 20.

____. 2012a. "Impôt: Marceau recule sur les gains de capital." *La Presse*, October 3.

____. 2012b. "Pauline Marois présente son Conseil des ministres." *Le Devoir*, September 19.

____. 2012c. "Grand Prix: Les policiers detiennent 'préventivement' une trentaine de personnes." *Le Devoir*, June 10.

____. 2012d. "Des juristes en toge marchent ce soir contre la loi 78." *Le Devoir*, May 28.

____. 2012e. "Grève étudiante: Comme la veille, le SPVM déclare la manifestation illégale dès le début." *Le Huffington Post Québec*, May 20. At <quebec.huffingtonpost.ca/2012/05/20/manifestation-nocturne-illegale_n_1531854.html>.

____. 2012f. "Projet de loi 78: Amendements, précisions et questionnements à l'Assemblée nationale." *Le Devoir*, May 18.

____. 2012g. "La FECQ aimerait que la CLASSE dénonce la violence." *La Presse*, April 22.

____. 2012h. "Marée étudiante dans les rues de Montréal." *Le Devoir*, March 22.

____. 2012i. "Les centrales syndicales appuient les étudiants en grève." *Le Devoir*, March 13.

____. 2011a. "Les étudiants se font entendre à Montréal." *Radio-Canada*, November 10. At <ici.radio-canada.ca/nouvelles/societe/2011/11/10/001-manifestation_etudiante-contre_hausses-frais_scolarite.shtml?plckFindCommentKey=CommentKey:43f81 96e-fd1f-44e4-88a4-a533024cfde7#!>.

____. 2011b. "Jean Charest met sur pied une commission d'enquête sur la construction." *Le Devoir*, October 19.

____. 2010a. "Charest menace de poursuivre Gérard Deltell à cause de ses propos." *Le Devoir*, November 17.

____. 2010b. "Budget: Le taux d'insatisfaction du Parti libéral atteint 77%." *Les Affaires* April 12.

Preston, Samuel. 1984. "Children and the Elderly: Divergent Paths for America's Dependents." *Demography* 21, 4 (November).

Professeurs contre la hausse. 2012. "Le visage de la honte." May 19. At <profscontrelahausse. org/communiques/le-visage-de-la-honte/>.

Purcell, Mark. 2008. *Recapturing Democracy: Neoliberalization and the Struggle for Alternative Urban Futures*. New York: Routledge.

Radio-Canada. 2013a. "Règlement P-6: pas d'itinéraire exigé pour une célébration de victoire du Canadien." April 17. At <ici.radio-canada.ca/regions/montreal/2013/04/17/007-hockey-p6-police.shtml>.

____. 2013b. "L'ASSÉ boycotte le Sommet sur l'enseignement." February 14. At <ici.radio-canada. ca/nouvelles/societe/2013/02/14/001-asse-sommet-boycott.shtml>.

____. 2012a. "Charest interpelle la majorité silencieuse." August 2. At <ici.radio-canada.ca/sujet/ elections-quebec-2012/2012/08/01/009-charest-debut-campagne.shtml>.

____. 2012b. "Jacques Duchesneau a lui-même dévoilé son rapport à une journaliste." June 14. At <ici.radio-canada.ca/nouvelles/societe/2012/06/14/001-commission-charbonneau-jour5.shtml>.

____. 2012c. "Rumeurs de loi spéciale: La FECQ en appelle à Jean Charest." May 16. At <ici.

REFERENCES

radio-canada.ca/nouvelles/societe/2012/05/16/004-etudiants-reactions-loi-speciale.
shtml?plckFindCommentKey=CommentKey:fe931efd-aa56-43ac-bf9a-4a478ed5ffa4>.

_____. 2012d. "Différentes mesures atténueront la hausse des droits de scolarité." May 6. At <ici.
radio-canada.ca/nouvelles/societe/2012/05/05/001-etudiants-manifestation-conseil-plq.
shtml>.

_____. 2012e. "Débat sur le financement des universités: Qu'est-ce que la taxe sur le capital?" May
4. At <ici.radio-canada.ca/nouvelles/Economie/2012/05/04/007-taxe-capital-quebec-
retour-analyse.shtml>.

_____. 2012f. "Négociations suspendues: Les étudiants solidaires." April 25. At <ici.radio-canada.
ca/nouvelles/societe/2012/04/25/001-conflit-etudiant-mercredi.shtml>.

_____. 2012g. "La FEUQ et la FECQ rencontrent la ministre Beauchamp aujourd'hui." April 22.
At <ici.radio-canada.ca/nouvelles/societe/2012/04/22/004-ministre-beauchamp-ren-
contre-feuq-fecq-discussions.shtml?plckFindCommentKey=CommentKey:6f329a21-e
c47-4e06-95d1-403e372addcb>.

_____. 2012h. "Le premier ministre Charest 'encourage' la violence, dit la FECQ." April 13. At <ici.
radio-canada.ca/nouvelles/societe/2012/04/13/003-bureau-beauchamp-saccage.shtml>.

_____. 2012i. "Frais de gestion des universités québécoises: De chiffres et leur signification."
April 12. At <ici.radio-canada.ca/nouvelles/societe/2012/04/12/007-gestion-epreuve-
universites.shtml>.

_____. 2012j. "Financement des universités: Les solutions de la FEUQ et de la FECQ." April 11. At
<ici.radio-canada.ca/nouvelles/societe/2012/04/11/002-feuq-feq-deux.shtml>.

_____. 2012k. "Grève étudiante: Charest et Beauchamp haussent le ton." April 11. At <ici.radio-can-
ada.ca/nouvelles/societe/2012/04/11/003-beauchamp-boycottage-etudiant.shtml>.

_____. 2012l. "Grève étudiante: Coups d'éclat dans plusieurs villes du Québec." March 28. At
<ici.radio-canada.ca/nouvelles/societe/2012/03/28/001-hausse-droits-scolarite-manif-
perturbation-mercredi.shtml>.

_____. 2011a. "Jean Charest offre les pleins pouvoirs à la commission Charbonneau." October
22. At <ici.radio-canada.ca/nouvelles/Politique/2011/10/21/003-charest-commission-
enquete-volte-face.shtml>.

_____. 2011b. "Collusion et corruption dans l'industrie de la construction." September 17. At
<ici.radio-canada.ca/nouvelles/national/2011/09/14/003-unite-anticollusion-rapport.
shtml>.

_____. 2011c. "Charest rebrasse les cartes." August 11. At <ici.radio-canada.ca/nouvelles/
Politique/2010/08/11/002-remaniement_officiel.shtml>.

_____. 2011d. "Budget du Québec 2011: Éducation." At <radio-canada.ca/nouvelles/budget/
qc2011/les_faits_saillants/education.shtml>.

_____. 2011e. "Les étudiants manifestent contre la hausse des droits de scolarité." March 18.
At <ici.radio-canada.ca/regions/quebec/2011/10/21/010-manifestation-etudiants-
vendredi.shtml>.

_____. 2011f. "Québec crée une unité anticorruption permanente." February 18. At <ici.radio-
canada.ca/nouvelles/societe/2011/02/18/001-unite-corruption-procureurs.shtml>.

_____. 2005. "Grève étudiante: L'entente est finale, maintient Fournier." April 5. At <ici.radio-
canada.ca/nouvelles/Index/nouvelles/200504/05/002-greve-etudiant-mardi.shtml>.

_____. 2004. "Charest plus populaire que son gouvernement." December 22. At <ici.radio-canada.
ca/nouvelles/Politique/nouvelles/200412/22/001-sondage-charest-plq.shtml>.

Radio-Canada and La Presse, canadienne. 2012. "Line Beauchamp démissionne,
Michelle Courchesne lui succède." May 14. At <ici.radio-canada.ca/nouvelles/
politique/2012/05/14/001-beauchamp-demission-etudiants.shtml>.

Ratel, Jean-Luc. 2006. *Le financement des universités québécoises: Histoire, enjeux et défis.* Québec

City: Confédération des associations d'étudiants et d'étudiantes de l'Université Laval (CADEUL).

Rebick, Judy. 2013. "A Generation That Is Deepening Democracy." *Inroads* 32 (Winter).

Renaud, Benoit. 2005. "Six grèves générales." In ASSÉ (ed.), *Recueil de textes sur l'histoire du mouvement étudiant.* Montréal: ASSÉ. (Orig. pub. 1996.)

Reuters. 2014. "Bernie Ecclestone Tells Court He Paid Banker to Buy Silence Over Tax Affairs." *Guardian*, July 15.

Revenu Québec. N.d. "Income Tax Rates." At <revenuquebec.ca/en/entreprise/impot/societes/taux_imposition.aspx>.

Ricard, François. 2012. "Une révolte étudiante qui rompt la routine d'une société devenue ennuyeuse." *Le Monde*, June 7.

Richer, Jocelyne. 2012. "Que chacun paye sa juste part, plaide Bachand." *La Presse*, March 11.

Robert, Martin. 2012. "The Organizations Behind Quebec's 2012 Student Strike." *Canadian Dimension* 46, 5 (September/October).

Robert, Véronique. 2012. "'Au nom de l'article 31, je vous arrête.'" *Voir*, June 28.

Roberts, Leslie. 1963. *The Chief: A Political Biography of Maurice Duplessis.* Toronto: Clark, Irwin & Company.

Robillard, Alexandre. 2010a. "Financement du PLQ: Bellemare dit avoir des preuves contre Charest." *La Presse*, March 23.

____. 2010b. "Amir Khadir dénonce les liens entre des ingénieurs et le PLQ." *La Presse*, March 18.

Robinson, Andy. 2011. "Spain's Indignados." *The Nation* June 27.

Robitaille, Antoine. 2012a. "Des idées en l'ère — Charest, chef gréviste." *Le Devoir*, May 19.

____. 2012b. "Déclaration de guerre aux étudiants." *Le Devoir*, May 18.

____. 2012c. "Beauchamp accusée de saboter l'entente." *Le Devoir*, May 7.

____. 2010a. "Financement du PLQ — Le DGE assigne Marc Bellemare à témoigner." *Le Devoir*, March 19.

____. 2010b. "Duchesneau dirigera une force anticollusion." *Le Devoir*, February 24.

Rocher, Guy. 2004. "Un bilan du Rapport Parent: Vers la démocratisation." *Bulletin d'histoire politique* 12, 2 (Winter). At <classiques.uqac.ca/contemporains/rocher_guy/bilan_rapport_parent/bilan_rapport_parent.pdf>.

Rocher, Guy, and Yvan Perrier. 2012. "Les droits de scolarité à l'université: 'Juste part' ou 'Lutte juste'?" Open letter, April 2. Available at <ledevoir.com/documents/pdf/droits_scola-rite_rocher.pdf>.

Roy, Arundhati. 2011. "We Are All Occupiers." *Guardian*, November 17.

Sabbagh, Clara, and Pieter Vanhuysse. 2006. "Exploring Attitudes Towards the Welfare State: Students' Views in Eight Democracies." *Journal of Social Policy* 35, 4.

Sadiki, Larbi. 2012. "January 25 and the republic of Tahrir Square." *Al Jazeera*, January 25. At <aljazeera.com/indepth/opinion/2012/01/20121259355661345.html>.

Salvet, Jean-Marc. 2012a. "Le gouvernement Marois modifie la taxe santé plutôt que de l'annuler." *Le Soleil*, October 10.

____. 2012b. "Méthodes de la SQ à Victoriaville: Allez en déontologie, dit Dutil." *Le Soleil*, May 10.

Sanschagrin, David, and Alain-G. Gagnon. 2014. "L'approfondissement du politique au Québec: Les partis politiques et la grève étudiante de 2012." In Marcos Ancelovici and Francis Dupuis-Déri (eds.), *Un printemps rouge et noir: Regards croisés sur la grève étudiante de 2012.* Montréal: Écosociété.

Santerre, David, and Judith Lachapelle. 2012. "Un total de 518 arrestations à la 30e manifestation nocturne." *La Presse*, May 23.

Savard, Alain, and Marc-André Cyr. 2014. "La rue contre l'État." In Marcos Ancelovici and Francis Dupuis-Déri (eds.), *Un printemps rouge et noir: Regards croisés sur la grève étudiante*

REFERENCES

de 2012. Montréal: Écosociété.

Schepper, Bertrand, and Laura Handal. 2012. *À qui profite le Plan Nord?* Montréal: IRIS. March.

Schwartz, Mattathias. 2011. "Pre-Occupied: The Origins and Future of Occupy Wall Street." *The New Yorker* November 28.

Serebrin, Jacob. 2011. "Who Are the Top 10 Highest Paid University Admins in Quebec?" *Macleans* May 25. At <oncampus.macleans.ca/education/2011/05/25/who-are-the-top-10-highest-paid-university-admins-in-quebec/>.

Seymour, Michel, Louis Dumont, Jean-Claude Marsan and Daniel Turp. 2012. "Hausse des droits contre dérives immobilières…" *Le Devoir*, February 15.

Shapiro, Samantha M. 2009. "Revolution, Facebook-style." *New York Times*, January 22.

Shields, Alexandre. 2013. "Restauration des sites miniers — les Québécois devront payer la note." *Le Devoir*, August 24.

Shields, Alexandre, and Melissa Guillemette. 2012. "1er Mai et carrés rouges." *Le Devoir*, May 2.

Silva, Margarida. 2011. "Southern Europe's Outrage." *New Presence: The Prague Journal of Central European Affairs*, Summer.

Simard, Valérie. 2012. "Manifestation étudiante: Le SPVM enquêtera sur l'intervention." *La Presse*, February 4.

Sioui, Marie-Michèle, and Patrice Bergeron. 2012. "Impôt santé: Le gouvernement Marois recule." *Journal Métro* October 10.

Sitrin, Marina. 2011. "Horizontalism: From Argentina to Wall Street." *NACLA Report on the Americas* 44, 6 (November).

Smith, Aaron, and Joanna Brenner. 2012. "Twitter Use 2012." *Pew Research Centre's Internet and American Life Project*. May 31.

St-Pierre, Renaud Poirier, and Phillippe Ethier. 2013. *De l'école à la rue*. Montréal: Écosociété.

Statistics Canada. 2011. "Focus on Geography Series, 2011 Census." At <statcan.gc.ca/census-recensement/2011/as-sa/fogs-spg/Facts-cma-eng.cfm?LANG=Eng&GK=CMA&GC=462>.

____. 2008. *Earnings and Incomes of Canadians Over the Past Quarter Century, 2006 Census*. Ottawa: Ministry of Industry. At <statcan.ca/census-recensement/2006/as-sa/97-563/index-eng.cfm>.

Stepanova, Ekaterina. 2011. "The Role of Information Communication Technologies in the 'Arab Spring.'" *PONARS Eurasia Policy Memo* 159 (May).

Sterne, Jonathan. 2012. "Quebec's #Casseroles: On Participation, Percussion and Protest." *Theory & Event* 15, 3 (online supplement). At <muse.jhu.edu/journals/theory_and_event/v015/15.3S.sterne.html>.

Stiglitz, Joseph. 2014. "Austerity Has Been an Utter Disaster for the Eurozone." *Guardian*, October 1.

Strapagiel, Lauren. 2013. "Canadian University Degrees Pricier Than Ever But Losing Value." *Postmedia News* August 26. At <o.canada.com/business/canadian-university-degrees-pricier-than-ever-but-losing-value>.

Switzer, Jane. 2011. "Judge Clears Protester, Assails 'Zealous' Toronto Police for G20 Tactics." *National Post* August 12.

Swyngedouw, Erik. 2011. "Interrogating Post-Democratization: Reclaiming Egalitarian Political Spaces." *Political Geography* 30.

Sylvestre, Marie-Ève. 2012. "Les arrestations préventives sont illégales et illégitimes." *Le Devoir*, June 12.

Teisceira-Lessard, Philippe. 2012a. "FECQ: Léo Bureau-Blouin passe le flambeau à Éliane Laberge." *La Presse*, June 1.

____. 2012b. "Fissures dans le mouvement étudiant." *La Presse*, May 28.

____. 2012c. "La FECQ appelle ses membres à débrayer." *La Presse*, March 2.

Tepe, Markus, and Pieter Vanhuysse. 2008. "Are Aging OECD Welfare States on the Path to Gerontocracy?" *Journal of Public Policy* 29, 1 (August).

Thériault, Carl. 2013. "La FEUQ perd 11% de ses membres." *Le Soleil,* October 6.

Tillard, Patrick, and Jasmin Miville-Allard. 2013. "Une clarté qui envahit." In Fermaille (ed.), *Fermaille: Anthologie.* Montréal: Moult Éditions.

Tormey, Simon. 2012. "Occupy Wall Street: From Representation to Post-Representation." *Journal of Critical Globalisation Studies* 5.

Tremblay-Pépin, Simon. 2013a. "Les médias et la hausse des frais de scolarité de 2005 à 2010 — 2ième partie." Institut de recherche et d'informations socio-économiques (IRIS) blog, February 5. At <iris-recherche.qc.ca/blogue/les-medias-et-la-hausse-des-frais-de-scolarite-de-2005-a-2010-2ieme-partie>.

____. 2013b. "Les médias et la hausse des frais de scolarité de 2005 à 2010 — 1ère partie." IRIS blog, February 4. At <iris-recherche.qc.ca/blogue/les-medias-et-la-hausse-des-frais-de-scolarite-de-2005-a-2010-%E2%80%93-1ere-partie>.

TVA Nouvelles. 2012. "Hausse des frais de scolarités: les grèves étudiantes déclenchées." February 14. At <tvanouvelles.ca/lcn/infos/national/archives/2012/02/20120214-142208.html>.

United Nations Office of the High Commissioner for Human Rights. 1976. *International Covenant on Economic, Social and Cultural Rights.* Entry into force January 3. At <ohchr.org/EN/ProfessionalInterest/Pages/cescr.aspx>.

Urbania. 2012. *Rouge,* Summer.

Valade, Maxence L. 2013. "Il y a un an, l'émeute de Victoriaville." *Le Devoir,* May 4.

Van Alstyne, Marshall, and Erik Brynjolfsson. 2005. "Global Village or Cyberbalkans? Modeling and Measuring the Integration of Electronic Communities." *Management Science* 51, 6 (June).

Vérificateur général du Québec. 2009. *Rapport du Vérificateur général du Québec à l'Assemblée nationale pour l'année 2008–2009: Tome II.* Québec City: Vérificateur général du Québec. March.

Vierstraete, Valérie. 2007. *Les frais de scolarité, l'aide financière aux études et la fréquentation des établissements d'enseignement postsecondaire.* Québec City: Ministère de l'éducation, du loisir et du sport (MELS).

Vradis, Antonis, and Dimitris Dalakoglou. 2011. "A Brief Timeline of Major Protests and Revolts in Athens between November 1973 and December 2010." In A. Vradis and D. Dalakoglou (eds.), *Revolt and Crisis in Greece.* Oakland, CA and Edinburgh: Occupied London/AK Press.

Woodsworth, Judith. 2009. "Universities, Business and the City: Taking Partnerships to a New Level." Address to the Cercle canadien de Montréal on October 18. At <cerclecanadien-montreal.ca/assets/files/Events_docs/judith_woodsworth_09-10_en.pdf>.

World Bank. 2012. "Climate Change Report Warns of Dramatically Warmer World This Century." November 18. At <worldbank.org/en/news/feature/2012/11/18/Climate-change-report-warns-dramatically-warmer-world-this-century>.

____. 1994. *Averting the Old Age Crisis.* Oxford: Oxford University Press.

Zabihiyan, Bahador. 2013. "L'appel de l'ASSÉ à manifester a été entendu." *Le Devoir,* February 27.

Žižek, Slavoj. 2002. *Revolution at the Gates: Žižek on Lenin.* The 1917 writings. London: Verso.

ACKNOWLEDGMENTS

A writer is only as inspired as his life is, and so I need to start by thanking those who fill my heart with the strength and passion to drive me forward. Marc, my brother, your unconditional love and faith in me are the ground beneath my feet. You share in all of my joys and successes, if for no other reason than we grew up together, and you've made me who I am. Julian, your emotional wisdom and easy embrace of life have somehow managed to rub off, and in the end, you taught me how to breathe. Thank you for eagerly soaking up every wine-drenched rant with the widest smile. Patrick, you knew I was a creator long before I ever knew it myself, and have supported me through every transformation. Thank you for inducting me into your crazy world. Lise, you've loved me like family since the earliest days. Thank you for always being there at a minute's notice. Whenever you need a village, you can count me in. Genie, Barbara, Hoa, Abram, Marc B., James: *Ostie que vous êtes beaux*, and I love you all more than you know. Keep on following your wild hearts. You certainly inspire me to follow mine. To my mother who taught me to be headstrong and assertive (I think I learned a little too well), and my father with his unending desire to help (even when I don't want it): Thank you for raising me with the freedom to discover the world on my own. I never let go of it.

This book was not the work of one writer alone. Daniel, this project could not have gotten this far without your full and steady support from start to finish. Your persistent questioning and experienced guidance throughout were truly invaluable, and this first-time author owes you a great debt of gratitude. Jason, no one's eyes are as fresh as yours, and your impulses and insights always keep me on my toes. Thank you for your heartfelt support and for being invested in the success of this endeavour as if it were your own. Errol, your unwavering support has been crucial, and I can't express enough appreciation for making this first book adventure such a genuine delight. Thank you for taking a chance on a wide-eyed novice and for allowing me to pursue the full breadth of my creative vision. Thank you, Mario, for embracing this project so eagerly. Your collaboration has enriched it as only you could have, and you share greatly in its success. Thank you Pascale Dufour, Jules Duchastel, Hugues Boisvert and John Peters for putting the time aside to lend your knowledge and expertise to this project. All of your feedback proved extremely constructive, and I am grateful to have been able to rely on such valuable insights. And lastly, I must express my sincere gratitude to *Jeunes volontaires* for its unhesitant backing of this project and to Emploi-Québec whose generous funding helped make this work a reality.

INDEX

INDEX

(see also labour union movement)

Syndicat de professionnelles et professionnels du gouvernement du Québec
(SPGQ), 74 (see also labour union
movement)

Table de concertation étudiante du
Québec (TACEQ), 67
Tahrir Square (see Egyptian revolution)
Thatcher, Margaret, 19, 35, 38, 51, 82,
129, 131, 156
There is no alternative (TINA) (see
Thatcher, Margaret)
tuition fees, 18, 27, 31-32, 35, 47-48,
72-73, 79, 81-82, 102, 130, 142-149,
152, 157, 159, 161 (see also free
university education)
effect on educational accessibility,
31-32
increases to, 5-7, 18-20, 23, 29,
31-32, 47-48, 56, 66-67, 70, 72-73,
79, 83-84, 88, 98, 107, 114-115,
133, 137, 142-148, 151, 157, 159,
161-162
regressive nature of, 84
tuition freeze, 6, 16, 18, 142
Tunisian revolution, 38
Turkish protests, 163
Twitter, 38-41, 77-78, 85–88, 108, 120,
126-127, 132, 153, 156 (see also
social media)

Union générale des étudiants du Québec
(UGEQ), 15-16, 19-21
unionism (see labour union movement)
Union Nationale, 13, 16, 162
Unité anticollusion (UAC), 59-60 (see also
Duchesneau Report)
United Nations (U.N.), 16, 96, 110, 122,
148
Unité permanente anticorruption (UPAC),
59-60
Université de Montréal, 15, 27, 32, 35,
Université du Québec à Montréal
(UQÀM), 16, 31, 77, 90, 92, 94, 107,
Université Laval, 69, 92
universities, 6, 14-16, 25-35, 50, 66, 73,

81, 94, 98, 102, 114-115 (see also
free university education)
university administrations, 28-31, 33,
92-93, 100-102, 107, 159-160
university diplomas, 142-143
value of, 34, 143-144
university presidents and rectors, 18,
23, 30-31, 35, 73, 102, 115 (see
also Conférence des recteurs et
des principaux des universités du
Québec (CREPUQ))
salaries of, 30-31, 73, 102

user fees, 6, 47, 55-57, 72
user-pay (see user fees)

Vaillancourt, Gilles, 59
vandalism, 68-69, 75, 79, 98, 106-107,
110
Victoriaville riot, 111-114
Villeneuve, Julien (see Anarchopanda)
violence (see police brutality; see vandalism)
violence and intimidation, 93, 96, 103,
124, 136

wealth inequality, 6, 13, 46, 57, 72, 83,
163
Woodsworth, Judith, 31, 35
World Social Forum, 21, 48
World Trade Organization (WTO), 38

Yo Soy 132, 163

Žižek, Slavoj, 37